PSYCHOPATHY
and DELINQUENCY

By WILLIAM McCORD, Ph.D.

Instructor in Social Psychology and General Education, Harvard University

and JOAN McCORD, Ed.M.

Research Assistant, Laboratory of Human Development, Harvard University

GRUNE & STRATTON   1956

New York   London

Grune & Stratton, Inc.
757 Third Avenue
New York, New York 10017

First printing—May 1956
Second printing—August 1964
Third printing—November 1970

Library of Congress Catalog Card Number 56-7935

International Standard Book Number 0-8089-0274-1

Printed in the United States of America (E-B)

Contents

ACKNOWLEDGMENTS

The authors wish to express their appreciation to the following publishers for permission to quote from these works:

Durham v. United States, published in the Federal Reporter, 1954, by the West Publishing Co.

A Judge Takes the Stand, by Joseph N. Ulman, published 1933 by Alfred A. Knopf, Inc.

Psychopathic States, by Sir David Henderson, published 1939 by W. W. Norton & Co., Inc.

The Crime of Imprisonment, by George Bernard Shaw, published 1946 by Philosophical Library, Inc.

Encyclopedia of Criminology, edited by Vernon Branham and Samuel Kutash, published 1949 by Philosophical Library, Inc.

Etiological Studies of Psychopathic Personality, by Anthony Smykal and Frederick Thorpe, published 1951 in Volume 7, Journal of Clinical Psychology.

Psychopathology and Treatment of Delinquent Girls, by Florence Powdermaker et al., published 1937 in Volume 7, American Journal of Orthopsychiatry.

Controls from Within, by Fritz Redl & David Wineman, published 1954 by The Free Press.

Herman Goering: Amiable Psychopath, by G. M. Gilbert, published 1948 in Volume 43, Journal of Abnormal and Social Psychology, by the American Psychological Association.

Wayward Youth, by August Aichhorn, published 1935 by The Viking Press, Inc.

Foreword

EVERY SOCIETY has its quota of trouble makers. Among the least understood, and perhaps most destructive, are the moral and emotional misfits known as 'psychopathic personalities.' Their warped natures frequently thrust them into the criminal segment of society. Even if they escape the law they bring misery and sorrow to their fellow men far out of proportion to their numbers.

The psychopath often has bland and pleasing external manners while on the inside he lacks those normal human sentiments without which life in common is impossible. The authors of this excellent volume describe him as an "asocial, aggressive, highly impulsive person, who feels little or no guilt and is unable to form lasting bonds of affection with other human beings."

While the existence of such 'moral insanity' has long been recognized, it is only in recent years that psychological and social science has given it sustained attention. Like other riddles of human personality its solution turns out to require the combined resources of genetics, child study, psychoanalysis, electro-encephalography, sociology, and psychotherapy—to name only some of the specialties involved. One merit of the present volume is its wide survey of contributions from these and kindred sources.

Labels are perilous things. To call a destructive person a "psychopath" does not, of course, prove that he belongs to a single well-defined nosological grouping. Indeed the first question to ask is whether psychopathy is nothing more than a semantic fiction. The authors face this question and decide in the negative. The syndrome, they say, is too well-marked and dependable for it to be shrugged off as a figment. If, then, we are dealing with a fairly unitary syndrome, does it have an identifiable cause? Here to be sure our knowledge falls short of providing a final answer, but the authors give a guarded affirmative reply, advancing a highly suggestive "neuro-social" theory of its origin.

Next the authors ask whether psychopathy can be treated successfully. Can normal sentiments of guilt and affection be planted and a modicum of self-control be instilled? It is now clear that severe punishment and half-hearted therapy do no good at all. But there

is hope in vigorous total-push methods of treatment if they are in-
augurated early enough—preferably no later than adolescence. Encouraging results have followed on the therapeutic efforts of Aichhorn, Bettleheim, Redl, and Papanek.

The most original contribution of this volume is its evaluation of
the type of milieu therapy practiced at the Wiltwyck School where
psychopathic delinquents are studied in comparison with other types
of young offenders. In order to carry through their evaluation the
authors have devised several ingenious measuring instruments to tap
relevant aspects of personality, including aggressive fantasy, guilt reactions, punitiveness of attitude, ego-ideals, and the boy's moral code.
In a well-controlled experiment the McCords find that children
diagnosed as psychopathic or as having behavior disorders actually
respond to therapy more favorably than do neurotic and psychotic
children. Whether the change is permanent cannot yet be told, but
the demonstration has special significance. It shows that young psychopaths if brought out of their emotional isolation can come to hold
more normal views of authority, of self-responsibility, and of social
relationships. The discovery serves as a warning to those who have
claimed without proof that psychopathy is incurable.

The authors ask whether psychopaths are legally insane or whether
they may be held legally responsible for their acts. All discussions of
this problem are necessarily inconclusive, but I find illumination in
the McCords' treatment of the matter. Given time and determination
we may yet find it possible to instill a normal structure of sentiments
into lives that start out as loveless, insensitive and destructive. The
full achievement, however will require further therapeutic discoveries
as well as reform in criminal procedures, starting perhaps with the
"treatment tribunals" advocated by Sheldon Glueck. Meanwhile we
must accept Justice Cardoza's summing up of the situation: "Everyone recognizes that the present (legal) definition of insanity has little
relation to the truths of mental life."

As a teacher I should like to add a further word. It has been my
experience that the field of criminology holds the precise balance of
intellectual and social challenge to which college students eagerly
respond. A well-written volume on the subject, particularly if it includes illustrative cases, and if it deals with the personal causation
of conduct, will have warm appeal. All these merits are found in

this text, together with an especially fine lesson in evaluation. The McCords' report of their original experiment can teach the student much concerning the approach of modern social science to the difficult task of measuring change in human character.

I am persuaded that this volume is the most comprehensive and most dependable source of information available on psychopathy. And by virtue of their original research the authors have pushed forward the frontiers of knowledge in a perplexing field.

GORDON W. ALLPORT

Preface

ANYONE WHO WRITES on the psychopathic personality faces a complicated, often puzzling task. First, he must disentangle the various
meanings of this ubiquitous term. The word "psychopath" has been
absorbed in everyday language and has been used as a label for men
as different as Whitaker Chambers and John Dillinger, Harvey Matu-
sow and Herman Goering. Then, if the student finds—as this book
contends—that there really is such a disorder as "psychopathy", he
must evaluate a mass of evidence concerning the nature, causes, and
treatment of the syndrome. This evidence is vast, sometimes conflicting, and continually growing. Between 1930 and 1940, twenty-eight
scientific articles appeared dealing with the problem. Between 1940
and 1955, this trickle of research became a torrent: 171 articles specifically dealing with psychopathy appeared and hundreds of others
produced facts relating to this strange disorder.

Why this sudden flood of research? Many factors combined to
produce it: the war brought thousands of psychopaths, with their
disturbing behavior, into the army; political developments in Germany focused attention on the relation of psychopathy to Nazism;
new techniques, like the E.E.G., allowed science a closer look at the
psychopath's neurology; the rising crime rate drew public concern
to the super-criminal psychopath. Most importantly, the ancient belief that psychopathy was an hereditary, innate lack of "moral sense"
went into a precipitous decline. The supposition, created by new discoveries and theories in the behavioral sciences, that psychopathy
might stem from the environment, opened new realms of investigation
and new hopes that the psychopath could be "cured."

A few men played an important role in changing the concept. Sir
David Henderson, the distinguished British psychiatrist, published
his comprehensive *Psychopathic States* in 1939; American psychiatrist
Hervey Cleckly followed in 1941 with *Mask of Sanity,* a book which
did much to show the influence of the disorder and its socially-caused
nature; and psychoanalyst Robert Lindner produced, in 1944, a
clinical portrait of treatment in *Rebel Without A Cause.*

Since this brief creative period, however, science has lacked a
synthesis of discoveries made in the last decade. One of the purposes
of this book is the compilation (and evaluation) of our knowledge
about the psychopathic personality, about his family life and his brain

ix

structure, and about his reactions to treatment and his cost to the community.

Another equally important purpose, however, is the evaluation of a treatment which can modify, if not cure, the psychopathic child—before he becomes a social menace. In "milieu therapy," as practiced at the Wiltwyck School (and by such men as Aichhorn, Redl, and Bettleheim), society may have an effective treatment. At least, our evaluation of this school's effect on disordered children indicates that the method achieves important changes.

Like any discussion of the psychopathic personality, this book has controversial elements. Some may disagree with our causal explanation (which stresses neurological and environmental influences); others may question the optimistic conclusions drawn from the Wiltwyck research and other reports on treatment; a few may debate the concept of "psychopathy" itself (and its independence from "culture-bound" judgments). But controversy is the seed-bed of discovery and a cause of scientific progress.

Dr. Sheldon Glueck and Dr. Gordon Allport of the Harvard faculty and Dr. Harry Levin of Cornell not only gave their advice and help, but also read the book in its various stages of completion. Dr. Glueck, with his wide experience as a criminological researcher, contributed substantially to the chapters on causation and legal policy. Dr. Levin's advice, particularly on the Wiltwyck research, its aims, statistics, and conclusions, greatly improved the project. Dr. Gordon Allport contributed unsparingly of his time and wisdom to every aspect of the book, from the definition of psychopathy to the recommendations concerning social policy. His discerning comments on the Wiltwyck chapter, his additions to the theory of causation, his correction of certain sentimental lapses, his suggestion of additional approaches and new insights—all were invaluable.

Ernst Papanek, director of the Wiltwyck school, made possible, encouraged, and helped to form the research on milieu therapy. Others on the staff of Wiltwyck, particularly Assistant Director Anna Chase, Head Counselor Francis Sims, and Senior Group Therapist Malcom Marx gave important help throughout the research. We feel deep gratitude to everyone at Wiltwyck—the counselors, the psychologists, the "Mennonites," the secretaries—for contributing their time and aid in the project.   WILLIAM McCORD
Cambridge, 1956   JOAN McCORD

1

Who is the Psychopath?

*This 'landowner' . . . was a strange type,
yet one pretty frequently to be met with,
a type abject and vicious and at the
same time senseless.*

DOSTOYEVSKY, describing Fyodor Karamazov.

A SWEATY CROWD jammed the courtroom and gaped at a slender, passive young man sitting in the dock. He seemed detached from the melee, bored by the complicated legal process. If the papers had not splashed his picture across the front pages few people would have known that this was the defendant, William Cook—"Billy the Kid"— brutal slayer of five human beings.

In his few years of life, Cook had been a terrible scourge to society. His youth had been spent in fights, homosexual orgies, and robberies. His adult life, short as it was, had culminated in the killing of a fellow robber, in the murder of an innocent man and wife and—most shockingly—in the shootings of their two children.

This was the day the crowd awaited. Today Billy Cook would "get what was coming to him." What could he possibly deserve but death? The crowd had little patience with the legal process that led to this moment. They despised the hair-splitting psychiatrists who had maintained that Cook was "mentally ill, although not insane." Few of the spectators understood the esoteric arguments among the expert witnesses. Three defense psychiatrists had asserted that Cook was "psychopathic." The prosecution agreed but added, to the joy of the crowd, "So what?"

As the judge read the sentence, a dissatisfied rustle swept through the crowd. Not death, but "300 years in Alcatraz" was Bill Cook's fate. Few heard or cared to hear what the judge so solemnly added: "Billy Cook is a symbol of society's failure."

To save itself from other Billy Cooks, society must come to under-

1

stand the psychopathic personality. Psychopathy, possibly more than other mental disorder, threatens the safety, the serenity, and the security of American life. From the ranks of the psychopaths come political demagogues, the most violent criminals, the riot leaders, sexual misfits, and drug addicts. Psychologist Robert Lindner has observed: "Hydra-headed and slippery to the touch though it is, psychopathy represents the most expensive and most destructive of all known forms of aberrant behavior."[1]

Just what is psychopathy? For 150 years, science has known of the psychopath's existence; for at least 140 years, scientists have quarrelled in defining his disorder.

Only a small minority has maintained that the psychopathic personality, as a distinct clinical syndrome, does not exist. One of these dissenters, psychiatrist Olof Kinberg, commented a few years ago: "[The concept] should be abrogated as theoretically unsatisfactory, practically misleading and destructive to scientific thinking."[2] Few of those who have dealt with criminals, who have worked in mental hospitals, or who have participated in social casework would agree with Kinberg. Indeed, most investigators believe that the concept not only has meaning, but that it is indispensable. Even Kinberg surreptitiously recognized that certain individuals require a special classification. "In the good old times," he admitted, "one exported such cases to the U.S.A. where most of them went to the dogs or were sent back by their consulates."[3]

Although most social scientists admit the existence of the psychopath, they have extraordinary difficulty in defining his disease. As a psychiatrist with long experience recently exclaimed: "I know an elephant when I see one, but damned if I can define one!"

Much of the difficulty with definition has, however, been superficial and overly stressed. Below their surface argument, most social scientists postulate a common core of psychopathy with which all would agree: *The psychopath is an asocial, aggressive, highly impulsive person, who feels little or no guilt and is unable to form lasting bonds of affection with other human beings.*

The lives of two typical psychopaths, William Cook and Joseph Borlov, illustrate in more human terms the abstract definition. William Cook has probably been the most thoroughly studied psychopath of our times. Not only did Cook submit to a full psychological examination (by Anthony Smykal and Frederick Thorne[4]) but he also wrote the complete story of his life.

Born in 1927, in a small Missouri town, Billy Cook never participated in the close family life of most Midwest farmers. His father, a pathological drinker, deserted Cook and the other children early in Billy's life. Although never brought to trial, Cook's father probably murdered his mother. When Billy was seven, he discovered her body. Later he described the event with a typical lack of emotion: " . . . one time my sister and me came home from playing at a yellow house and found her dead, laying on a cot. She had a large gash in the head."[5]

A juvenile court judge split the orphaned family, sending Billy to a foster home. His new "mother," a brutal nymphomanic, initiated Billy into the sordid side of sexual experience. When Billy finally ran away from the foster home, he was caught by the police and shipped to the Missouri Training School. He later wrote: "The training I got there was how to steal cars and pick locks."[6]

Paroled, Cook lived with his elder sisters who shifted him from town to town. One brother-in-law taught him the burglar's skills and often took him on drinking sprees which ended in brothels. Another relative got a farming job for the boy, then cheated him out of his earnings. No one wanted him. His "family life" ended when a sister forced him into prison by declaring he had broken parole.

In prison, Cook developed into a confirmed homosexual and built up a record as a trouble-maker. Upon release, he participated in several robberies and worked at odd jobs. Cook soon drifted westward—stealing when he could, working when he had to. An older man picked him up in a stolen car and offered to "pull some jobs." Cook turned him down, shot him, stole the car, and continued west.

When this car broke down, he hailed another, threatening the driver with his pistol. Cook later recalled: "I got in the car with these people. Moser was their name. I told them what had happened and I didn't want their money or anything. All I wanted was to get away."[7]

The car raced across the Southwest with Cook holding a gun on the driver, his wife, and their two children. At a New Mexico gas station Moser attacked Cook, pinning his arms to his sides. Cook struggled free, forced the family back into the car, and made them resume the drive. Soon Cook, frightened by the attack, murdered all four. He stopped the car just long enough to stuff the bodies into an abandoned mine shaft.

Cook reached California, but the police had begun a six-state search and an alert local sheriff arrested him. In a last desperate attempt, Cook kidnapped the sheriff in a police car and dashed across the Mexican border. In a Tiajuana cafe, Mexican soldiers caught him. Securely tied, he was thrust on board a plane destined for the United States. The Mexican soldiers, jubilant over their victory, shot volley after volley into the air as the plane left the ground.

In a California jail, two psychologists gave Cook an intensive examination. Their tests (the Rorschach and T.A.T.) showed the killer to be basically immature, completely isolated from the human world, and impoverished in his emotional life. Because he couldn't profit from experience, he reacted to frustration with hostility and fury. Unable to identify with others, he seemed constantly preoccupied with "his feelings of rejection and underprivilege."[8]

The psychologists asked Cook to make several drawings of the human figure. After "blind analysis," another expert concluded that the drawer had an extremely low frustration tolerance; was explosive; preoccupied with sex; and psychopathic.[9]

His examiners pointed to early rejection as the probable cause of his disorder: ". . . here was a child who suffered an intensive exposure to *all* of the pathogenic factors which are accepted by modern psychiatry as being etiological to conditioned character disorders."[10]

Billy Cook exhibited a character unrestrained by guilt and barren of love—a personality so impulsive, so warped, that every frustration resulted in explosive, murderous aggression.

Another typical psychopath, Joseph Borlov,[11] covered his disorder with a more sophisticated veneer. I first met Borlov as his counselor and teacher in a segregated unit of San Quentin Prison. He was a handsome man, slender, wavy-haired, and always immaculately garbed in the prison dress. The English accent to his speech, his theatrical gestures, his well-timed sense of the dramatic tabbed him as an actor, which once he was. Nothing on the surface revealed his career as a forger, robber, liar, homosexual—and ultimately, murderer.

Because he felt no compunction about lying, it is difficult to disentangle Borlov's real life from his fabrications. The facts seem to be these: Born in 1900 as an illegitimate child in St. Petersburg, Borlov escaped the Bolshevik Revolution when his father took him to Paris. In France, his father deserted him. A vacationing American couple adopted him and brought him to the United States. During the twenties and early thirties Borlov lived by playing chorus parts in musicals and "walk-ons" in Broadway plays. Small robberies, forged checks, and fees as a homosexual prostitute supplemented his income. Borlov later described these years with a grandiose disregard for facts:

> In 1925, I first went to work for Florenz Ziegfield at the New Amsterdam in New York. The show was crummy; Marilin [sic] Miller, the star. I had a couple of bits in the show. Two years later, Ziegfield featured me in the Follies—I had arrived. For the first time in some years. I had a feeling of security—no more tank towns—I was eating regularly. After a few seasons with the Follies my old impatience and dissatisfaction appeared. I wanted to act; then I heard that Maude Adams and Otis Skinner were going to return from retirement and tour with a company in "Merchant of Venice." This was for me. I made tracks for Long Island to beard Otis Skinner in his own den. Fortunately for me, he had never heard of me—and was very nice. I fixed his sink. I think it was the sink that got me the part. Anyway, I was hired at the salary of sixty-five smackers a week. I was getting $1500 from Ziegfield. So much for money!

Everything, or almost everything, that Borlov described about this period in his life was a lie, but intelligence shines through the fabrication. Actually, he never played with Marilyn Miller, Otis Skinner, Maude Adams. Instead, his biggest income came from petty robberies; his greatest triumphs, from female impersonations.

After several arrests in New York, Borlov drifted west to California. Late in 1940, in a drunken spree, he forged $8,000 in bogus checks. Arrested in Santa Barbara, Borlov was tried and sentenced to San Quentin for five years. Released in 1952, Borlov "went wild" in San Francisco. He robbed several grocery stores, successfully charged $500 worth of perfume to a non-existent account at Magnin's, and, in another burglary, shot a man to death.

During his imprisonment, several psychiatrists examined Borlov and agreed in diagnosing him as a psychopathic personality. His impulsive outbursts of aggression, his narcissism, and his lovelessness singled him out as pathologically different from other men. His lying indicated the possible existence of hallucinations. Yet all who knew him agreed that Borlov, unlike the psychotic individual, did not for one minute believe his own lies. He lied, the psychiatrists agreed, because he enjoyed it. If pressed, he would affably admit his prevarications.

His warped mind, although completely asocial, was capable of sparkling analysis. As philosophically as any academician, Borlov could rationalize the failings of his fellow criminals:

A diseased mind will some day be cured by medicine—probably surgery —but never by conversation nor statistics. All crime is a product of environment, usually of civilization. No man is bad nor is any man evil—everyone is forced into a pattern by society. The very people who condemn his mistakes create his future crime. Since entering this particular prison, I have met many men—some are mentally ill—others just ignorant, while some are the victims of their own desires. Many sincerely know they have made a mistake and will not recreate one. Too many of them are of the belief that they must outsmart the authorities, the law, their captors. The pity of it: they don't have the mental equipment for the task they have set themselves.

Unfortunately for society, Borlov had the "mental equipment" for his task. He had the intelligence but no inner control. He had insight into his fellows but not into himself. He could talk of "guilt," of "misdeeds," of "mistakes," but the words were mere abstractions. Borlov could kill without guilt, lie without compunction, and steal without remorse. He said to me, when I left the prison: "A lot has happened to me, a lot more will happen. But I enjoy living and I am always looking forward to each day. I like laughing and I've done a lot. I am essentially a clown at heart—but a happy one. I always take the bad with the good."

Neither Borlov nor Cook would think of themselves as sick men— nor would society, its judges, its police, or its wardens. Yet beneath superficial differences, Borlov and Cook suffered from the same disorder. Whether brilliant or stupid, whether sophisticated or primitive, whether born to the purple or "on the wrong side of the tracks," psychopathic personalities have the same symptoms of maladjustment. All those who (to their sorrow) have dealt with psychopaths would recognize the following fundamental profile:

I. THE PSYCHOPATH IS ASOCIAL

Society cannot ignore the psychopath, for his behavior is dangerously disruptive. He may be robbing a store or knifing another man; he may be peddling drugs or forging a check. No rule, however important, stops him. Since the bizzare, erratic behavior of the psychopath antagonizes society, he is often found in the social waste baskets: the prisons or the mental hospitals.

Because his behavior is so threatening, many people lose sight of the disorder which causes it. Much of psychology's confusion over the psychopath can be traced to a basic mistake: equating deviant behavior with the psychopathic personality.

The actions of the psychopath are only outward symptoms of a sick mind. Many other deviants—the professional criminal, the gang criminal, the sexual aberrant—exhibit dangerous behavior, but they do not share the character structure of the true psychopathic personality. Moreover, the definition of deviant behavior varies from culture to culture. Borlov's homosexuality might have been honored in ancient Greece and Cook's murders might have been overlooked if his victims had been known German spies in the last war. Deviant behavior, then, is an inadequate criterion of psychopathy. At most it may indicate the existence of a psychopathic character structure.

In almost every culture, the psychopath can be found. What he does will differ; what his society condemns will vary—but the purposeless rebel, the unsocialized misfit, the person who feels no guilt in breaking social mores can be found everywhere. Consequently, any adequate study of the psychopath must look beyond asociality.[12]

II. The Psychopath is Driven by Primitive Desires

The psychopath has the same desires as other men. He requires food, water, and sleep; he wants sex, self-esteem, and power.[13] The psychopath differs, however, in his demand for immediate fulfillment of every passing desire.

Hobbes said: "The wicked man is but the child grown strong." The psychopath is like an infant, absorbed in his own needs, vehemently demanding satiation. The average child, by the age of two, compromises with the restrictions of his environment. He learns to postpone his pleasure and to consider his mother's needs as well as his own. The psychopath never learns this lesson; he does not modify his desires, and he ignores the needs of others. In most respects, the pychopath is Narcissus, completely absorbed in himself, craving only his own pleasure.

Much of the psychopath's asociality can be traced to this quest for immediate pleasure. F. A. Freyhan observed: "The psychopath . . . is unsocial rather than anti-social."[14] He does not purposefully attack society, but society too often blocks his way to fulfillment.[15]

It seems probable, though not provable, that the psychopath has a dominating need which most human beings have to a more modified degree: a desire for excitement and variety. The average man wants excitement but he also wants security. He seldom sacrifices his security in a search for change. The psychopath, however, often seems willing to sacrifice everything for excitement. His satisfactions have always been fleeting and highly changeable from childhood through maturity. Consequently, he seems to know no greater pleasure than constant change, and the search for excitement at any cost becomes an important motive.[16]

But if the psychopath develops a desire for excitement which other men do not have, he does not develop another important need: the "self-actualizing" or "creative" need. As Fromm, Horney, Riesman, and Maslow have pointed out, the drive for autonomy and self-fulfillment motivates the psychologically healthy person. This search for self-actualization appears only when other basic needs (love, self-esteem, safety) have been fully satisfied. Continually preoccupied with his primitive desires, the psychopath never reaches this higher level of human motivation.

III. The Psychopath is Highly Impulsive

Everyone wishes at some time during his life to ignore his responsibilities, restrictions, and duties. Once in a great while the normal person gives in to this whim, but the psychopath does so continually. His life seems an erratic series of unconnected acts, first leading one way, then another. Chornyak has quipped that with the psychopath, "The lid is off the id."[17]

Borlov, for example, often left his night club engagements to take whirling rides in fast automobiles. The clubs would fire him; he would get another bit part. Again and again he repeated this pattern. Billy Cook held a great many jobs, but never for more than two months: he couldn't stand the restrictions and boredom of regular work.

Unlike the normal person, or even the average criminal, the psychopath's adventures often seem purposeless. Even his crimes are rarely planned. He robs a store in a whim of the moment, not after careful consideration. He flits from woman to woman with volatile passion, never feeling prolonged attraction.

The psychopath has no stable goals. His life is dominated by fleeting desires which leave no space for farsighted planning. After many years of experience with criminal psychopaths, psychologist Robert Lindner observed: "Determined progress toward a goal—unless it is a selfish one capable of immediate realization by a sharply accented spurt of activity—the dynamic binding together of actual strands, is lacking."[18]

Lauretta Bender, a child psychiatrist who examined 800 psychopathic children, concluded that the most prominent trait of the psychopathic syndrome was "diffusely unpatterned impulsive behavior."[19]

IV. THE PSYCHOPATH IS AGGRESSIVE

The psychopath's asociality most often expresses itself in brutal aggression. He is not the passive neurotic who hurts no one but himself, nor the anxious psychotic who withdraws from human contact. The psychopath's uninhibited search for pleasure often clashes with the restrictions of his society; the conflict frequently results in aggressive action.[20]

A notorious Baltimore murder illustrates the psychopath's quick-triggered aggression. Two men held up a milk wagon. Both carried loaded guns. The driver resisted. One criminal did not pull his gun. The other robber, a psychopath, used his gun to shoot and kill the driver. The panic which any animal experiences when faced with serious frustration more often causes the psychopath to react with aggression.

Why is the psychopath so inordinately aggressive? His childhood may account for the phenomenon. The psychopath is usually severely rejected, physically beaten, and emotionally deprived by his parents.[21] As a child, then, he suffers from almost constant frustration. Today most social scientists believe that aggression is always caused by frustration (although frustration may cause other reactions too).[22]

It may be that the psychopath, because of this severe childhood frustration, spends the rest of his life working out his aggressive feelings. No one, however, has actually proven that the psychopath has a more intense aggressive "drive."[23] It seems more probable that a lack of inhibition rather than a heightened "drive" accounts for the psychopath's aggressive behavior.

The critical difference seems to be this: the psychopath is highly aggressive because he has never learned more socialized ways of dealing with frustration. The normal man has learned to control aggression. He reacts to frustration with sublimation, with constructive action, with withdrawal—less often with aggression. The psychopath, on the other hand, characteristically reacts to frustration with fury.

Psychopathic aggression may be the result of early reward for such behavior. Often, the psychopath gained attention through aggression when other methods failed. Admittedly, the attention was usually retaliatory, but many a child prefers punitive attention to total neglect.

Does aggression make the psychopath any happier? Objectively, it seldom solves his problems and often increases them. But, subjectively, does hurting others somehow give the psychopath an inner satisfaction? Robert Lindner believes that it does. He feels that the psychopath's aggression is an attempt to overcome anxious fearfulness: "Typical psychopathic manifestations are tensional discharges aimed at restoring a disturbed organismic balance."[24] Lindner's "homeostasis" theory must postulate a rather high degree of tension within the psychopath.

Yet most observers would maintain that the psychopath has relatively little anxiety, worry, or inner conflict. Bender, for example, found her psychopathic children to be without anxiety. "There are conflicts, and frustration is reacted to immediately by temper tantrums."[25] This does not mean that the psychopath adjusts to frustration. Lindner to the contrary, the psychopath's aggressiveness seems more a conditioned response to external obstacles than an attempt to resolve inner tensions.

Some scientists believe that the psychopath is confused by his own behavior. Kirson Weinberg has observed: ". . . the psychopath frequently seeks others to limit his random aggressions. . . . Actually he too is puzzled by his waywardness and unwittingly may want to put limits to his random, appetite-fulfilling and destructive behavior."[26] Our experience partially confirms Weinberg's observation—but only up to a point. The psychopath may temporarily seek control over his indiscriminate aggression, but this desire, like so many others, soon passes. Any control, however mild, again irritates him and he rejects it. One psychopathic convict we knew pleaded for psychiatric help, yet abandoned his psychologist after the first two interviews and returned to his old patterns of aggressive narcissism.

V. THE PSYCHOPATH FEELS LITTLE GUILT

When the normal man violates the moral strictures of his culture, a gnawing uneasiness grips him: his conscience hurts. But the psychopath—and this is a crucial trait—has few internalized feelings of guilt. In the usual sense, the psychopath has no conscience. He can commit any act with hardly a twinge of remorse.

William Cook illustrates the psychopath's guiltlessness through his dispassionate description of three murders: "The two little kids started crying, wanting water. I gave them some and she (their mother) drove a while—and I turned around and started shooting in the back seat and then turned back and shot her. She fell over against me and onto the floor."[27]

In the world of psychopathy, William Cook is no exception. After quenching the children's thirst, he shot them. It is this heartlessness of the psychopath which most strikingly sets him apart from the normal human being. The psychopath has the same desires as others; he dresses and talks in the same way. Yet a most important human element is missing: the sense of guilt.

Not only does this deficiency of guilt set the psychopath apart from the normal man, it also distinguishes him from other cultural deviants. Non-psychopathic criminals, for example, internalize an "underworld code of morality." For them, there can be "honor among thieves." If he breaches this code, the "normal" criminal feels remorse. The psychopath however, has few values—neither those of society nor those of a gang. Dreikurs ascribes this to a lack of (Adlerian) common sense: ". . . our thinking in common, our participation in general ideas, in values and morals accepted by the whole group to which we belong."[28] The Freudian labels the trait as an under-developed "super-ego." Both interpretations point to the psychopath's lack of inner controls. This guiltlessness is one of the central features of psychopathy.

Some psychopaths exhibit a deceptive shell of remorse, but the shell is empty. They talk of morality but inside they feel none, and their words do not hinder their actions. Borlov, for example, philosophized about his "tears" and the "lessons of the Bible":

> Life can at times be a problem—and a laugh. For me, there have been a great many laughs and the tears only made the laughter sweeter—a very little tragedy offsets and highlights the good. But all men, whatever their fate, could take a good lesson from the Bible—the fundamental truths of religion must guide us all.

Yet Borlov could steal and kill with conscienceless abandon. Sometimes his unconcern showed through the hyperbole:

> There have been times when they (society) have been frantic—but I, amid the riot I have created, remain calm and usually collected. I have always landed right side up—from the Village to the Hotel Pierre.

Hervey Cleckly, a neuro-psychiatrist, has noted this cleft between the psychopath's understanding of morality and his amoral actions. Cleckly believes that the psychopath suffers from "semantic dementia," a severe form of dissociation between rational faculties and emotional inner control.

At first glance, there seem to be areas in which the psychopath is detained by conscience. Weinberg asserts: ". . . he does internalize in mild or marked degree such elementary restraints as incest, murder of his parents, cannibalism, and dress."[29] Yet in several of these areas of "elementary restraint," the psychopath has no desires pressing him into deviance. The desire to be a cannibal, for example, is by no means innate; it is a learned cultural custom which psychopaths in our society do not acquire.[30]

Nevertheless, psychopaths—or at least some psychopaths—do adhere to some of the customs of our culture. They brush their teeth, they drive on the right side of the road, and they wear clothes. Why, then, do they not develop a mature conscience, feelings of guilt, or consistent life goals?

Gordon Allport has made a distinction between two types of learning, "opportunistic" and "propriate," which may explain this feature of psychopathy.[31] All human beings learn "opportunistically." That is, they absorb through continual conditioning a sub-system of habits and "tribal conformities" which help them to adjust to their world. Psychopaths, too, go through this brute learning process. As a result of punishment and repetition, they apparently develop the rudiments of social behavior. It is in another area, "propriate learning," where psychopaths seem deficient.

Most human beings pass beyond the "opportunistic" stage. They develop a "proprium,"[32] a style of life, an inward unity, which is uniquely theirs. Here the psychopath falters. For various reasons—particularly, as a later chapter shows, because of his warped childhood—the psychopath apparently does not learn "propriately." He fails to develop a consistent self-image, or long-range goals, or, most importantly, a mature conscience. He does not pass beyond the animally-conditioned stage of learning.

The vast majority of social scientists have found that the psychopath, whatever crime he may commit, feels little guilt. This consensus of opinion cuts across theoretical orientations. Sociologist Weinberg concluded: ". . . the psychopath can experience shame but slight guilt."[33] Psychologist Robert White says that the psychopath "does not accept blame for his conduct nor feel shame about it."[34] British psychiatrist Sir David Henderson, after long experience in the treatment of psychopaths, concluded: "They rarely if ever show any particle of remorse. . . ."[35] From the viewpoint of psychoanalysis, J. Thornton summarized this striking psychopathic trait: "The chief distinguishing feature in psychopathic personality is nothing but a conspicuously defective or else completely under-developed super-ego."[36]

Like the beast in Tennyson's "In Memoriam," the psychopath "takes his license in the field of time, unfettered by the sense of crime."

VI. The Psychopath Has a Warped Capacity For Love

The psychopath has often been characterized as a "lone wolf." He seems cold and compassionless. He treats people as he does objects: as means for his own pleasure. Though he may form fleeting attachments, these lack emotional depth and tenderness, and frequently end abruptly in aggressive explosions.

Joseph Borlov was such a lone wolf. He had worked with partners, but only for particular crimes. He had several homosexual "affairs," but none lasted. He had taken a wife, but soon deserted her. In prison, Borlov gained the reputation of cold unapproachability.

This warped capacity for love is so obvious that most social scientists regard it as the core of the psychopathic syndrome. A. H. Maslow connects lovelessness with the psychopath's aggression: "I have found it helpful in understanding psychopaths to assume that they have no love indentifications with other human beings and can therefore hurt them or even kill them casually, without hate, and without pleasure, precisely as they kill animals who have come to be pests."[37]

Maslow, along with some other writers, makes the questionable assumption that the psychopath is incapable of love. Certainly his shallow and volatile relations show a severely blunted capacity for affection, but there are indications that the capacity, however under-developed, still exists.

Recent therapeutic experiments show that the psychopath does seem to identify with his therapist.[38] A few therapists have reported the establishment of rapport with the psychopath. If the psychopath actually lacked the capacity for love, such rapport would be impossible.

Some observers maintain that the psychopath does not need love. "In the psychopathic personality," Maslow wrote, "the needs for being loved and loving have disappeared and, so far as we know today, this is a permanent loss. . . ."[39] Maslow bolsters his conclusion by citing animal research showing that certain basic instincts can be permanently extinguished through severe frustration. According to this theory, severe rejection has extinguished the psychopath's need for love.

There is, on the other hand, evidence showing that the normal child's need for love is not diminished by rejection. Instead, his striving for love actually seems to increase when the need is unsatisfied.[40]

Whether because he is incapable of forming them, or because his experience has not shown him how to form them, the psychopath wards off close attachments. Perhaps, as some psychoanalysts maintain, the psychopath fends off close relations because he fears being hurt. In any case, his lovelessness sets him apart as a uniquely isolated individual.

VII. THE PSYCHOPATHIC SYNDROME

Putting all the foregoing traits together, we see a picture of a dangerously maladjusted personality:

The psychopath is asocial. His conduct often brings him into conflict with society. The psychopath is driven by primitive desires and an exaggerated craving for excitement. In his self-centered search for pleasure, he ignores restrictions of his culture. The psychopath is highly impulsive. He is a man for whom the moment is a segment of time detached from all others. His actions are unplanned and guided by his whims. The psychopath is aggressive. He has learned few socialized ways of coping with frustration. The psychopath feels little, if any, guilt. He can commit the most appalling acts, yet view them without remorse. The psychopath has a warped capacity for love. His emotional relationships, when they exist, are meager, fleeting, and designed to satisfy his own desires. These last two traits, guiltlessness and lovelessness, conspicuously mark the psychopath as different from other men.

In this chapter we have discussed each of these traits separately. Although necessary for a clear analysis, such separation tends to create an artificial, unconnected picture of the psychopathic personality.[41] Another case study of a typical psychopath may serve to draw these disparate strands into a unified portrait of the psychopathic character structure.

In 1953 I spent many hours with Howard Dever, [42] discussing his life and future. Throughout our interviews he talked freely, controlling the situation with a glib stream of sophisticated conversation. His business suit, his conservative tie, and his clipped mustache proclaimed him as a successful young man "heading for the top." The setting of our talks—the Boston Psychopathic Hospital where Dever underwent observation before his trial for fraud, robbery, and impersonation—belied this promise.

Dever was born thirty-five years ago in a rural Vermont village. He hated the town and dismissed his childhood years with: "I got into trouble a lot, but they never put me in jail—not for a night." He disparagingly described his parents as "dull, stupid farmers." He pictured his father as a taciturn, forbidding person preoccupied with a country bank. His mother—"colorless, weak, lethargic"—didn't have the "gumption" to oppose his father's episodic rages. He added: "My parents really weren't so bad, though we were never close. They sent me money."

Although abnormally aggressive throughout childhood, Dever's official criminal record began during his high school years. His first job, when he was fourteen, ended abruptly as the town grocer caught Dever stealing $50 from the cash register. Despite his father's intervention, Dever's reputation as a "sneaky kid" grew until most townsmen ostracized him: "I became the scapegoat for everything that happened. Inspector Crooker would pick me up even if I wasn't doing a thing, just sitting on the curb."

At sixteen, Dever ran away to New York, where he led a life of larceny and dope peddling. His Manhattan career ended in 1941, when the Army drafted him. After three weeks in a Missouri boot camp, Dever went A.W.O.L. Military Police retrieved him in Vermont and sent him to a large Army prison at Vincennes. He hated the Indiana heat, his "crooked" companions, and the rough handling of Army police. "But I was lucky," he jovially admitted, "I was assigned a real Chicago lawyer for my court-martial. Boy, was he a slicker. He sent to Missouri for my company records, proved my name was still on the roll during my A.W.O.L., and got me released."

Immediately after his acquittal, Dever walked from the court room and again deserted. Retrieved, he repeated the pattern. His record shows fourteen absences without leave.

The Army shipped Dever overseas. In England, after more desertions, he was sent to the Oxford psychiatric hospital. From there too, Dever escaped. Each episode involved alcoholic orgies in London, fist fights, and bizarre aggressive behavior. The baffled doctors tried insulin shock, electric shock, and sodium amytal analysis. These brought temporary improvement.

Dever was released and (through a military bureaucrat's mistake) given a plush assignment as a clerk in "Torch" headquarters. During the day, he intermittently fulfilled his duties as a filing clerk. At night, he retired to his own London flat (in direct violation of Army regulations). During his evening wanderings through Piccadilly, Dever met an English girl whom he later married.

In one of the last Nazi bombing raids, an explosion smashed one of Dever's legs. Given a medical discharge, Dever headed back to America—leaving his wife on the day she delivered their first child. Several months later, his wife traced him to New York. She flew across the Atlantic and (after an emotional reunion) forgave him. Dever swore eternal faithfulness.

A week later he left for Florida without notifying his wife: "I met a guy in a bar and he said he wanted to pull some jobs in Florida; would I go along? I said 'O.K.' but I forgot to tell my wife. She didn't know where I was but she took me back when I came home. It wasn't that I didn't like her—we got along O.K. I just had other things to do."

Dever's asocial behavior continued with almost monotonous regularity. He entered the automobile black market for a while, then moved to the selling of fraudulent bonds. He committed many burglaries and topped his career in Boston with the impersonation of an F.B.I. officer and the forging of a $5,000 check.

At the time of our talks, Dever faced trial in Boston on a fifteen-count indictment. New Jersey, Florida, and New York awaited his extradition. Summarizing his life, Dever said: "Hell, I didn't need the money. I just would get an idea and I'd go out and do it. Maybe I hurt somebody doing it, but I've had fun."

A comparison of Howard Dever with William Cook or Joseph Borlov shows the basic similarity in their character structures. Their malformed personalities expressed themselves in superficially different ways: Borlov, in pathological lying;[43] Cook, in brutal aggression;[44] Dever, in sophisticated "confidence" crimes.[45] Beneath these symptoms, however, they possess the same basic traits: an inability to control aggressive impulsiveness, persistent anti-sociality, a craving for primitive satisfaction, and a striking lack of guilt with a seriously defective capacity for loving others.

"Borderline" cases who combine certain psychopathic traits with other mental aberrations can, of course, be found. Unless an individual exhibits the two critical psychopathic traits—guiltlessness and lovelessness—he should not be categorized as psychopathic.

NOTES

1. LINDNER, ROBERT. Psychopathy as a Psychological Problem. In P. L. Harriman: *Encyclopedia of Psychology.* New York Philosophical Library, 1948, p. 508.

2,3. KINBERG, OLOF. On the Concept of "Psychopathy" and the Treatment of So-called "Psychopaths." *Theoria,* 12:169-180, 1946.

4-10. SYMKAL, ANTHONY, AND THORNE, FREDERICK C. "Etiological Studies of Psychopathic Personality. *Journal of Clinical Psychology,* 7:299-316, 1951.

11. "Joseph Borlov" is a pseudonym. Since Borlov's future has not been settled as irrevocably as Cook's, it would be unfair to reveal his true name. The facts of his case are, however, presented without alteration. Quotations from him are taken from his letters.

12. In 1930, G. E. Partridge advocated the term "sociopath" in place of "psychopath." His definition of the "sociopath" emphasized social maladjustment to the exclusion of other criteria. See paper, Current Conceptions of Psychopathic Personality, *American Journal of Psychiatry,* 10:54, 1930. By lumping many varied types of criminals, sexual deviants, drunkards, and even unsavory politicians, into one mass, such thinking buries the very real differences among them.

Sir David Henderson, an influential British writer, unfortunately described psychopaths as those "who throughout their lives, or from comparatively early age, have exhibited disorders of conduct of an anti-social or asocial nature." See *Psychopathic States,* New York, W. W. Norton, 1939. Henderson qualified this definition and compiled an excellent study of the psychopath's character. Yet his words, used out of context, further muddled an already confused field.

13. S. B. Maughs, after intensive study of 5 psychopaths, concluded that their sexual desires were less pressing than the average man's. See A Concept of Psychopathy. *Journal of Criminal Psychopathology,* 3:329-356, 465-499, 1942.

14. FREYHAN, F. A. Psychopathology of Personality Functions in Psychopathic Personalities. *Psychiatric Quarterly,* 25:469, 1951.

15. Phyllis Greenacre traced the psychopath's primitive drive for pleasure to distortion in his "sense of reality" and his perception of cause and effect. She maintained that the psychopath does not comprehend what course will ultimately satisfy him—so he takes immediate, often disastrous, action to satisfy his desires. See Problems of Patient-Therapist Relationship in the Treatment of Psychopaths, *Handbook of Correctional Psychology,* edited by ROBERT LINDNER and ROBERT SELIGER. New York, Philosophical Library, 1947.

16. The psychopath, says Greenacre, views the world as "magical." The insecurity of his childhood and the volatile inconsistency of his parents gives

the psychopath a distorted view of reality. Because of the parents' changing whims, "What works for the child at one time, completely fails at another." Thus, the psychopath's life has been one of constant surprises.

17. CHORNYAK, J. Some Remarks on the Diagnosis of the Psychopathic Delinquent. *American Journal of Psychiatry,* 97:1331, 1941.

18. LINDNER, ROBERT. *Rebel Without a Cause—The Hypnoanalysis of a Criminal Psychopath.* New York, Grune & Stratton, 1944, p. 3.

19. BENDER, LAURETTA. Psychopathic Behavior Disorders in Children. *Handbook of Correctional Psychology, op. cit.* (note 15), p. 373.

20. Sir David Henderson believes that "inadequate" and "creative" psychopaths exist, as well as the typical aggressive psychopath. (*Op. cit.,* note 12.) The "inadequate" type, according to Henderson, is narcissistic, immoral, emotionally blunted; but he is passively, rather than aggressively abnormal. The "creative" type is eccentric, impulsive, often egocentric. It seems more likely that such people belong to other diagnostic categories (acting-out neurotic, neurotic, or "cultural deviant"). Henderson's evidence will be more fully analyzed in a later chapter.

21. See chapter on causation.

22. See J. DOLLARD, L. DOOB, N. E. MILLER, O. H. MOWRER, and R. R. SEARS: *Frustration and Aggression.* New Haven, Yale University Press, 1939.

23. See GORDON ALLPORT: *The Nature of Prejudice.* Cambridge, Addison-Wesley, 1954, chap. 22. A criticism of the concept of an instinctive aggressive drive.

A recent study indicates that the psychopath's aggressive need is no more intense than that of the average delinquent. See JULES D. HOLZBERG, and FRED HAHN: The Picture-Frustration Technique as a Measure of Hostility and Guilt Reactions in Adolescent Psychopaths. *American Journal of Orthopsychiatry* 22:776-797, 1952.

24. LINDNER, ROBERT. Psychopathic Personality and the Concept of Homeostasis. *Journal of Clinical Psychopathology and Psychotherapy,* 6:511, 1945.

25. Bender, *op. cit.* (note 19), p. 363.

26. WEINBERG, KIRSON S. *Society and Personality Disorders.* New York, Prentice-Hall, 1952, p. 269.

27. Smykal and Thorne, *op. cit.* (note 4), p. 311.

28. Quoted in MILTON GURVITZ: Developments in the Concepts of Psychopathic Personality. *British Journal of Delinquency,* 2:96, 1951.

29. Weinberg, *op. cit.* (note 26), p. 268.

30. The psychopath may not have the incestual desire which many psychoanalysts believe to be universal. See Freyhan (*op. cit.,* note 14) for evidence that the psychopath feels unconcern rather than hatred for his parents. For a conflicting opinion (i.e., that the psychopath does hate his parents), see D. STAFFORD-CLARK, DESMOND BOND, and J. W. L. DOUST: The Psychopath in Prison: a Preliminary Report of a Cooperative Research. *British Journal of Delinquency,* 2:117-129, 1951.

31. For a complete discussion of this complex problem of social learning,

see G. W. ALLPORT: *Becoming: Basic Considerations for a Psychology of Personality.* New Haven, Yale University Press, 1955.

32. Gordon Allport depicts the "proprium" as consisting of a variety of functions and properties: a bodily sense, self-identity, "ego-enhancement" (self-seeking), "ego-extension" (the feeling that certain objects and loved ones belong to the person), rationality, a self-image, "propriate" (ego-involved) striving, and the "knowing faculty" (that part of the self which judges and observes the other functions). In at least three of these areas—consistent self-image, propriate motivation, and the "knowing faculty"—the psychopath seems pathologically deficient.

33. Weinberg, *op. cit.* (note 26), p. 266.

34. WHITE, ROBERT. *The Abnormal Personality.* New York, Ronald Press, 1948, p. 403.

35. Henderson, *op. cit.* (note 12), p. 67.

36. THORNTON, NATHANIEL. The Relation Between Crime and Psychopathic Personality. *Journal of Criminal Law, Criminology, and Police Science,* 42, 1951.

37. MASLOW, A. H. *Motivation and Personality.* New York, Harper, 1954, p. 173.

38. Research in this area is reviewed in a later chapter.

39. Maslow, *op. cit.* (note 37), p. 131.

40. Recent research by the Harvard Laboratory of Human Development indicates that rejection leads to more "dependent" behavior, a greater striving for love. See R. SEARS, E. MACCOBY, and H. LEVIN: *Patterns in Child Rearing.* Evanston; Row, Peterson, 1956.

41. In 1952, the American Psychiatric Association replaced the term "psychopathic" with "sociopathic." We have continued to use the label "psychopathic personality" because its use in the last seventy-five years has made it more familiar.

42. A pseudonym.

43. Pathological lying, while often associated with the disorder, is not a universal trait of the psychopath. Persistent lying can come from causes other than psychopathy.

44. Cook's aggression was more brutal than that of most psychopaths. But no psychopath controls his aggression for any extended period of time. Although the psychopath may temporarily contain aggression for a particular objective, he will explode later under different circumstances.

45. Some psychopaths appear charming. This superficial social poise is by no means a necessary correlate of the disorder. Even those psychopaths who do have a pleasant exterior cannot long hide their inner aggressiveness or guiltlessness, nor can they form deeper relations than can other psychopaths.

2

From Moral Insanity to Psychopathy

[The concept] is an attempt to return to belief in demon possession . . .

J. ORDRONAUX, 1873

Psychopathy has now emerged as the most important of the great transitional groups of mental disorders.

EDITORS, British Journal of Delinquency, 1951

"Enraged at a woman who had used offensive language to him, he precipitated her into a well."[1] With these words, a French doctor of the early 1800's introduced an unusual case which had long puzzled him. His patient, the son of a "weak and indulgent mother," came from a powerful noble family. As a child, he had been given everything he wanted; as an adult he had inherited a fertile estate. Although highly privileged, the patient could never satisfy his desires. Obstacles aroused terrible fury: when a dog got in his way, he kicked it to death; when his horse jerked at the reins, he whipped it unmercifully. The patient's mania had worsened until, in a fit of exasperation, he had "precipitated" a peasant woman into a well.

Pinel, the psychiatrist, took charge of the patient when he arrived at the famous Bicetre. Since none of the usual psychiatric classifications seemed to describe the symptoms, Pinel concluded that this patient suffered from "manie sans délire."

With Pinel's description and diagnosis, the concept of psychopathy began. Pinel's patient (who probably was not a true psychopath) initiated a flury of psychiatric speculation. Psychiatrists throughout Europe had often encountered such individuals, but Pinel was the first to build a conceptual scheme of the disease. Pinel's "manie sans délire" was more inclusive than the modern concept of psychopathy, for it mixed together a welter of very different disorders—paranoia, the "epileptoid personality," neurotic hysteria—as well as some cases of true psychopathy.[2]

Confused as it was, Pinel's article shed new light on previously unexplained phenomenon. Other psychiatrists, interested in Pinel's observations, reported their experiences with such personalities. In England, Dr. J. C. Pritchard coined the phrase "moral insanity" to describe those in whom: ". . . . the moral and active principles of the mind are strongly perverted or depraved; the power of self-government is lost or greatly impaired and the individual is found to be incapable, not of talking or reasoning upon any subject proposed to him, but of conducting himself with decency and propriety in the business of life."[3] Although Pritchard's 1835 definition came closer to the modern picture of psychopathy, he too included such disorders as manic-depressive psychosis under the label.[4]

In 1878, Gouster presented the first clinical picture of the symptoms found in "moral insanity": long-standing "moral perversion"; a delight in mischief, excitement, and passion; "enfeebled judgment"; and certain abnormal physical proportions.[5]

Gouster's early description of the psychopath drew heavily from the more general work of Cesare Lombroso, an Italian doctor. One of Lombroso's catagories, the "born criminal," strikingly resembles the modern concept of the psychopath. Lombroso described the "born criminal" as a "moral imbecile": guiltless, highly aggressive, boastful, impulsive, peculiarly insensitive to social criticism and physical pain. He believed that "born criminals" could be identified by physical stigmata. He depicted such criminals as atavistic throwbacks to a more primitive stage in human evolution. Although much in his well known work—particularly his causative theories—has been disproved, his study has had profound influence.

In the 1870's the concept of "moral insanity" had gained wide popularity and general acceptance within the medical world. By maintaining that a specific faculty, the moral sense, had become diseased, it seemed to explain the disturbed behavior of certain highly aggressive patients.

Though medicine accepted the new concept, religion and law rejected it with horror. "Moral insanity," lawyers felt, would destroy the basis for criminal responsibility. Ministers detected a planned attempt to subvert free will and turn the world back to "paganism and license."

As early as 1812, the American psychiatrist Benjamin Rush outlined the problem in this philosophic battle, a battle involving issues beyond the scope of psychopathy alone. After treating cases which we would today call psychopathic, Rush admitted: "How far the persons whose diseases have been mentioned should be considered as responsible to human or divine laws for their actions, and where the line should be drawn that divides free agency from necessity, and vice from disease, I am unable to determine."[6]

Rush's quandary was one which we face today, but the civic leaders of his century had a ready answer: "The only disease to which the moral nature is subject," said Professor Ordronaux, *"is sin."*[7] Ordronaux and other defenders of the faith saw a sinister motive behind the idea of moral insanity. Ordronaux believed the concept was "an attempt to return to belief in demon possession of the Middle Ages and a reversion to superstition."[8] A Dr. Elwell expressed common opinion: The idea was fostered by a "class of modern German pagans, who are trying with what help they can get in America to break down all the safeguards of our Christian civilization, by destroying, if possible, all grounds for human responsibility."[9]

The dispute reached its climax in the highly publicized trial of President Garfield's assassin. Guiteau, the murderer, went before the courts in 1881. His defense lawyers called in several psychiatrists who diagnosed Guiteau as morally insane—therefore, not responsible for his acts. The prosecution produced other psychiatrists who disagreed and testified that Guiteau, since he "knew the difference between right and wrong," should be executed. Guiteau lost his case. The defenders of righteousness were jubilant and criminal responsibility had been temporarily upheld. The trial, of course, settled nothing concerning the issue of moral responsibility, which is still very much alive today.

Throughout the nineteenth century, investigation into causes and treatment of psychopathy, as well as other mental disorders, was buried in speculative dispute. Those few who thought about the problem concerned themselves with theoretical, almost theological questions like: "Can the moral sense be diseased and the intellectual faculty remain unimpaired?"

Yet the nineteenth century did witness the first faltering attempts to characterize this highly disturbing personality. Because of loose classification and lack of research, psychiatric pioneers accomplished little, but they stimulated an intellectual movement which, by the early nineteen hundreds, had begun to build a store of observational data.

The turn of the century witnessed an upsurge of research and an important shift of interest. Scientists abandoned theoretical conflicts, turning to observation of the psychopath himself. Because of its unpleasant connotation, the term "moral insanity" was replaced by "psychopathic inferiority," a label invented by Koch in 1888. Koch implied that the disorder was caused by a constitutional predisposition. In time, "constitutional psychopathy" gained wide use.

Careful observers set about refining the concept and giving it a specific meaning. Meyer, in 1912, excluded neurotics from the category.[10] Mercier, in 1913, won official recognition (through the British Mental Deficiency Act) that conduct disorders were one particular variety of insanity.[11] And Birnbaum, in 1914, pointed out that criminal behavior *per se* was not psychopathy, nor did psychopaths necessarily exhibit intellectual defects.[12]

By the end of the first World War psychiatrists had reached a consensus that psychopathy was a special disorder manifested in "strong vicious or criminal propensities on which punishment has had little or no deterrent effect."[13] Although they agreed on this definition (which today would be rejected as too general), they could not agree on the causes of the disorder. Some (like Mercier) emphasized intellectual deficiency; others (like Birnbaum) pointed to "pathological emotionality"; while still others (like Meyer) continued to postulate a constitutional inferiority.

In America, the first person to initiate an empirical study of the psychopath was Bernard Glueck, a psychiatrist at Sing Sing Prison. Glueck posited that the criminal act, in every instance, is the resultant of the interaction between a particularly constituted personality and a particular environment.[14] In 1918, he investigated 608 Sing Sing convicts, 18.9 per cent of whom were psychopaths. Glueck found that the psychopaths had the greatest recidivism, the highest proportion of drunkenness and drug addiction, and the earliest onset of antisocial behavior.

Stimulated by Glueck's study, other scientists examined the psychopath himself. On both sides of the Atlantic, the psychological make-up of the psychopath became an important issue. Cyril Burt in Eng-

land, Augusta Scott and Alice Johnson in America studied the motives and character of the psychopath. Of these early studies, John
Visher's work in 1922 has best withstood the test of time. Visher
selected fifty cases of psychopathic personality from a veterans' hospital and subjected them to intensive psychological examination. He
found that normal hospital treatment had no effect on the men and
that many had neurotic parents. Most importantly, Visher presented
an almost modern picture of the psychopath's character traits: extreme impulsivity, lack of concentration, marked egotism, and abnormal projection. The most critical disability of the patients centered
around a guiltless, uninhibited social nihilism.

In the 1930's two new intellectual currents redirected the study
of psychopathy. One movement had begun with Bolsi's discovery,
in 1924, that encephalitis can result in psychopathic symptoms. Bio-
logically-oriented psychiatrists hailed Bolsi's findings as proof that
organic malfunctions wtihin the brain accounted for the psychopath's
quirks. Accepting this premise, many medical men turned from the
study of the psychopath's behavior and personality to a study of his
brain. Some of this work uncovered information about the psychopath's neurology which has proved highly useful; but, by assuming
that the cause of psychopathy had been discovered, this biological approach hindered the exploration of other possibilities.

The 1930's also marked the spread of the psychoanalytic school.
Americans and Europeans, oriented toward Freudian, Adlerian, or
Jungian interpretations, felt that the neurological school ignored many
facets of the psychopath's character. They proceeded to elaborate
their own theories. Coriat depicted the psychopath as a perennial
child, a basically immature person who had never resolved the
Oedipus conflict.[15] Wittels conceptualized the psychopath as "stuck"
at the phallic stage of development.[16] Partridge pushed the psychopath's original maladjustment back even further into childhood; he
described the disorder as a permanently fixated concentration on oral
needs.[17]

Of all the psychoanalysts who dealt with the issue, Franz Alexander
has had the greatest influence. In 1930, his paper on the "neurotic
character" was interpreted by many as relegating psychopathy to a
subordinate category, as one among many neuroses.[18] He described
neurotic characters as 'living out their impulses," as "solving intense
inner conflict" by "acting out," and as seeking gratification on an

"alloplastic" plane (i.e., discharging instinctual tension by changing the environment). For Alexander, the "neurotic character" was a regressed, self-injuring person, dominated by father-hatred and typified by an underdeveloped ego.

Today, most social scientists believe that Alexander's theory depicts the personality of the acting-out neurotic rather than the true psychopath. Alexander's emphasis on inner tension and conflict as dominating motives fails to jibe with the modern acceptance of the psychopath as uncontrolled by conscience, free of anxiety, and driven by a craving for primitive pleasure.

In the 1930's, the neurologists contributed knowledge of the psychopath's brain,[19] and the psychoanalysts developed explanatory hypotheses. Meanwhile, another group, the "classifiers," confused the issues.

German psychiatry had long delighted in systematized classification. In 1888 Kraepelin had proposed a "typology" of psychopathy and had divided the disorder into seven sub-types: the excitable, the unstable, the impulsive, the eccentric, the liars and swindlers, the antisocial, and the quarrelsome. Obviously, Kraepelin brought together an uncongenial variety of mental disorders and social deviance. In the context of the nineteenth century, with psychology in its youth, such a mixture was understandable.

But in the 1930's, after years of careful definition and research, little excuse could be made for systems which lumped a bewildering variety of hysterics, compulsives, sex deviants, and borderline psychotics under the title of "psychopathic personality."

Eugene Kahn's book, written in 1931, defined such a potpourri: "By psychopathic personalities we understand those personalities which are characterized by quantitive peculiarities in the impulse, temperament, or character strata."[20] Based on this definition (or rather, lack of definition), Kahn launched into a "clinico-descriptive" classification of "psychopaths." Among them, he included the "nervous," the "anxious," the "sensitive," the "hyperthymic." Only one of his many types, the "cold autists," seems to approximate the modern definition of psychopathy: "They suffer from moral feeble-mindedness. . . . They know as a rule what right and wrong is but they do not feel it."[21]

As causative factors, Kahn postulated a mysterious "anlagen" which corresponded to various "leptosomatic body builds." The very obscurity of the book impressed many. It passed through several editions and exercised a wide influence in psychiatry.

Some writers revolted against the confusion by rejecting the entire concept. "The term psychopathic personality, as commonly understood, is useless in psychiàtric research," wrote one psychiatrist in 1944. He continued: "It does not refer to a specific behavioral entity. It serves as a scrap-basket to which is relegated a group of otherwise unclassified personality disorders and problems."[22]

Other scientists—Henderson, Cleckly, Karpman, Lindner—argued that psychopathy was a distinct disorder. For them, the problem was redoing the job that had been started in the early 1900's: investigating, clarifying, and specifically defining psychopathy.

Each attacked the problem in his own way: Henderson, by classifying the clinical symptoms of the psychopath; Cleckly, by gathering case studies; Karpman, by investigating the thought-processes and dreams of the psychopath; and Lindner, by analyzing patients under hypnosis. All four developed similar conceptualizations of the disease.

In 1939 Sir David Henderson's book, *Psychopathic States,* was published in England and in America. Henderson's discussion of the "aggressive psychopath" had profound influence, particularly in Britain. He clarified the distinction between the "epileptoid personality" and the psychopath. He analyzed the connection between the psychopath's motives and the dangerous manifestations of the disorder: crime, alcoholism, and drug addiction. And he noted the close connection between the psychopath's asociality and his lack of guilt.

Certain sections of the book created wide controversy and brought sharp criticism. He linked suicide with psychopathy, overlooking the psychopath's lack of depressive tendencies. He maintained that a psychopathic character underlay some psychoses, ignoring contradictions between the psychopathic and psychotic disorders. He postulated an "inadequate" type of psychopath, apparently confusing psychopathy with certain types of neuroses.[23]

Another of Henderson's theories, his association of genius and psychopathy, provoked further dispute. Henderson felt that a brilliant but erratic person, like Lawrence of Arabia, should be considered a "creative psychopath." He pointed to Lawrence's impulsivity, his erratic mood changes, and his taste for aggressive action as signs of psychopathy. Henderson overlooked Lawrence's undermining shyness, his hatred for the horrors of war, and most importantly his pervading guilt and desire for expiation: "The craving to be famous, and the horror of being known to like being known [disturbed me]; I was standing court-martial on myself."[24]

Lawrence may have been a neurotic or a saint, or both, but he does not seem to have been a true psychopath.[25] A towering intelligence can be associated with psychopathy, but the achievements which we usually consider as the signs of genius seem incompatible with the extreme impulsivity, aggression, and guiltlessness of the psychopath.

Henderson tended to overextend the concept; Hervey Cleckly, an American psychiatrist, tried to limit it. His book, *The Mask of Sanity*,[26] written in 1941, produced the most complete clinical description of the decade. Cleckly, too, emphasized the personality traits of guiltlessness, incapacity for "object love," emotional shallowness, egocentricity, purposelessness, and impulsivity. In addition, he introduced some new observations on psychopathic characteristics. He perceived the charm with which psychopaths sometimes conceal their asociality; he recognized the psychopath's characteristic inability to learn from experience; and he pointed out the psychopath's tendency to seek external control, sometimes punishment, for his behavior. Cleckly asserted that psychopaths could be found not only in prisons but also in society's most respected positions: as doctors, lawyers, politicians, and even as psychiatrists.

Because "psychopathy" had been so widely misused, Cleckly suggested replacing the term with "semantic dementia" (i.e., a disorder characterized by a split between word and action). He pointed out that psychopaths can understand the strictures of society and parrot them with skill, but they dissociate what they say from what they do.

The label "semantic dementia" had merit, yet it stressed one symptom of the disorder, ignoring other essential elements: undeveloped conscience, aggressiveness, and inability to identify with others. Because most social scientists could not agree that "semantic dementia" was the fundamental symptom (and because "psychopathy" had been used for many years), Cleckly's new concept never gained wide popularity.

Like Cleckly and Henderson, Benjamin Karpman, chief psychotherapist of St. Elizabeth's Hospital, devoted himself to the clarification of the psychopath's personality structure. Karpman described the same general picture, but added material derived from intensive analyses of the psychopath's dreams, his thought processes, and his capricious character. In a series of articles published throughout the third and fourth decades of this century, Karpman drew upon his clinical experience for fascinating case studies of the psychopath under treatment.

In 1941 Karpman attempted to draw a distinction between two varieties of psychopathy: "idiopathic" and "symptomatic." With the "idiopathic" psychopath, "psychopathic behavior is the central feature . . . and the core of his personality . . . it is found impossible to elicit anything suggestive of psychogenesis."[27] With the "symptomatic" psychopath, psychogenic causes could easily be discovered. In its original form, Karpman's division could have had important practical consequences: it could have separated those for whom there was a known treatment (symptomatic) from those for whom no treatment had been discovered (idiopathic).

In later articles, Karpman postulated that "symptomatic" cases were neurotics "parading" as psychopaths, and that "true" psychopathy never resulted from emotional causes.[28] True psychopathy, according to Karpman, always came from an unmeasurable "constitutional acquisitiveness and aggression."[29]

Karpman's exclusion of psychogenic causes from psychopathy seemed to many social scientists an unjustifiable obstacle to further analysis of both causes and treatment. Hervey Cleckly, among others, attacked Karpman's classification: "I cannot, however, follow him in the assumption that, when he or any other investigator does not succeed in finding basic conflict and a dynamic pattern behind pathologic behavior, such factors can be regarded as nonexistent."[30]

Robert Lindner, an American psychoanalyst, observed the same character structure in the patients whom he treated. Lindner's experiments immeasurably broadened knowledge of the psychopath's physiology, childhood, and personality.

While some scientists worked with the definition and theory of psychopathy, others laboriously attacked specific segments of the problem. Throughout the depression, research on causation flourished, and numerous workers produced evidence concerning the psychopath's brain waves, the functions of his cortex, his childhood experiences, the characterists of his family, and the effects of early social isolation upon his personality.

With the coming of the second World War and the military draft, managing the psychopath assumed new dimensions. In the armed forces his behavior soon brought the psychopath to the attention of the Medical Corps, the correctional services, and even the General Staff. Numerous articles appeared dealing with the problems of segregation, diagnosis, and treatment.

By the end of the war, social science had come to realize the importance and the danger of the psychopath. The work of Karpman, Henderson, Cleckly, and Lindner laid foundations for the growing research into causation and treatment. At long last the dispute about whether the psychopath really existed had come to rest.

Although a few demurred, most observers felt that the psychopath differed so markedly from the normal criminal, the neurotic, or the psychotic that he must be thought of as having a separate disorder. From those who treated the psychopath came the stoutest defense of the concept. The American psychiatrist Chornyak commented: "Those of us who work in psychiatric clinics and in courts . . . continuously have to deal with this type of abnormal personality."[31] And an English psychiatrist, E. T. O. Slater, said in 1946: "If we were to drop the term altogether, we should be obliged to invent an equivalent or to overlook a whole series of clinically very important phenomenon."[32]

By 1951, the editors of the influential *British Journal of Delinquency* could, without fear of criticism, devote an entire issue to psychopathy and announce: ". . . Psychopathy has now emerged as the most important of the great transitional (borderline) groups of mental disorders . . . it occupies a fixed intermediate position in a hierarchy of developmental disorders. . . ."[33]

At mid-century, social science underwent another shift of emphasis. The problem of definition seemed close to solution, and the issues of causation had been clarified by research; but the treatment of the psychopath remained an obscure field.

Scientists coming from all branches of psychology, psychiatry, and sociology increasingly focused their attention on treatment. Physicians experimented with barbiturates, dilantin sodium, shock therapy, and lobotomy. Social workers called on the techniques of group therapy and psycho-drama. A handful of psychoanalysts hesitatingly applied their methods, and psychologists attempted therapy ranging from informal counseling to hypnoanalysis.

Significant findings came from those who worked with maladjusted children. Few of the pioneers in child therapy concerned themselves exclusively with the psychopathic child. Yet, by the 1950's, observers felt that the work of Aichhorn, Bettleheim, Redl, and Papanek offered considerable hope for the psychopathic child.[34]

Along with the greater emphasis on treatment, the early 1950's marked the emergence of another significant trend: a linking of psychopathy with politics. Nazi concentration camps had stirred the world's interest both in those who directed the horrors and in those who committed them. Although the central motive of most of the storm troopers (e.g., Colonel Hoess) seemed to be fanatical obedience, some psychologists discerned a psychopathic tone in some of the Nazis.

G. M. Gilbert, chief psychologist of the Nuremberg trials, described Herman Goering as an "amiable psychopath." Gilbert pointed to Goering's brutal, loveless childhood as typical of the psychopath's background. Goering's father was a stern Prussian official who valued military discipline above all else. Goering's earliest memory was of "bashing his mother in the face with both fists when she came to embrace him after a prolonged absence. . . ."[35]

As a child, Goering loved excitement, the glaring splash of military uniforms, and early exhibited his taste for sadistic brutality. Uncontrolled behavior and vicious attacks on his sisters led his parents to shift Goering from school to school. His mother predicted: "Herman will either be a great man or a great criminal!"[36]

In his youth, Goering's drive for glory, his brutality, his emotional impulsiveness, and his aggressiveness "found its most desirable expression in the military prerogatives of his culture."[37] Goering's recklessness earned him the distinction of being one of Germany's top air aces in World War I, but his uncontrolled greed brought him into illegal wartime adventures. He took illicit leaves, accepted bribes, and established a clandestine army supply company.

After the war, he married a rich Swedish countess. Despite his newly found wealth, Goering missed the excitement of war. Attracted by Hitler's militancy, Goering was swept into the Nazi party. He moved from honor to honor as president of the Reichstag, head of Nazi industry, and chief of the Luftwaffe. His objective was expressed in a Reichstag speech:. "I am not here to exercise justice, but to wipe out and exterminate!"[38]

Goering's spectacular rise to power provided him with the means of satisfying his craving for pleasure. He turned to drug addiction, mistresses, and "Roman" orgies. As Germany collapsed, Goering pranced through his palace, Karinhall, dressed in a toga, with painted fingernails and lips.

With the fall of Germany, Goering, along with the other Nazi leaders, went on trial for his part in the war crimes. Gilbert, who came to know Goering during the trial, noticed a singular lack of guilt. After seeing a documentary film of mutilated bodies from a concentration camp, for example, Goering commented only: "It was such a good afternoon, too, until they showed that film—They were reading my telephone conversations on the Austrian matter and everybody was laughing with me—and then they showed that awful film, and it just spoiled everything."[39]

Before ending his life with poison, Goering left this message for the West: "You Americans are making a stupid mistake with your talk of democracy and morality. . . . Don't think that Germans have become more Christian and less nationalistic all of a sudden . . . you can take your morality and your repentance and your democracy and stick it up!"[40]

Many features of Goering's personality fit the psychopathic syndrome: his asociality, his impulsive craving for pleasure, and his guiltlessness; but other traits seem atypical (e.g., his ability to carry out the long range plans necessary in administrative tasks). Yet, Herman Goering illustrates a frightening possibility: with luck, with the right social and political conditions, a psychopath could gain control over a nation's destiny. Robert Lindner has soberly warned: "The psychopath is not only a criminal, he is the embryonic storm trooper."[41]

Other investigators in the early 1950's traced a predilection of criminals for a political ideology centered around ethnocentrism, admiration of power, authoritarianism, and conservatism. The writers of *The Authoritarian Personality* found that convicts were generally more anti-democratic than any other segment of the population.[42] Naturally, we do not equate criminality with psychopathy, but it seems probable that the psychopath's aggression, his lack of respect for others, and his intermittent need for outside control of his behavior would predispose him to an authoritarian ideology. A recent comparison of delinquents with normal children showed that this anti-democratic trend appears even in childhood.[43]

Reviewing the history of "psychopathy" shows that a small group of investigators, with only a few setbacks, have built an impressive ladder of verified knowledge:

In the early 1800's, Pinel, Pritchard, and Lombroso first described and labeled the "morally insane."

In 1878, Gouster presented the first complete delineation of the psychopath's symptoms.

In the early 1900's, Meyer, Birnbaum, and others excluded irrelevant disorders from the concept.

In 1918, Glueck studied the behavior and characteristics of the psychopath in prison.

In the 1920's and 1930's, numerous scientists empirically attacked the problem of causation.

In the 1940's and the 1950's, many investigators experimented with the full-scale studies of the psychopath's psychology and introduced the modern concept of the disorder.

In the 1940's and the 1950's, many investigators experimented with the treatment of the psychopath and connected his disorder with other social and political problems.

By mid-century, no investigator of the psychopathic personality had to begin entirely anew; he could draw upon the accumulated theories and research of 150 years. Perhaps the most important achievement of these investigations has been the establishment of psychopathy as an independent personality syndrome. As the editors of the *British Journal of Delinquency* commented in 1951: "It is no longer possible to maintain without fear of brisk contradiction that the concept of psychopathy is a psychiatric fiction covering inadequacies in clinical classification. . . ."

Yet this research has not solved the problem of causation. The British editors continued: ". . . fifty years of sporadic investigation of the subject have resulted in little more than a profusion of contending generalizations . . . our understanding of psychopathy is still rudimentary and our researches wretchedly inadequate."[44] The disparate strands of evidence need to be drawn into a unified whole.

Moreover, these years of research have failed to cope with the psychopathic disorder. Therapy awaits further scientific investigation.

The structure of the psychopath's personality needs deeper study. There is some, but not enough, knowledge of what goes on inside the psychopath's mind, how he differs from other deviants, and how he can be correctly diagnosed.

NOTES

1,2. KAVKA, JEROME. Pinel's Conception of the Psychopathic state: an Historical Critique, *Bulletin of the History of Medicine.* 23:461-468, 1949.

3. Quoted in DAVID HENDERSON: *Psychopathic States.* New York, W. W. Norton, 1939, p. 11.

4. PRITCHARD, JAMES C. *A Treatise on Insanity.* Philadelphia; Haswell, Barrington and Haswell, 1835.

5. GOUSTER, MONTZ. Moral Insanity. *Revue Des Sciences Medical* (abstracted in *Journal of Nervous and Mental Disease*, 5:181-182, 1878).

6. Quoted in Henderson, *op. cit.* (note 3), p. 13.

7. ORDRONAUX, JOHN. Moral Insanity. *American Journal of Insanity*, 29:p. 313, 1873.

8,9. Quoted in S. B. MAUGHS: A Concept of Psychopathy: Historical Development. *Journal of Criminal Psychopathology*, 2:345, 1941.

10. GURVITZ, MILTON. Developments in the Concepts of Psychopathic Personality. *British Journal of Delinquency*, 2:88-102, 1951.

11. Maughs, *op. cit.* (note 8).

12. BIRNBAUM, KARL. The Psychopathic Criminal. *Journal of Nervous and Mental Disease*, 2:543-553, 1917.

13. This is the description settled upon in the British Mental Deficiency Act of 1913.

14. See also BERNARD GLUECK, A Study of 608 Admissions to Sing Sing Prison. *Mental Hygiene*, Vol. II, 1918, 85-151.

15. Maughs, *op. cit.* (note 8).

16. WITTELS, F. The Criminal Psychopath in the Psychoanalytic System. *Psychoanalytic Review*, 24:276-291, 1937.

17. Maughs, *op cit.* (note 8).

18. ALEXANDER, FRANZ. The Neurotic Character. *International Journal of Psychoanalysis*, 11:292-313, 1930.

19. See chapter on Causation.

20. KAHN, EUGENE. *Psychopathic Personalities.* New Haven, Yale University Press, 1931, p. 62.

21. *Ibid.,* p. 348.

22. PREU. The Concept of Psychopathic Personality. In J. M. HUNT: *Personality and the Behavior Disorders,* Vol. II, Ronald Press, 1944, p. 933.

23. See chapter on diagnosis.

24. Henderson, *op. cit.* (note 3), p. 99.

25. Although RICHARD ALDINGTON, in *Lawrence of Arabia, A Biographical Enquiry* (London, Collins, 1955) emphasizes Lawrence's negative qualities, the biography gives little evidence of psychopathy.

26. CLECKLY, HERVEY. *The Mask of Sanity.* St. Louis, C. V. Mosley, 1941.

27. KARPMAN, B. On the Need of Separating Psychopathy into Two Distinct Clinical Types: the Symptomatic and the Idiopathic. *Journal of Criminal Psychopathology*, 3:137, 1941.

28. CURRAN, D. AND MALLINSON, P. Psychopathic Personality. *Journal of Mental Science*, 90:266-286, 1944.

29. KARPMAN, B. Seven Psychopaths: a Correlative, Non-Statistical Study of Predatory Crime. *Journal of Clinical Psychopathology and Psychotherapy*, 6:299, 1944.

30. Quoted in A. CRUVANT, and LEON YOCHELSON: The Psychiatrist and the Psychotic Psychopath; a Study in Interpersonal Relations, *American Journal of Psychiatry*, 106:594-498, 1950.

31. CHORNYAK, J. Some Remarks on the Diagnosis of the Psychopathic Delinquent. *American Journal of Psychiatry,* 97:1327, 1941.

32. SLATER, E. T. O. Psychopathic Personality as a Genetical Concept. *Journal of Mental Science,* 94:277, 1948.

33. Editors, *British Journal of Delinquency,* 2:77, 1951.

34. See chapters on treatment.

35. GILBERT, G. M. Herman Goering: Amiable Psychopath. *Journal of Abnormal and Social Psychology,* 43:211, 1948.

36. *Ibid.,* p. 213.

37. *Ibid.,* pp. 213-214.

38. *Ibid.,* p. 218.

39. *Ibid.,* p. 226.

40. *Ibid.,* p. 228.

41. LINDNER, ROBERT. *Rebel Without a Cause.* New York, Grune & Stratton, 1944.

42. ADORNO, T. W., and others. *The Authoritarian Personality.* New York, Harper, 1950.

43. McCORD, WILLIAM, AND McCORD, JOAN. Authoritarianism and Prejudice Among Delinquents. (Unpublished paper, 1953.)

44. Editorial, *British Journal of Delinquency, op. cit.* (note 33), p. 78.

3

The Problem of Diagnosis

Everyone is forced into a pattern . . .
JOSEF BORLOV, San Quentin
convict.

THE CONCEPT OF psychopathy has been greatly clarified during the past one hundred years. Unfortunately, however, the studies seldom influenced workers in the field: the police court judges, the wardens, the prison psychologists. Each of these workers used his own definition of the disorder, so the practical task of uniform diagnosis remained.

Conflicting published reports illustrate this diagnostic dilemma. At one Illinois state prison, 98 per cent of the inmates were labeled "psychopathic." At another midwestern prison, psychiatrists diagnosed only 5 per cent as "psychopathic."[1] The diagnosis of sex-offenders offers another example of this confusion: 52 per cent at New York's Bellevue Hospital were called "psychopathic," but only 15 per cent who appeared before the New York's courts' psychiatric clinic were so titled.[2]

Obviously these institutions meant different things when they spoke of psychopathy. Much of the confusion arises from viewing all antisocial behavior as psychopathic. Many investigators, particularly those who make unusually high estimates of psychopathy, seem to use antisocial behavior as their only diagnostic criterion.

Deviant behavior alone is, of course, an inadequate standard. It obscures the critical distinction between the psychopath and other deviants, complicates the study of causation, and hinders experimentation in therapy. Both the study and the treatment of psychopathy require rigid classification.

Some contemporary psychiatrists have proposed that diagnosis of psychopathy be based entirely on causative factors. Unfortunately, those who advocate such a criterion cannot agree about its causes.

35

Karpman, for example, maintains that the psychopathic label should be applied only when the individual's disorder has "idiopathic" (presumably constitutional) causes. "In the true psychopath," he wrote, "we have instinctive antisocial behavior which is without any motive except that associated with constitutional acquisitiveness and aggression."[3] Karpman never defines "constitutional acquisitiveness," nor does he show how it differs from those drives which he would term "neurotic" (i.e., "the search for security, the satisfaction of the ego, or the struggle for power").[4]

Ralph Rabinovitch, another psychiatrist, apparently agrees with Karpman that the diagnosis of psychopathy should be based on causation. He does not agree, however, that psychopathy is caused by a constitutional predisposition. Just as stoutly as Karpman would limit psychopathy to constitutional causes, Rabinovitch would confine it to psychogenic causes. In direct contrast to Karpman, Rabinovitch believes that the "definitely known cause" of the disorder is childhood emotional deprivation.[5]

These two opposing positions present the inadequacy of a causative standard for diagnosis. Despite diagnostic confusion, most researchers agree upon the existence of a distinct psychopathic syndrome. Furthermore, recent studies have shown that psychological tools can successfully distinguish the psychopath from other individuals. These studies have turned to personality structure as the key to diagnosis.

One group of investigators used projective tests, particularly the Rorschach, in an attempt to establish reliable diagnostic tools. Robert Lindner initiated this movement in 1943 with a study of convicts. He administered the Rorschach to 40 "normal" criminals and 40 psychopathic criminals. The psychopathic group had originally been determined by the prison psychiatric staff on the basis of clinical interviews.[6] In their Rorschach protocols, the two groups exhibited profound qualitative differences.[7] The psychopaths showed an intense explosiveness, an almost complete egocentricity, general superficiality, and an avoidance of threatening material.[8]

Stimulated by Lindner's discovery, other researchers used the Rorschach in their investigations of the psychopath's personality structure. Heuser, in 1946, found the same qualities (shallowness and violent upheavals) in the responses of 28 psychopathic soldiers. In addition, Heuser's protocols showed the men to be "ruled by basic instinctual and sexual desires," lacking inner controls, and unable to learn from experience.[9]

In 1947 Bowlus and Shotwell confirmed the Rorschach findings of Lindner and Heuser in a study of 12 psychopathic girls at the Pacific Colony.[10]

While some scientists worked with Rorschach analyses,[11] others investigated the application of the Thematic Apperception Test and the Picture Frustration Test. In 1943 Kutash administered the T.A.T. to 60 psychopathic morons. Their most frequent responses showed aggression, eroticism, fear of death, an unconscious desire for punishment, "separation anxiety" (fear of rejection by society or family), and "ambition conflicts."[12]

In 1952, Holzberg and Hahn used the Picture Frustration Test on 17 psychopathic boys and a control group of normal delinquents in a reform school. Although the psychopathic boys appeared no more extra-punitive than other delinquents, they seemed to have much less inhibition of aggression when faced with the disapproval of authority figures.[13]

Handwriting analysis, too, has been tried in the search for diagnostic aids. In 1935 Naegelsbach compared the handwriting of 59 "aggressive psychopaths" to 30 "inadequate psychopaths" (probably acting-out neurotics). He believed that the powerful, free, and large writing of the aggressive cases reflected their overstimulation, excitability, and force.[14] Naegelsbach's provocative paper did not cite his methods for selecting psychopathic cases. Consequently, it has had little practical influence in clarifying the problem.

One of the most challenging attempts to differentiate the psychopath from the normal person was initiated by Simon, Holtzberg, and Unger. In 1951 these scientists investigated Cleckly's hypothesis that psychopaths learn social values, but do not act in accord with them when conflict arises between primitive desires and social restrictions. They administered a completion test to 22 psychopathic women and 22 student nurses at the Long Lane School.[15] Test items followed this pattern:

Rhoda's friend at the office asked her to stay late and help her out. Rhoda had planned to go to the movies that night. She told her friend:
   a. She had made other plans.
   b. She would stay.

The psychopathic women significantly more frequently chose the response which disregarded the wishes of others.

Social science in the last decade has been concerned not only with showing which personality traits characterize the psychopathic syndrome, but also finding which traits do not.

Intelligence has frequently been proposed as a standard for diagnosis. Observers in the early 1900's (e.g., Mercier) believed that the psychopath was mentally defective. More recently, scientists (e.g., Henderson) have emphasized intellectual brilliance as typical of the syndrome. In 1947 Milton Gurvitz laid the dispute to rest by proving that the psychopath is neither a dullard nor a genius. In a comprehensive examination of 3,649 inmates of a federal prison, Gurvitz found that the 851 psychopaths had the same I.Q. distribution as the non-psychopathic convicts. Moreover, neither group significantly differed from the intelligence range of normal Americans.[16]

Some psychiatrists have used "incurability" as a major criterion of psychopathy.[17] This "diagnostic" standard has obstructed therapeutic experimentation in psychopathy as it did in "dementia praecox."[18] When dementia praecox was assumed incurable, research stagnated. Gradually, a few studies showed that the disease could be successfully treated. The "incurable" connotation of dementia praecox was abandoned but, in its time, it did great harm. Recent research indicates that the judgment of "incurability" is just as inapplicable in the study of psychopathy. The psychopath, though difficult to treat, is not incurable.[19]

Although the post-war period has witnessed a flurry of new discoveries about diagnosis, the problem has not been completely solved. The psychological tests applied during the last decade should be of considerable value, but tests are needed which tap the psychopath's basic symptoms: his apparent guiltlessness and his difficulty in relating to others.[20]

Impulsivity, aggressiveness, egocentricity, though symptomatic of the psychopath, do not distinguish him from other deviants. The paranoid can be ruthlessly aggressive, the neurotic can be narcissistic, and a manic-depressive psychotic can be purposelessly impulsive. The psychopath's underdeveloped conscience and his inability to identify with others differentiate him from other deviants.

The next decades will probably produce adequate tests of guilt and relational ability, but until that development, clinical judgment must carry the major burden in diagnosis. Tests can help, but the scientist's perception of the over-all personality structure provides the most dependable criterion. Again, we should emphasize that total personality, rather than a single behavioral feature, is the key to diagnosis. A comparison of the psychopath with other deviants should highlight the unique pattern of his personality.

The psychopath certainly differs from the psychotic. Yet, at times, the two disorders have been confused. Not only have psychopaths been misdiagnosed as psychotic,[21] but, as a recent study by Bernard Glueck, Jr., has shown, psychotics have been mislabeled as psychopaths.[22] Glueck, director of the Sex Research Project at Sing Sing, subjected 200 sex offenders to a thorough psychological examination. Most of the men had been diagnosed (at some period in their lives) as psychopathic personalities. Deeper analysis indicated, however, that the convicts actually suffered from a type of schizophrenia. Under well-developed defenses, the sex offenders had subtle delusions, mild depression, and anxiety arising from basic conflict. In addition, most of these sex "psychopaths" felt guilty about their crimes.[23]

As Glueck's study illustrates, psychotics have a variety of symptoms. They all, however, possess a "serious loss of contact with reality."[24] The psychotic withdraws from frustration and creates a private delusional world. Self-reference pervades his thinking, and hallucinations surround him. Sometimes the psychotic undergoes extreme depression (involutional melancholia), sometimes an exalted grandiosity (hebephrenic schizophrenia). Often, he has delusions of persecution (paranoia). In some psychotic varieties, he alternates stupor with frenzy (manic-depressive psychosis).

Whatever the form, psychosis differs from psychopathy in that the psychotic generally withdraws from reality, but the psychopath attacks;[25] the psychotic usually creates a world of hallucinations, but the psychopath does not; and the psychotic often feels intense guilt (or at least intense anxiety), but the psychopath never does.

The distinction between neurosis and psychopathy seems equally clear. The neurotic, like the psychotic, feels intense anxiety and inner conflict. He is continually under tension, chronically dissatisfied, and often (although not always) rigid and inhibited. The neurotic attempts to solve this conflict in a variety of ways: by repression, by regression, or by other protective mechanisms. He may develop a phobia (an unreasoning fear of certain symbols), an obsession (a persistent idea oppressing his thoughts), an hysteric symptom (paralysis, anesthesia), or he may revert to severe anxiety attacks if all defenses fail.

The neurotic tries to assuage his inner disturbance with unrealistic means. He does not, like the psychotic, sever his contacts with reality. He can still function in society and can still take care of himself. The degree of social adjustment best marks the hazy dividing line between "insanity" and neurosis.

The personality of the psychopath differs greatly from that of the neurotic: the neurotic feels intense inner anxiety, and the psychopath has little; the neurotic is often oppressed by guilt, and the psychopath has apparently none; the neurotic can usually maintain bonds of love, but the psychopath seldom can; the neurotic usually represses his hostility, but the psychopath rarely does.

In fact, psychopathy is almost the antithesis of neurosis. In terms of emotional sensitivity, the neurotic is "thin-skinned," the psychopath is "thick-skinned."

Recent research has indicated the incompatibility of the two disorders.[26] In 1944 Mason studied 636 military criminals and discovered that the psychopathic criminals had the least neurotic characteristics. From the Army's point of view, Mason concluded, the neurotic was the better risk.[27]

Although the psychopath is radically different from the average neurotic, he is not so easily distinguished from the "acting-out neurotic."[28] Like other neurotics, the "acting-out neurotic" feels chronic inner conflict. Instead of repressing his feelings, the acting-out neurotic tries to resolve the conflict through anti-social behavior. Usually such behavior runs in episodic spurts. For a time he maintains a sullen, depressed demeanor, but when anxiety and tension increase unbearably, he explodes into aggressive attacks.[29]

Many so-called "sex-psychopaths" are really acting-out neurotics. Their behavior stems from compulsion, hysteria, and depression, which can be appeased only through action.[30] The psychopath is often sexually deviant, but he seldom becomes fixated on a particular object. He is sometimes homosexual, sometimes heterosexual. He is willing to try anything, but no compulsion forces him to do so. Unlike the typical sex offender, he does not concentrate on one bizzare form of gratification.

The psychopath is often confused with the acting-out neurotic.[31]

This confusion is understandable since (superficially) their symptoms are so similar. The case history of a neurotic San Quentin convict, "Jack Baker,"[32] should help to differentiate between acting-out neurosis and psychopathy.

Jack Baker was born in a rural community in New York. Because of his parents' harsh treatment, Baker ran away from home when he was twelve. Police captured him and returned him to his parents. They committed him to a reform school. Although the school had no walls, Baker refused to run away because he had given his word that he would remain.

At the age of fifteen, he began "hoboing" around the nation, supporting himself by farm work and burglaries. During this period, he "rolled" drunks, robbed apartments, and was continually in fist fights. He drifted to California and began stealing cars which he then sold to a fence. In 1949 he was strolling on the Long Beach "Pike" looking for pickpocket prospects. He stopped before a "hell-fire and brimstone" preacher whose eloquence convinced him that he should reform.

Baker turned himself in to the Los Angeles police. They telegraphed his parents, offering to return the boy to New York, but the parents refused to accept him. At nineteen, Baker was too old for reform school. Therefore, he was sent to San Quentin for burglary and theft.

Baker recorded his impressions of San Quentin:

When you arrive, you are dazed and sort of numb to any feeling. You are led into the inside of the towering grey walls, then out a gate into a lovely garden. "Ah," you sigh, "this isn't bad after all." But you are soon stripped of clothes and assigned to the West Block as a "fish." . . . You have a cell partner. He's a nice guy. He shows you how to pick locks. You are alone with your dreams and no one pays any attention to you.

Some of the men get to ridiculing you. They call you "Punk." . . . That night, your cell-mate gives you a knife. You thank him and think he is trying to act like a movie character. Your cell-mate asks you why you don't line up with so and so, so you do. Now you are happy. Self-consciousness flees when you are with your new friends. You can face those guys who call you "Punk." Up to now, you have been quiet and never in trouble, always a good worker. . . .

But now you must impress your new friends and prove to yourself that you are afraid of nothing. So you begin robbing cells, staying out of school, refusing to work, getting smart with the guards, sneaking in the show, getting up for seconds. And your friends went with you.

Now you've been caught. You stand naked with the loot before you.

(Everything you do in here seems to be an occasion for disrobing you.)
So, up to the shelf you went. After that, you go to the Hole. Finally,
you are sent to the South Block Segregation. There, a big Negro tries to
con you. He has a knife. You cry with shame. You ask Smith to send you
back to Old Prison Segregation. He tells you to go fight the Negro. You
can't believe it. The man must know that you could be killed. The next
morning you did fight the nigger, but you couldn't seem to hurt him and
he kept backing you up. . . .

As Baker's story indicates, he became one of the prison "tough
guys." But his toughness did not come from guiltlessness or from callous disregard for others. Baker is not a psychopath. He feels tre-
mendous guilt, he is "self-conscious," and he "cries with shame." A
further excerpt shows Baker's confusion and anxiety:

Ever since I can remember, everything concerning sex has been embar-
rassing to me. Why this is so I have never been able to learn. As I grew
older, I began to desire relations with women, but because of my acute
embarrassment, those relationships I did have with them were unsatisfactory. I hate myself for these thoughts. I feel the desire to gratify my sex
impulses, while at the same time, I feel disgust for such things and at
myself for being so weak.

Baker has the neurotic symptoms of permeating anxiety and intense inner conflict; yet he reacts with aggression rather than repression. This characteristic marks him as an acting-out neurotic.

The acting-out neurotic has, in common with the psychopath, the
behavioral symptoms of aggressiveness and asociality. But, unlike the
psychopath, the acting-out neurotic possesses strong guilt feelings,
and is plagued by intense anxiety.

Psychotics and neurotics, acting-out neurotics and psychopaths are
all psychologically disordered people. In one way or another their
personalities have become maladjusted. Often they come into conflict with the demands of society. Yet not all personality maladjustment results in behavior deviance (a neurotic compulsiveness, for
example, is almost a prerequisite for the successful scholar).

Not all deviance, on the other hand, results from a disordered
personality. Many criminals and delinquents, though socially maladjusted, are psychologically healthy people. In a recent study of
delinquents, in fact, Sheldon and Eleanor Glueck found that 48.6 per
cent had no conspicuous mental pathology.[33]

Increasingly, social science has recognized that criminality cannot
be equated with psychopathy.[34] In 1951 British investigators com-

pared psychopathic and non-psychopathic convicts, using clinical interviews, E.E.G. examinations, and psychological tests. The psychopaths exhibited much greater resentment of parents (particularly of fathers), insensitivity to moral appeals, inability to profit from punishment, and a complete lack of long-range goals. They revealed more neurological difficulties, more abnormal E.E.G. patterns, and greater proclivity for serious crimes. The psychopaths differed so significantly from the other criminals that the investigators concluded: "The psychopath in prison is a clinical entity distinct from other prisoners."[35]

The total pattern of the psychopath's personality differentiates him from the normal criminal. His aggression is more intense, his impulsivity more pronounced, his emotional relations more shallow. His guiltlessness, however, is the critical distinguishing trait. The normal criminal has an internalized, albeit warped, set of values. If he violates these standards, he feels guilt. The words of a professional criminal, reported by a psychologist at San Quentin, portray these sub-cultural mores:

> I befriended this man, gave him money. He was down and out and I helped him get on his feet. I introduced him to my friends. I taught him the trade. I always insisted that he get a good-sized cut of the proceeds. He was quite happy. He was now well off. In one of the jobs, he was caught together with several others. I escaped. All the others kept their peace. He squealed on me. . . . Such an action is almost incomprehensible to me.[36]

The first step in the cure of any disease is accurate diagnosis. Great progress has been made. The development of psychological testing and the contributions of comparative studies have illustrated the gulf which separates the psychopath from the normal criminal, from the neurotic, and from the psychotic.

In order to cure his disorder, the psychopath must be recognized as having a unique personality syndrome of aggressiveness, guiltlessness, affectional shallowness, and extreme impulsivity. Techniques which help the psychotic or the neurotic do not work equally well with the psychopath. Nor do causal explanations which have fitted other disorders apply to psychopathy.

Some of the same men who have clarified the concept of psychopathy have addressed themselves to the challenging problem of causation. The last thirty years have marked a proliferation of theories and a smaller, but still impressive, amount of evidence concerning the cause of psychopathy. It is with this issue that the next chapter deals.

NOTES

1,2. SUTHERLAND, EDWIN. Sexual Psychopath Laws. *Journal of Criminology, Criminal Law, and Police Science*, 40:543-554, 1950.

3,4. KARPMAN, B. Seven Psychopaths; a Correlative, Non-Statistical Study of Predatory Crime. *Journal of Clinical Psychopathology and Psychotherapy*, 6:299, 1944.

5. RABINOVITCH, RALPH. Psychopathic Delinquent Children—1949 Round Table. *American Journal of Orthopsychiatry*, 20:223-265 (April), 1950.

6. Lindner, Heuser, Bowlus, and Shotwell used approximately the definition of psychopathy as that presented in Chapter 1.

7. Although Lindner found marked qualitative differences in the protocols, he did not find any quantitative differences between the answers of the two groups.

8. LINDNER, ROBERT. The Rorschach Test and the Diagnosis of Psychopathic Personality. *Journal of Criminal Psychopathology*, 5:69-93, 1943.

9. HEUSER, K. D. The Psychopathic Personality: Rorschach Patterns of 28 Cases. *American Journal of Psychiatry*, 103:105-112, 1946.

10. BOWLUS, D. E., AND SHOTWELL, ANNA. A Rorschach Study of Psychopathic Delinquents. *American Journal of Mental Deficiency*, 52: 23-30, 1947.

11. Sheldon and Eleanor Glueck in their significant study of causation, *Unraveling Juvenile Delinquency*, also used the Rorschach as a diagnostic tool for differentiating various forms of mental pathology. Since their study concerned other problems, they have not as yet published an analysis of the psychopathic delinquents' responses.

12. KUTASH, S. B. Performance of Psychopathic Defective Criminals on the T.A.T. *Journal of Criminal Psychopathology*, 5:319-340, 1943. Kutash selected his cases primarily on the basis of intense anti-social behavior and egocentricity. He probably included acting-out neurotics in the sample.

13. HOLZBERG, JULES, AND HAHN, FRED. The Picture-Frustration Technique as a Measure of Hostility and Guilt Reactions in Adolescent Psychopaths. *American Journal of Orthopsychiatry*, 22:776-797, 1952. They used intense behavioral aggression as the major standard for selection.

14. NAEGELSBACH, H. Zur Graphologischen Beurteilung Psychopathischer Talle. *Z. Angew. Psychol.*, 49:258-269, 1935.

15. SIMON, BENJAMIN, HOLTZBERG, JULES, D., AND UNGER, JOAN. A Study of Judgment in the Psychopathic Personality. *Psychiatric Quarterly*, 25:132-150, 1951. The psychopathic women were selected in accord with Cleckly's "clinical profile," one which closely agrees with the description of the psychopath in Chapter 1.

16. GURVITZ, MILTON. Intelligence Factor in Psychopathic Personality. *Journal of Clinical Psychology*, 3:194-196, 1947.

17. KARPMAN, B. Psychopathy in the Scheme of Human Typology. *Journal of Nervous and Mental Disease*, 103:276-288, 1946.

18. The unfortunate connotation of "constitutional incurability" adhering to the label "psychopathy" was one of the major reasons why the American

Psychiatric Association replaced the term with "sociopathy" in 1952. See *Handbook of Mental Disorders,* Boston, 1952.

Many psychologists are reluctant to prejudice a child's future by labeling him a psychopath. If the standard of incurability is abandoned, the term is no more opprobrious than "neurotic," "behavior disorder," or "psychotic."

19. See chapter on treatment.

20. The Picture Frustration Test and the completion test described above have potential value in diagnosing the psychopath's guiltlessness. Research in this area has been sporadic, and the usefulness of the tests has not been established. In Chapter 6 we describe a test of guilt feelings which can be applied to child psychopaths and may help to solve this diagnostic problem.

In testing "affectional ability," structured situations have sometimes been used. Such a method is cumbersome, and other methods need to be devised.

21. See J. L. NELSON and J. ZIMMERMAN: Psychopathic States with Psychotic Reactions. *Psychiatric Quarterly,* 14:49-60, 1940. Also J. M. CALDWELL: The Constitutional Psychopathic State: I. Studies of Soldiers in the U. S. Army. *Journal of Criminal Psychopathology,* 3:171-179, 1941.

22. GLUECK, BERNARD, JR. Psychodynamic Factors in the Sex Offender. *Psychiatric Quarterly,* Jan. 1954.

23. In a later article, Dr. Glueck apparently extends his findings with sex offenders into a general criticism of the concept of psychopathy: "The classical hallmarks of the psychopath, his lack of anxiety and guilt, are no longer valid diagnostic criteria, since we have been able to demonstrate a great anxiety and guilt in individuals so diagnosed." See BERNARD GLUECK, JR.: Changing Concepts in Forensic Psychiatry. *Journal of Criminal Law, Criminology, and Police Science,* 45:125 (No. 7), 1954. Glueck ably demonstrated the inapplicability of the psychopathic label to his group of sex-offenders, but his evidence does not seem to contradict the numerous studies which indicate the *true* psychopath's guiltlessness.

24. WHITE, ROBERT. *The Abnormal Personality,* New York, Ronald Press, 1948, p. 490.

25. The paranoid psychotic is often aggressive, but at the same time, he withdraws from reality.

26. See SOL LEVY and others: Personality Factors in a State Prison. *Journal of Clinical and Experimental Psychopathology,* Jan.-Feb. 1952.

SHELDON and ELEANOR GLUECK, in their study of delinquency causation, found a significantly higher proportion of neuroticism in non-delinquent boys than in delinquent boys. See their *Unraveling Juvenile Delinquency,* Cambridge, Harvard Press, 1950, p. 240.

27. MASON, I. An Index of the Severity of Criminalism or Psychopathy. U. S. Army Medical Dept. *Bulletin,* 75:110-114, 1944.

28. The category of acting-out neurosis has recently gained recognition among such prominent investigators as Karpman, Alexander, and Weinberg.

See B. KARPMAN: The Sexual Psychopath. *Journal of Criminal Law, Criminology, and Police Science,* 42:184-198, 1951. Also F. ALEXANDER: The Neurotic Character. *International Journal of Psychoanalysis,* 11:292-313, 1930. Also KIRSON WEINBERG: Acting-out Disorders. *Society and the Personality Disorders,* New York, Prentice-Hall, 1952.

29. Acting-out neurotics and psychopaths have sometimes been confused with brain-damaged patients. Brain damage can result in aggressive, impulsive, irritable behavior; but, alone, it does not result in the peculiar guiltlessness or emotional callousness of the psychopath. Differential diagnosis is actually relatively simple in the case of brain-damaged patients. Advances in psychological testing and E.E.G. analysis have provided techniques for separating the brain-damaged person from other personalities.

30. See Karpman: The Sexual Psychopath, *op. cit.* (note 28).

31. The causative studies of both Levy and Greenacre seem to be dealing with acting-out neurotics rather than psychopaths. See DAVID LEVY: *Maternal Overprotection.* New York, Columbia Press, 1943. Also PHYLLIS GREENACRE: Conscience in the Psychopath. *American Journal of Orthopsychiatry,* 15:495-509, 1945.

32. A pseudonym. Quotations are from personal communications.

33. Glueck and Glueck, *op. cit.* (note 26), p. 239.

34. See R. B. VAN VORST: An Evaluation of the Institutional Adjustment of the Psychopathic Offender. *American Journal of Orthopsychiatry,* 14:491-493, 1944. Also H. CASON and M. J. PESCOR: A Statistical Study of 500 Psychopathic Prisoners. *Public Health Reports,* 61:557-574, 1946.

35. STRAFFORD-CLARK AND OTHERS. The Psychopath in Prison: a Preliminary Report of a Cooperative Research. *British Journal of Delinquency,* 2:117-129, 1951. Prison psychiatrists selected the psychopathic cases on the basis of Henderson's definition of the psychopath. Henderson emphasized recurrent asocial conduct, lack of guilt, and unresponsiveness to treatment. Therefore, it is not surprising that the investigators discovered repeated convictions and rejection of the "lessons of punishment," in their psychopaths. Other differences cannot, however, be explained as due to the selection of cases. Resentment of fathers, ill-defined goals, and impulsiveness have no necessary correlation with anti-social conduct.

36. CORSINI, RAYMOND. Criminal Psychology. In VERNON BRANHAM AND SAMUEL KUTASH: *Encyclopedia of Criminology.* New York, Philosophical Library, 1949, p. 114.

4

The Causes of Psychopathy

The child is father of the man . . .

WORDSWORTH

"WE ARE ALL BORN PSYCHOPATHS," Harry Lipton recently observed, ". . . we are born without repressions." The new-born child has no inhibitions. He expresses his rage with complete freedom. No inner control moderates his impulsivity. Certainly, the new baby has no guilt feelings. In these traits at least, all men *are* born psychopaths.

Yet almost immediately the normal baby moves out of his "psychopathic stage." The baby soon develops a need for love and perhaps a need to give love. The baby learns to control his impulses and to adjust himself to the demands of his environment. Within six months he begins to react to frustration with more effective means than sheer fury. In time, after developing inner controls, the normal baby acquires "human nature."

Why do a few children (our psychopaths) never make this transition into "humanness"? Why have they such inadequate internalized controls? Why can they not form "loving" relations? Why, as adults, do they continue to react to frustration with infantile aggression?

A great many attempts have been made to answer these questions. Some scientists have looked at reflexes, others at brain formation, others at electro-encephalographic patterns, others at ancestral history, and still others at parental treatment. With these approaches, and many others, science has tried to solve the psychopathic mystery.

Why does one man develop a psychopathic character while another man does not? We do not yet have a definitive answer, but the past decades of research have not been altogether fruitless. We know a great deal more about the psychopath than we did twenty-five years

47

ago: We know something about the electrical impulses within the psychopath's brain, we know more about his early family life, and we know a great deal about the general results of affectional isolation.

Theoretical bickering has often obscured the goal of research. Many of those who have studied the psychopath have insisted that only their particular line of investigation could furnish a satisfactory answer to the problem. Often, "studies" of psychopathic causation have been circular arguments which eventually prove the *a priori* judgments of the authors. There has been little exchange of information among the various theoretical "schools," and no synthesis of their discoveries. Since the psychopath, like all men, is both a biological and a social organism, many approaches must be used in studying his disorder.

I. THE HEREDITARY APPROACH

Some scientists have sought the causes of psychopathy in hereditary factors. In various ways they have attempted to prove that the disorder results from an inherent predisposition. Such "Victorian" psychiatrists as Pritchard, Pinel, and Kraepelin postulated that an inborn defect, an hereditary lack of "moral sense," caused "moral insanity." Is there any evidence for this belief?

Some investigators hoped that genealogical research would link psychopathy and heredity. G. E. Partridge, in 1928, meticulously traced the lineage of 50 psychopathic personalities. He discovered that 24 of the cases had ancestors "in a direct line" who showed psychopathic traits.[1]

Other investigators tried this same type of study. In 1939 an Ecuadorean psychiatrist investigated psychopathic personalities in the Quito Prison and found a high incidence of epilepsy and alcoholism in their parents.[2] In 1946 a team of American scientists discovered that 54 per cent of their psychopathic patients had ancestral histories involving epilepsy, "maladjusted personality," or alcoholism.[3] And, in 1947, Dr. Peter Mohr examined the case histories of 226 psychopaths admitted to the Swiss Königsfelden asylum and found that 68 per cent had maladjusted ancestors.[4]

Many modern observers, impressed with these figures, insist that psychopathy must be an hereditary disorder. Yet, the figures give only meagre support to such a generalization.

The "hereditary" studies characteristically defined their "psychopathic" subjects in vague terms ("erratic, anti-social, eccentric").

Consequently, various disorders were confused under the amorphous label of psychopathy. Their analyses did not provide for comparative standards. In fact, the same proportion of normal people seem to have "hereditary defects" as do psychopaths.[5] A recent study of normal people revealed that 57 per cent had a "positive family history of neuropathic taint."[6] Finally, they have not isolated the relative influence of heredity from that of environment. The child raised by maladjusted parents may become psychopathic. This fact alone does not show whether heredity or an insecure home life causes the disorder.

Franz Kallman's study, in 1930, produced provocative findings concerning heredity versus environment. Kallman showed that the children of psychopaths have a higher percentage of psychopathy than the siblings of psychopaths. Apparently, the incidence of the disorder does not follow the closest lines of blood kinship, and other factors must play the dominant role. Kallman believed that the children of institutionalized psychopaths fall prey to the disorder because their family status declined when the parents were incarcerated.[7]

In the 1930's other investigators attempted to appraise the influence of nature and nurture by comparing the life histories of twins. The most prominent of these scientists, Johannes Lange and A. J. Rosanoff, hoped to demonstrate the dominant influence of heredity by proving that identical twins had more similar personalities than fraternal twins. At least one in each pair was known to have a criminal record. Lange discovered that 77 per cent of the identical twins and only 12 per cent of the fraternal pairs had similar prison histories.[9]

During the same year, in America, A. J. Rosanoff analyzed the criminality of four hundred pairs of twins. Rosanoff also noted a greater incidence of both identical twins being delinquent than of both fraternal twins. Rosanoff found the similarity in identical twins 1.4 times that of fraternal twins—as compared to Lange's 6.4 ratio.[10]

Neither Lange nor Rosanoff, however, adequately established the identical relation of the "identical" twins.[11] Critics of their work believe they had no valid basis for their conclusions. Even more importantly, both relied upon numerous agencies (of dubious reliability) for information regarding their subjects. Furthermore, analysis of Rosanoff's study reveals that the "identical" twins who had been raised in separate families had less similar criminal records.

Thus, neither study convincingly demonstrates heredity's influence on criminality. Even if identical twins do behave more similarly, this may be due (as Edwin Sutherland has pointed out) to the very similar treatment that they receive as children.

More recently, scientists have applied the "twin" method specifically to the study of psychopathic causation and have discovered no definite connection between heredity and psychopathy. Slater thoroughly studied the life histories of nine pairs of twins. Some were psychopathic, some neurotic. He found that only two of the pairs possessed similar personality traits.[12]

Historically, the hereditary approach has been closely associated with the "constitutional school." Hooton, Kretchmer, and Sheldon have attempted to demonstrate a relation between physique and character. Although their work does not necessarily presuppose hereditary causation, most of the constitutionalists have postulated an hereditary basis for both physique and character.

The constitutionalists have been concerned with criminality in general, rather than with the specific problem of psychopathy.[13] Lombroso's work with Italian criminals pioneered this approach to criminal causation. Hooton's *Crime and the Man*[14] and Sheldon's *Varieties of Delinquent Youth*[15] carried it on with more sophisticated techniques. Their attempts to establish a typical criminal body-type have exerted little influence in criminology, primarily because their findings were contradictory. Hooton, for example, concluded that the criminal was physically inferior to the "normal" man. Sheldon maintained that the delinquent has a "mesomorphic" (muscular, athletic, tightly-knit) body and was, therefore physically *superior* to the average boy.

The recent work of Sheldon and Eleanor Glueck represents the most rigorous attempt to relate bodily constitution to delinquency causation. The Gluecks compared the body types of five hundred juvenile delinquents with five hundred non-delinquents. They discovered that delinquents were generally superior in gross body size, exhibited a more homogeneous build, and (following an initial lag) developed rapidly after the fourteenth year. The Gluecks found 60 and one-tenth per cent mesomorphs among the delinquents.

Unlike other scholars, the Gluecks did not assume a necessary relation between constitution and heredity. Nor did they portray the bodily physique as the dominant cause of delinquency. Rather, they pictured bodily constitution as but one factor among many dynamisms which influence behavior.[16]

Although the Gluecks' analysis shed light on delinquency causation, it was not designed as an investigation of psychopathy. As yet, no research shows a specific relationship between physique and the psychopathic personality.[17] Consequently, this facet of the disorder remains a mystery.

At the present time, it is untenable to maintain a direct causal connection between heredity and psychopathy. In fact, research has produced evidence which contravenes this belief. The work of Kallman and the Royal Medico-Psychological Association has (tentatively) shown:

> Psychopathy does not follow the lines of closest blood kinship: the children of psychopaths have a higher incidence of developing the disorder than do the siblings of psychopaths.

> The ancestors of psychopaths apparently have the same incidence of hereditary "taint" as the ancestors of normal people.

In a recent study of the psychopath's ancestors, Hervey Cleckly concluded: " . . . any consistent or even suggestive history of familial inferiority is notably lacking in the present series."[18]

Heredity cannot yet be excluded as a causal factor. With more adequate delineation,[19] with more rigidly controlled experiments, and with more sensitive measurement, an hereditary link may possibly be established. Given our current knowledge, however, the extravagant claims of the geneticists must be questioned.

II. THE NEUROLOGICAL APPROACH

For more than a century, medicine has known that injuries to the brain can result in anti-social behavior. For more than three decades, some scientists have hoped to trace psychopathy to a defective brain.

In the famous "crowbar case" of 1848, a man who had been hit on the head changed from a law-abiding citizen to a "childish kind of crook: profane, obstinate, and given to outbursts of temper."[20] Often, in the history of medicine, damaged brains have caused striking transformations in behavior.

Reports of surgical operations on the brain include similar changes in behavior. The current fashion of excising the frontal lobes sometimes turns patients into egocentric, aggressive misfits. The controversial operations of Walter Freeman and James Watts first demonstrated that prefrontal lobotomy caused certain patients to shed their social controls, their inhibitions, and their long-range goals.[21]

Brain operations do not always have the same results. Sometimes people become more inhibited, or intellectually retarded, or greatly depressed. Recent experiments have shown that the aggressive pattern occurs in almost every case when one specific area of the brain is damaged: the hypothalamus.

In 1944, after studying cases of verified lesions of the hypothalamic area, B. Alpers concluded that the aggressive behavior of his patients had markedly increased. In addition, "obvious anti-social tendencies and partial or complete loss of insight" occurred.[22]

Experimental operations on animals further pointed to hypothalamic damage as a cause for "anti-sociality." Fulton and Ingraham, for example, made surgical incisions injuring the hypothalamic region of healthy, friendly cats. Immediately after the operation, the cats' behavior changed from playfulness to violent, impulsive, "sham" rage. Patting their backs produced snarling aggressiveness.[23] A similar experiment with dogs, involving removal of the entire thalamic area, brought about a condition of chronic anger.[24]

Disease, as well as injury, can cause an increase in anti-social conduct. In 1939 British neurologist David Henderson reported that victims of encephalitis, chorea, and epilepsy sometimes "became transformed; those who, previously, were models of virtue and good behavior are changed into libertines and ne'er do wells."[25] In 1942, after analyzing a great many post-encephalitic children, Lauretta Bender concluded that the disease increased aggressiveness and decreased the patients' anxiety concerning his uninhibited behavior.[26]

The similarity between the behavior of a brain-damaged person and the psychopath—in aggressiveness, impulsivity, and lack of inhibition —suggested a path for new investigation. The analogous behavior might be indicative of deeper similarities. In fact, many scientists believed that early brain damage might prove to be the cause of psychopathy.

The rapid development of electro-encephalography permitted a partial test of this hypothesis. The new instrument made possible the tracing of electrical impulses within the brain. Early experiments soon demonstrated that brain-damaged individuals had a high incidence of abnormal waves: sharp spikes or unusually slow undulations. If the psychopath exhibited an aberrant pattern, this might indicate that he, too, suffered from a defective brain.

D. Hill and D. Watterson were the first to measure the electrical pattern with the psychopath's brain. In 1942 they tested 104 patients in a mental hospital, dividing them into "aggressive psychopaths" (aggressive, anti-social, guiltless, impulsive) and "inadequate psychopaths" (egocentric, immoral, but non-aggressive).[27] Sixty-five per cent of the "aggressive psychopaths" evidenced abnormal E.E.G. patterns, in contrast to 32 per cent among the "inadequate psychopaths."[28]

In the same year G. Bradley measured the brain waves of child "behavior disorders." Some of these children exhibited the psychopathic traits of aggressiveness, guiltlessness, and inability to relate to others. Bradley, too, found that 65 per cent had abnormal tracings.[29]

Using the same method, Silverman examined 75 "psychopaths" in a federal prison. He found that 53 per cent had definitely abnormal patterns. An additional 26 per cent had "borderline" tracings.[30] A year later, and using a larger sample of criminal subjects, Silverman repeated the experiment and obtained approximately the same results: 75 per cent of his cases had either borderline or definitely abnormal brain waves.[31]

Three additional studies seemed to corroborate the assumption that brain disorder played a prominent role in psychopathy. In 1945 the British psychiatrist Sessions-Hodges examined 70 "psychopaths": he declared that all had abnormal E.E.G. tracings.[32] In 1946 a team of American scientists (Gottlieb, Ashley, and Knott) reported that 58 of 100 "psychopaths" had abnormal patterns.[33] And, in 1947, Rockwell and Simmons reported their study of 10 "psychopaths," all of whom exhibited abnormal brain waves.[34]

A comprehensive analysis of 1,000 normal individuals, in 1943, showed that only 15 per cent had abnormal patterns.[35] Therefore, the studies which found that over 50 per cent of the psychopathic subjects had abnormal tracings[36] encouraged many to believe that a cause for the disorder—a defective brain—had been discovered.

Other research tempered the original enthusiasm. Simons and Diethelm, in 1946, studied 69 criminal "psychopaths" and concluded that only 27 per cent showed definitely abnormal brain waves.[37] In 1947 another research team compared a group of "constitutional psychopaths" to a group of normal individuals. They found no appreciable difference between the E.E.G. patterns of the two groups.[38] And Milton Greenblatt, in 1950, reviewed 380 cases of "psychopathy" at the Boston Psychopathic Hospital. He reported an incidence of 30 per cent aberrancy, only slightly higher than that in a normal population.[39]

These conflicting findings reflected the researchers' vague standards in selecting their cases. Many personality types had been commingled, and the research lost much of its reliability. Unless neurologists give careful, specific descriptions of their subjects' personalities, the E.E.G. examinations do not clarify the issue of causation.

One study of the psychopath's brain waves did adhere to a clearly delineated standard, in establishing psychopathy. Carried out in 1946, this research by Ostrow and Ostrow involved the E.E.G. analysis of 440 inmates of the Federal Prison Bureau's Medical Center.[40] Sixty-nine convicts were extraordinarily impulsive, unable to accept social limitations, and showed seriously warped empathetic abilities. Only these were labeled psychopathic. The Ostrows compared the E.E.G. patterns of the psychopaths with those of homosexuals, epileptics, schizophrenics, and imprisoned conscientious objectors. Within each group, the Ostrows found:

Diagnosis	Percentage of Abnormal Patterns
Psychopathy	50
Homosexuality	56
Epilepsy	98
Schizophrenia	80
Conscientious Objectors	65

Careful diagnosis, made after thorough review of case histories and intensive clinical interviews, adds weight to the Ostrows' findings. Their tests indicate a high degree of abnormality not only among psychopaths, but also among other imprisoned deviants.[41] Perhaps the most interesting implication of their work is that the type of personality abnormality could not be deduced from the E.E.G. pattern. Certainly the conscientious objector's personality differs from that of the psychopath, just as the psychopath's differs from the schizophrenic's. Yet, many men in each of the groups seem to have damaged neural structures.

Although not conclusive, the Ostrows' research stands as the most rigorous of the neurological studies.

Despite confusion, the past years of E.E.G. examinations have removed some of the mystery surrounding the psychopath's neurological processes. Failing to differentiate psychopathy from other disorders, the research nevertheless indicates the strong probability of a greater proportion of abnormal E.E.G. patterns among psychopaths than among the normal population. The exact incidence of abnormality has not yet been established. Obviously the highly tentative E.E.G. studies fall short of proving that psychopathy is caused by a defective brain.

Seeking further evidence of physical abnormality in psychopaths, neurologists looked for those abnormal reflexes, tics, and tremors which often signal the existence of neural disorder. Silverman, in 1943, was the first scientist to examine psychopaths for external signs of brain disorder. Silverman found that 21 of 75 criminal "psychopaths" had pathological reflexes and severe tremors.[42]

In 1945, after investigating 70 criminal "psychopaths," Sessions-Hodges noted that 76 per cent had disfunctional signs, in contrast to only 9 per cent in a control group of 50. The psychopaths exhibited a flickering movement of fingers and an equivocal plantar response.[43]

In 1951 a group of British prison psychiatrists compared criminal "psychopaths" (prisoners who seemed unresponsive to treatment) with non-psychopathic convicts. They divided the psychopaths into three groups: those who had a history of epilepsy, those who had a history of head injury, and those who had neither disorder in their background.[44] Surprisingly, the psychopaths who were free from epilepsy and brain injury had the highest proportion of neurological symptoms:

Diagnosis	Percentage exhibiting neurological "signs"
Non-psychopathic criminals	25
Psychopaths with epileptic history	36
Psychopaths with head-injury history	46
Psychopaths without epilepsy or head-injury	52

Yet, after their study of 69 psychopaths, Simons and Diethelm had concluded: "No defects in the function of the nervous system were found. There was no evidence of any structural change in the patients' brains."[45]

Like the E.E.G. studies, the examination of physical symptoms suffered from inadequate diagnosis of psychopathy. The investigators almost certainly included non-psychopaths in their samples, thus preventing a reliable gauging of abnormal symptoms.

One study of the psychopath's physiology was based on more satisfactory criteria. In 1943, Robert Lindner experimented with criminals in an attempt to detect the reactional differences of psychopaths. Lindner compared 103 non-psychopathic, first term prisoners in a federal institution to 105 psychopathic inmates. Diagnosed after clinical interviews, the psychopaths were egocentric, rejected authority, lacked insight, and had knowledge of—but did not internalize—social regulations.

Lindner used an electric shock as the basis of his experiment. One minute before the shock, a bell gave warning. From the sounding of the tone until two minutes after the shock, instruments recorded galvanic and respiratory reactions, as well as dorsal pedis pulse. Only the galvanic response significantly distinguished the psychopathic from the non-psychopathic criminals. Before the shock, the psychopaths showed less tenseness; during and shortly after the shock, they exhibited greater anxiety. Yet the psychopaths more quickly reverted to their normal physiological functioning.[46]

Lindner believed that psychopathic impulsiveness could be traced to his discovery that they are "poised more delicately and are more responsive to alterations in the situation." Perhaps, too, the lack of continued anxiety in this test situation might help explain why psychopaths fail to internalize social controls: physiologically, they do not protract the tenseness induced by a punishing situation.[47]

Although Lindner's study portrayed a new facet of the psychopath's physical structure, it furnished no evidence of organic brain disorder. Still seeking indications of neurological defect, some psychiatrists examined psychopaths' medical histories for possible causative factors.

Silverman's study, in 1943, had noted that 36 per cent of the psychopathic cases showed medical histories indicative of cerebral lesions. His cases had had such diseases as dystocia, tumors, birth trauma, and childhood head injury.[48] Gottleib, Ashley, and Knott found that 38 per cent of their psychopathic subjects had, as children, experienced anoxia, convulsions, or head injury.[49] The Strafford-Clark team discovered that 45 per cent of their criminal psychopaths had a history of epilepsy or head injury.[50] A. M. Shotwell, on the other hand, examined 12 "psychopaths" at the Pacific Colony and found no history of early brain damage.[51]

Like other attempts to relate psychopathy to brain damage, inadequate diagnosis hampered these studies. The incidence of early brain disease among psychopaths cannot be determined if many disorders are indiscriminately included in the sample.

Though recognizing the inadequacies of the neurological studies, a few provisional generalizations seem justified:

Compared with normal people, a greater proportion of psychopaths exhibit signs of neurological disorder (tremors, exaggerated reflexes, tics).

Psychopaths are probably more physiologically responsive to physical changes in their environment.

Compared with normal people, a greater proportion of psychopaths have a history of early diseases which damage the brain.

No scientists maintain that brain damage invariably causes psychopathy. Yet, from this cursory evidence, some theorists have concluded that all psychopathy is caused by neural disorder. Most frequently, they have indicated encephalitis, sub-clinical epilepsy, or a defective hypothalamus as the precipitating cause.

Those who champion encephalitis present the weakest case. No investigator has demonstrated a high incidence of encephalitis in psychopaths, but a few, detecting behavioral similarities of aggressiveness and anti-sociality between encephalitics and psychopaths, have claimed a causal connection. Yet, in 1950, after thorough reviews of the lives of 154 individuals who had undergone post-vaccination encephalitis, a German research group found no evidence for believing that psychopathic, or even criminogenic, consequences resulted from the disease.[52]

The belief that epilepsy causes psychopathy rests on a dubious analogy. Both epileptics and psychopaths exhibit "unstable emotionality" and "aggression resembling psychic seizures." In addition, abnormal E.E.G.'s appear in both psychopaths and epileptics. Similarities undoubtedly exist; but these causal theorists have still to explain why so few psychopaths have a verified history of epilepsy, why so many psychopaths have normal E.E.G. patterns, and why so few epileptics develop psychopathic personalities.

Citing recent experiments with dilantin sodium, some psychiatrists maintain that the psychopath must have a "sub-clinical" variety of epilepsy.[53] Epileptic seizures of some types can be reduced through dosages of dilantin sodium, and two recent studies have tentatively indicated that the psychopath may also respond favorably to the drug.[54] Therefore, these theorists assert, epilepsy and psychopathy are two forms of the same disorder. This reasoning (from treatment to cause) is tenuous, particularly since experiments using dilantin sodium with psychopaths are inconclusive.

Although there seems little justification for blaming either encephalitis or epilepsy for psychopathy, more substantial evidence connects the disorder with a defective hypothalamus. Modern neurological research has shown that the hypothalamus governs various internal mechanisms within the human body. In addition, the hypothalamus (along with cortical areas) plays an important part in the establishment of normal associational patterns. When the hypothalamus is damaged, the patient almost invariably becomes unstable, aggressive, and "anti-social." Consequently, several scientists have suggested that the hypothalamus is the brain area responsible for inhibition: that if it is damaged, or "inherently" defective, a psychopathic character results.[56]

Since a history of hypothalamic injury has been discerned in only a minority of psychopaths, the theory must postulate that brain damage occurred in the intrauterine stage, or that the hypothalamus was hereditarily defective. The theory rests on the behavioral similarity between the psychopath and the brain-injured person. The apparently higher incidence of E.E.G. abnormality, of physical symptoms of brain disorder, and of histories of head injury lend it credence. Yet the few autopsies known to have been performed on psychopaths do not confirm the theory.[57] Before being accepted as an explanation of psychopathy, the hypothalamic theory must be subjected to further research. There is evidence that the hypothalamic area does control inhibition and therefore, damage to this area may contribute to psychopathy.

Because of a confused interpretation of psychopathy, neurological research has been somewhat unsatisfactory. Epileptics, neurotics, and psychotics have been included in several of the studies, and may account for much of the neural abnormality attributed to psychopaths. Nevertheless, more psychopaths seem to have defective neural structures than would be expected in a normal population.

III. THE ENVIRONMENTAL APPROACH

An ancient German legend tells of a brutal experiment performed by Emperor Frederick II. In the 1400's the Emperor ordered that a group of babies be raised at his court. The infants received everything they wished—except love. Frederick forbade any demonstrations of affection. The children, so the legend says, all died.

Perhaps lack of love can kill. Today, most social scientists would view early emotional deprivation as at least a seriously warping experience. The research in psychoanalysis and social psychology has shown that childhood relationships play a paramount role in the formation of adult personality.

An increasing number of social scientists have applied the philosophy and methods of dynamic psychology to the study of psychopathy. The last two decades of research have amassed an impressive fund of knowledge about the psychopath's early social relations. In the search for the causes of psychopathy, social science has tapped two major sources of information: the study of psychopaths' childhood experiences, and the examination of rejected or isolated children. In this twofold approach, some investigators look to the psychopath himself and attempt to distinguish the environmental factors which caused his unique character syndrome. Others analyze the love-starved child and try to ascertain whether early emotional deprivation leads to a psychopathic personality.

A reform school psychotherapist, G. E. Partridge, was the first scientist to study the early environmental influence on psychopaths. In 1928 Partridge thoroughly examined 12 psychopathic delinquents. All the boys hated their parents, but more importantly, all of the boys had been rejected as young children.[58]

Five years later, Elizabeth Knight, a social worker, noticed similar rejection in her study of aggressive boys. Knight compared the family backgrounds of 9 extremely aggressive children with those of 9 very submissive children. The mothers of all the aggressive boys rejected their children; the mothers of the submissive lads appeared overprotective. An overtly punitive atmosphere dominated the homes of aggressive cases; the homes of the submissive children, on the other hand, were "harmonious."[59]

In 1940 Minna Field turned up further provocative evidence about environmental causation. After rigorous analysis of 25 children at the State Psychiatric Institute, Field found that 23 had been rejected by their parents. Field traced the children's aggressive and destructive behavior to the influence of their maladjusted parents, particularly the mothers. None of the mothers were "well integrated," and none had been loved by their parents.[60]

B. L. Haller's research, 1942, also pegged rejection as a causative factor. Haller demonstrated that a majority of 52 "psychopaths" paroled from a mental hospital had either been neglected or rejected as children.[61] Haller concluded, after interviewing the psychopathic patients, that they had a subconscious overattachment to their mothers. Although his findings have not been confirmed, there is reason to expect that the severely rejected child wants (even more than the normal child) to have his mother's affection.

Other studies in the 1940's appeared to find an entirely different familial constellation in the background of psychopaths. Due to confusion in diagnosis, S. A. Szurek, W. L. Heaver, and Phillis Greenacre found that the "psychopath" was rejected, if at all, only by his father. His mother, on the other hand, was highly indulgent and subconsciously approved of the child's deviant behavior.

Szurek, in 1942, initiated this theory when he reported his experience with the treatment of "psychopathic" children. Szurek cited one of his cases, a highly aggressive six-year-old, as evidence. The little boy kicked his playmates, struck his cousin with a hammer, chased other children with a knife, and attacked his teachers. Interviews with the boy's mother showed her to be emotionally involved with the child, extremely anxious, and over-protective. Szurek found that the mother got "deep pleasure from martyr-like submission to his whims and her smothering impulses towards him."[62] Separation from the mother caused a noticeable improvement in the boy's behavior. From this evidence, Szurek concluded that the unconscious encouragement of the mother caused "psychopathic" traits in the child.

The work of Heaver and Greenacre tended to confirm, at least in part, the conclusions of Szurek. In 1943 Heaver studied 40 patients at a New York hospital, and discovered that the majority had neglectful, but materially indulgent, mothers. The fathers were stern authoritarians, unconcerned with their children.[63] In 1945 Phyllis Greenacre reported her analysis of 9 "psychopaths." All the psychopaths had "stern, respected, and often obsessional fathers . . . remote, preoccupied, and fear-inspiring." The patients' mothers were frivolous, pleasure-loving, and continually seeking adulation from their contemporaries.[64]

Unfortunately, Szurek, Heaver, and Greenacre mislabeled acting-out neurotics as "psychopaths."[65] Their patients were aggressive and anti-social. They did not, however, exhibit the psychopathic traits of guiltlessness and warped emotions. Though provocative as analyses of causative factors in neurosis, the findings shed little light on true psychopathy.

More accurate diagnosis marked the work of Robert Lindner. In 1944, Lindner hypnoanalyzed 8 criminal psychopaths. After many hours of treatment, the patients revealed an "abrupt cessation of psychosexual development before the successful resolution of the Oedipus conflict." All had experienced brutal parental treatment.[66] Lindner hypothesized that the psychopathic child develops a deep hatred for his father. Instead of resolving the Oedipus complex (as do normal children) through identification with the father, the psychopathic child turns bitterly against his father. Lindner believed that his patients, deprived of parental identification and a stable superego, had transplanted their hatred to a symbol: society.

Subsequent studies substantiated the belief that psychopathy flourishes in an atmosphere of rejection. In 1947, after examining the familial records of "anti-social characters," British psychoanalyst Kate Friedlander found that severe emotional deprivation precipitated their behavior.[67] Three years later, American psychiatrist R. D. Rabinovitch reviewed his therapeutic experience with child psychopaths and concluded that a "gross limitation of mothering" caused the disorder.[68] In 1952 John Bowlby reported that his research with "affectionless characters" showed a high incidence of familial rejection in their backgrounds.[69] Although using different labels, Friedlander, Rabinovitch, and Bowlby dealt with the guiltless, affectionless, asocial psychopath.

Hence, the last decade of British and American research spun a consistent web of psychopathic causation. In study after study, emotional deprivation appeared to have precipitated a psychopathic personality structure.[70]

Perhaps the most definitive work was done by Lauretta Bender. In her clinical work at New York's Bellevue Hospital, Bender examined hundreds of child psychopaths. She found similar personality symptoms in all: diffuse impulsiveness, an inability to feel guilt, manipulation of morality without emotional meaning, and an "inability to identify themselves in a relationship with other people." Furthermore, her study indicated that all the psychopathic children had experienced emotional deprivation, neglect, or discontinuous affectional relationships. Bender believed that early emotional starvation, particularly during the first three years, leads to psychopathy. "We know that the critical time," she wrote, "is the first three years, especially the first year; any significant break in parent relationships or any period of deprivation under five years may be sufficient to produce this personality defect."[71]

Although questioning Bender's emphasis upon very early childhood, social scientists welcomed her clinical research as an additional substantiation of environmental causation. Bender and other investigators attributed the psychopath's inability to maintain close relations with others to early rejection. Bender found that the psychopath, as a child, had little experience with normal relationships, little opportunity for identification, and virtually no satisfaction of his craving for love.

Without identification, most social theorists believe, no child can evolve a mature conscience. One theory is that the normal child internalizes his parents' values because he fears the loss of their love. When his parents have no love to offer, the child does not fear its withdrawal. The unloved child becomes the unsocialized adult because he was not rewarded with affection. Physical punishment may bring temporary obedience, but when the threat of punishment no longer exists, no residue of conscience remains.

Although theoretically compact, the case for environmental causation is inconclusive. Much of the research confounds psychopathy with other disorders, thus weakening the evidence. In the more rigorous studies, the number of cases was not extensive. Nevertheless, the careful work of Lindner, Friedlander, Rabinovitch, Bowlby, and Bender has consistently shown that psychopaths, as children, were either neglected or rejected by their parents.[72]

While some scientists studied the psychopath himself, others investigated a related problem of great significance. It seems appropriate to ask: "Does rejection *necessarily* result in psychopathy? If not, what other factors make the critical difference?" Analyses of emotionally deprived children help to answer these questions.

Psychologist W. W. Newell, in 1934, examined 33 rejected children from the Cleveland Public Schools. He found the children extraordinarily aggressive, and their aggression seemed to be proportionate to the amount of overt rejection shown by the parents.

Two years later Newell added 42 cases to the original 33, and included a control group of 82 children (every pupil in one of the third grades and one of the fifth grades in a Baltimore public school). After prolonged observation Newell categorized the children in terms of their behavior: aggressive, submissive, mixed, or stable. Again, he observed a high proportion of aggression in the rejected children. His results gave the pattern:

Behavior	Percentage of Rejected Children	Percentage of Control Children
Aggressive	29	5
Submissive	29	29
Mixed	41	11
Stable	0	55

Not only did Newell find that rejection often led to aggression, he also found an interesting difference in the reactions of boys and girls: "Boys are aggressive when either—or both—parent's handling is consistently hostile. Girls are aggressive when either—or both—parent's handling is ambivalent, or when the father is hostile."[73]

In 1937 psychiatrist David Levy sought further verification of the effects of affectional deprivation. Levy studied rejected children undergoing treatment at New York's Institute for Child Guidance. He, too, found a high incidence of aggression. In addition, he discovered that the children lacked emotional depth and were severely handicapped in their ability to learn from experience—characteristics important in the development of psychopathy."[74]

Research by Percival Symonds, in 1939, confirmed the earlier findings. Symonds matched 31 pairs of children by age, sex, grade in school, social background, and intelligence. One of each pair was rejected by one or both parents; the other was accepted by both. Symonds' staff recorded information concerning the children's behavior, personality, and attitudes. Tabulation uncovered significant differences between the two groups: accepted children seemed "stable, well socialized, calm"; but "rejected children . . . showed much emotional instability, an excess of activity and restlessness, are generally antagonistic toward society and its institutions, and show apathy and indifference."[75]

The early studies of rejected children indicated that rejection causes socially destructive traits: aggression, inability to learn from experience, lack of emotional response, and antagonism toward society. Mildred Burgum, in 1940, set herself the task of determining constructive traits which might be traced to rejection. She studied 25 rejected children who had developed such admirable personality traits as

self-assurance, self-reliance, and "independence." This unusual reaction to rejection might, she believed, be due to several factors: high
intelligence, the child's desire to escape from the home, or possibly
the child's experience that "independence" brought him some approval.

Despite the fact that Mrs. Burgum specifically selected subjects who
exhibited constructive characteristics, she found only 8 who responded
to affection, and but 5 who could be considered "responsible." The
majority reacted "with destructive aggression, defensive escapes, or
personality and conduct disorder."[76]

Lewis Wolberg, in 1943, gleaned further evidence of the effects of
rejection. He examined 33 children being treated for extreme emotional disorders. Although not initially selected as rejected children,
he found they had all been rejected by their parents. Some of the
children showed a desperate need to cling, to be reassured and fondled.
Others desired complete seclusion and avoided all interpersonal relations. Twenty-eight of the children manifested extreme aggression,
temper tantrums, and destructiveness (even homicidal attempts). Of
even greater significance in the study of psychopathic causation, Wolberg found that "most of the rejected children seemed never to have
developed the capacity of delaying immediate gratification for future
pleasures; and the experience of deprivation mobilized tensions of
an almost uncontrollable nature."[77]

In 1945 the Fels Research Institute sponsored an extensive analysis
of parent-child relations. Over a period of $2\frac{1}{2}$ years, Fels' observers
visited the homes of 124 families. After long analyses, they classified
parents as acceptant, casual, or rejectant. Among the 31 rejectant
homes, they found two distinct varieties: nonchalant disinterest in
the child's welfare, and actively hostile dominance of the child. All
of the rejecting parents were hostile, unaffectionate, and disapproving.
Conflict, quarrels, and resentment pervaded the atmosphere.

The Fels Institute's research demonstrated a high correlation between parental treatment and child behavior. Children raised in
the rejectant environment usually showed extreme hostility, a "highly
emotional non-conformism," and a marked resistance to adults. Although the rejected children usually reacted with aggression, some
of them turned to other types of behavior: over-dependence, withdrawal, or precocious self-sufficiency. The severity of rejection seemed
to make the difference: the "actively" repressed children responded
with the most severe symptoms, the greatest emotionality, and the
least inner control.[78]

Also in 1945, Schactel and Levi administered Rorschach tests to 50 nursery school children who had been brutally treated by their parents.[79] They, too, found that rejected children responded sometimes with positive self-reliance, but more frequently with hostile truculence. Some of these very young children seemed definitely psychopathic:

> Johnny is extremely scattered, disorganized, and excitable . . . although he longs for expansion and adventure, he is quickly bored. He has virtually no fear, guilt, or conscience; rather, he is daring, incalculable.

Schactel and Levi noted that rejection molded the child's attitude, even at this early age, toward all human beings: "They accept the fact that they are not loved . . . (and) view all relations in terms of getting something from others . . ."[80]

By mid-century, studies of the rejected child had clearly demonstrated the relation between rejection and behavior disorder. In recent years the Harvard Laboratory of Human Development has carried out a comprehensive examination of the effects of child training on personality. The researchers interviewed 379 mothers and observed their nursery-age children in various play situations. They concluded that rejection significantly increases both aggression and dependency.[81] The Harvard Laboratory admitted the difficulty of measuring rejection; yet, in cases where *any* signs of rejection could be discovered, the children were more aggressive toward their parents, as well as more clinging and demanding of attention.

The Harvard research emphasized the fact that rejection usually, but not always, increases aggression. Frequently the rejected child exhibits the psychopath's syndrome of uncontrolled hostility, excessive impulsivity, low guilt, and apparent incapacity for love. Some rejected children respond differently, repressing their hostility, isolating themselves, and withdrawing from reality.

Studies of unloved children temper the claims that rejection, by itself and in every case, results in a psychopathic personality. Certainly, analysis of psychopaths has demonstrated almost overwhelming rejection in their childhood backgrounds. Yet studies of rejected children have clearly shown that lack of love does not *inevitably* cause psychopathy. Psychopaths were rejected as children, but not all rejected children become psychopaths.[82]

The severity of rejection may be the key *differentia specifica*. Several studies of the rejected child (e.g., the Fels' investigation) indicated that aggression and guiltlessness increase with greater parental rejection. The greater the deprivation of love, the more psychopathic the child's personality. Aggression increased with more pronounced rejection in the Newell studies, as well.

Several recent investigations of isolated children—children raised away from normal human love or social control—support such an interpretation.

In the past few years investigators have examined the effect of institutional isolation on personality. Between 1935 and 1945 William Goldfarb published a series of reports on this problem. In 1945 he compared 70 children who had been reared in institutions for their first three years with 70 children who had lived in foster homes from infancy through childhood.[83] Goldfarb found decided distortions in the institutionalized children: a serious lack of inhibition, an insatiable longing for love, and "incomprehensible cruelty to other children, foster parents, and animals." Goldfarb believed that institutionalization had "primitivized" the children: "This tendency to meagerness of feeling for other humans is complemented by the absence of normal anxiety following acts of hostility, cruelty, or unprovoked aggression."[84]

Institutionalized children attracted the attention of another psychiatrist, Lawson Lowrey. In 1940 Lowrey analyzed 28 children who had lived in an institution for the first three years of their lives. These children, too, showed an inability to relate to others, hostile aggressiveness, infantile behavior, and "unsocial" attitudes. Surprisingly, Lowrey discovered that this "isolation personality" occurred only when the children had been institutionalized before the age of two years.[85]

In England, Anna Freud and Dorothy Burlingham examined these "infants without families." The children, observed in a wartime nursery, were isolated from their parents and deprived of familial love. Freud and Burlingham noticed anti-social tendencies and stunted inner controls in their cases. They theorized that the children's consciences failed to develop because they lacked the ability to identify with adult love objects. Without emotional attachment, the children could not internalize adult demands or restrictions.[86]

John Bowlby's recent work has closely linked affectional isolation and psychopathy.[87] Bowlby analyzed cases of early deprivation, and concluded that "isolated" children are seriously handicapped in the later formation of affectional bonds. Due to this defect, the child develops other socially maladjusted traits. Bowlby's studies led him to conclude: "Certainly it would appear that the more complete the deprivation in the early years, the more isolated and asocial the child . . ."[88]

There have been few cases of *total* infant isolation which might serve to check Bowlby's conclusion. One of the most extreme cases was discovered, in 1940, by child welfare officials. A child of five had spent her short life tied to a chair with her arms locked above her head. The girl was the illegitimate progeny of a young woman who lived with her stern, fundamentalist parents. The Grandfather secluded the baby in a closed room. After the child's discovery, sociologist Kingsley Davis attempted to trace the influence of isolation upon the child's personality.

In any usual sense of the word, the child had no personality. Five years old, she could not walk, talk, or feed herself, and she just barely responded to loud noises made near her. After transfer to an institution, the girl showed little improvement. But after being moved into a foster home, where she was given affection, she began to walk up stairs, talk, and feed herself. She remained wild, unable to form relations, and extremely retarded.[89]

Other children raised away from human contact—Sanichar, Kamida, and the "girl of Songi"—showed the same symptoms as Davis's case. These extraordinary individuals never "became human." Their isolation was so complete that even the "socialization" necessary for psychopathy did not occur.

The social isolation of the institutionalized child, although severe, is not absolute, and many institutionalized children resemble the adult psychopath.[90] Apparently, severe affectional isolation predisposes a child to psychopathy, but absolute isolation results in total retardation.

IV. A Neuro-Social Theory of Causation

"If we cannot see clearly," Freud once said, "at least we can see the obscurities clearly." His dictum describes contemporary knowledge of psychopathic causation. Twenty-five years of research have resulted in disparate, often conflicting, explanations. Yet, beneath theoretical disputes lie some established facts and a few probable hypotheses.

The "hereditarians," the neurologists, and the "environmentalists" have each contributed a share to this growing pool of knowledge. Although they failed to establish a congenital cause for psychopathy, the hereditary "school" has shown that:

Psychopaths apparently have the same proportion of "tainted" ancestors as do normal people.

Psychopathy does not follow the lines of closest blood kinship, and thus is probably caused by non-hereditary factors.

Through analyses of brain waves, reflexes, and medical histories, the neurologists have tentatively established that:

Injury to the frontal lobe region or the hypothalamus results in aggression and anti-sociality.

Many psychopaths exhibit physical signs of brain disorder.

Proportionally, more psychopaths than normal people have a history of early brain diseases.

The psychopath's physiology responds more quickly to physical changes in the environment.

The environmentalist research has contributed many important insights. Through their analyses of rejection and affectional isolation, as well as their studies of the psychopath himself, the environmentalists have indicated that:

The vast majority of psychopaths have been rejected in childhood.

Aggression is the dominant reaction to rejection.

Rejected or institutionalized children often, but not invariably exhibit the psychopathic syndrome. They lack normal guilt feelings, they are impulsive, aggressive, pleasure-seeking, and they seem incapable of relating to other people.

Each of the three schools has, in general, conducted its research and defended its theories without regard to other findings, but none of the theories has satisfactorily shown a cause for psychopathy.

In the 1930's the "hereditarians" insisted that psychopathy resulted from genetic defects. Yet, psychopathy does not follow the Mendelian law, psychopaths do not have a higher incidence of "queer" ancestors, and "twin studies" failed to establish an hereditary base for the disorder.

In the late 1930's and early 1940's the neurologists proclaimed that organic brain damage caused psychopathy. Yet only a minority of psychopaths reveal abnormal brain waves, only a few psychopaths have a history of head injury or early brain disease, and only some psychopaths show physical symptoms of brain disorder. Furthermore, abnormal brain waves appeared equally frequently in certain other types of deviants.

By mid-century, the environmentalists' theory reigned supreme. Psychopathy, they maintained, resulted from childhood rejection. Yet, not all rejected children developed into psychopathic personalities.

Each causal theory, alone, has fundamental defects which invalidate its claims. Some observers have therefore concluded that the causes of psychopathy can never be known. Such pessimism, however, is unjustified. The last twenty years of research indicate that a combination of neurological and social insights can produce a plausible, if not definitive, explanation of the disorder.

Because all psychopaths have been at least mildly rejected, rejection seems to be prerequisite in the development of the syndrome. But not all rejected children become psychopaths. Thus rejection, while necessary, is not a sufficient cause. Either a particular type of rejection or some additional factor must tip the balance toward psychopathy. Studies of rejected and institutionalized children have shown a correlation between severity of rejection and psychopathy. Severe rejection, though not complete isolation, seems to account for many cases of psychopathy.

The evidence of neural defect in some psychopaths warrants the conclusion that brain damage plays a causative role. Injury to the forebrain sometimes deletes restraints, increasing impulsive and aggressive actions. But brain damage alone does not result in the distinctive characteristics of the psychopath: guiltlessness and lovelessness. Neural malfunction seems to be the catalyst which, in some cases, turns a rejected child into a psychopath. The proclivity for psychopathy found even in mildly rejected individuals, if aggravated by a neural system incompatible with inhibition, develops into the psychopathic syndrome.

Thus, there seem to be two causes. First, *severe rejection, by itself, can cause psychopathy*. Second, *mild rejection, in combination with damage to the brain area* (probably the hypothalamus) *which normally inhibits behavior, causes psychopathy*. This theory, we believe, reasonably synthesizes the superficially conflicting discoveries about the psychopath.[91] Rejection, sometimes severe and sometimes complemented by neural defect, plays the paramount role. The psychopathic syndrome evolves from this rejection.

The psychopath's *inability to maintain close relations* seems due to his inexperience with affectional bonds. As a child, the psychopath was consistently rebuffed. He did not experience the satisfactions which accompany emotional attachment. Since he never developed ties of affection, he never acquired the ability to "empathize."[92]

Because he early learned that the world offered him no love, the psychopath reacts to other human beings with suspicious indifference. He doubts the sincerity of those who may seek to establish close relations.

Though the psychopath might wish to develop an emotional attachment, he lacks the necessary techniques. His erratic, uninhibited, and aggressive behavior drives people from him.

Failure to develop a conscience flows logically from the psychopath's lovelessness. Almost all social scientists believe that the internalization of moral controls takes place primarily through the child's identification with his parents. The child and the parents strike an unconscious bargain: in return for the child's conformity to social restrictions, the parents give the child love. If the child fails to conform, disapproval follows.[93] In time, the child looks ahead to the consequences of his acts. If he is about to misbehave, a gnawing fear warns that his parents might stop loving him. Thus, the inner anxiety eventually achieves an internalization of the parent's morality. The child has developed a rudimentary conscience.[94]

There is, of course, a more positive aspect in this development of inner controls: not only does the child fear withdrawal of love, he also identifies with his parents. He loves them, and he wishes to emulate them. As Gordon Allport has pointed out, children who fear the loss of love develop the concept of "must," but the "ought" of behavior comes only through identification with parents and other moral symbols.[95]

In a rejectant environment, love, the central element, is missing. Because the rejected child does not love his parents and they do not love him, no identification takes place. Nor does the rejected child fear the loss of love—a love which he never had—when he violates moral restrictions.

Without love, the socializing agent, the psychopath remains *asocial*. And if love is too weak to countermand brain lesions which make socialization difficult, the child becomes a psychopath.

Since there is no real conscience in the psychopath, he allows uninhibited expression to whatever aggressive urges he has. *Aggression* seems intensified in the psychopath, although recent research with psychopathic children indicates that their aggressive drives are no more pressing than the normal person's.[96] Since he does not have strong emotional ties, the psychopath does not understand the effects of his aggression on other people.[97]

Impulsivity is also intimately connected with early rejection. As a child, parental love did not compensate the psychopath for moderating his behavior and, in at least some cases, neurological disfunctioning weakened his inhibitory faculties. Thus, as an adult, his impulsivity is unchecked.

Although inconsistent and purposeless behavior is a product of impulsivity, it may also be due to a deficiency in the psychopath's ego. Harrison Gough (among many others) believes that the normal person's self-concept arises through emotional interaction with other people.[98] The child records the evaluations of those around him and gradually absorbs these into his feeling toward himself. If these early evaluations are missing or are inconsistent, the child is unable to develop a coherent attitude about himself. Absence of long-range goals and erratic impulsivity may be due to the psychopath's under-developed attitude toward his "self."[99]

The psychopath's *pleasure seeking,* like his other traits, seems primarily due to his early experiences. His emotional frustration, in all probability, increased the intensity of his desires. Because he so seldom experienced it, the psychopath craves pleasure with heightened intensity. Uninhibited by either conscience or attachment to others, the psychopath seeks immediate satisfaction for his whims.

Aggression, pleasure seeking, and impulsivity cause the psychopath to violate society's rules. These traits, in turn, come from deeper deficiencies: warped ability to form relations and consequent lack of conscience.

Thus, the psychopathic syndrome can be traced to early deficiency in affectional relations. Extreme emotional deprivation, or moderate rejection coupled with neural damage to inhibitive centers, best account for the development of psychopathy. The theory reconciles the two major discoveries: that all psychopaths are, in some degree, rejected, and that many psychopaths have a neural disorder.[100]

Although the neuro-social theory seems the most plausible explanation of the psychopathic personality, it requires the confirmation of empirical research.[101]

V. THE EFFECTS OF SOCIAL AND CULTURAL FORCES

In addition to individual causative factors, some consideration should be given to the cultural forces which may contribute to psychopathy. The scanty research of the past few years indicates that four social factors influence psychopathy: social crisis, the class structure, technological complexity, and cultural attitudes toward children.

Insofar as emotional deprivation causes psychopathy, social crises (e.g., war and depression) can be expected to increase the incidence of the disorder. At such times social functions, including child rearing, are impeded. Families often separate, depriving children of their normal quota of love. Even in united families, pressures on adults often disrupt relations.

Studies of children isolated from their parents during wartime tentatively support the interpretation. Freud and Burlingham examined English nursery school children who had been separated from their parents. The children showed a great deal of anti-social behavior, a seriously underdeveloped conscience, and a lack of identification with adults.[102]

Rosemary Pritchard and Saul Rosensweig also investigated the effects of war stress on London's children. The children usually reacted with aggression, pilfering, truancy, and disorganized behavior. The researchers also found that the war led to an increase in neurotic and psychosomatic difficulties.[103]

Tracing the effects of war, Szondi analyzed refugee children who had lived in concentration camps. He too noted intolerance for frustration, increased aggression, hypomania, and impulsivity.[104]

These few pieces of research certainly do not prove that war directly increases psychopathy. They do, however, suggest that the effects of social crises, particularly those which precipitate separation at an early age, predispose the victims to a psychopathic character.

Other research indicates that class structure, at least in America, may have some influence on the incidence of psychopathy. The Fels Research Institute and the Harvard Laboratory of Human Development have attempted to relate parental attitudes to social class. The Fels group discovered that rejectant parents came primarily from lower economic levels and lacked education.[105]

The Harvard study, too, showed a correspondence between rejection and socio-economic class. After interviewing 379 mothers about their child-rearing attitudes, the researchers found that "upper-lower" class women more often rejected their children than did the "upper-middle" class. The lower class mothers were significantly less demonstrative of their affection, cooler in relations with their children, and more overtly rejecting. Lower class fathers had significantly less warm relations with their children.[106]

The lower class attitude seems to be a result of economic position. A family barely "making ends meet" probably does not welcome the birth of new babies. Although these two studies did not attempt to link psychopathy with social class, a logical implication of their findings is that psychopathy has a higher incidence in the lower class. If rejection causes psychopathy and lower-class mothers more often reject their children, there should be a correspondingly higher incidence of the disorder.[107]

Over twenty years ago Mandel Sherman and Thomas R. Henry conducted a cultural analysis which tentatively indicated that psychopathy, unlike other mental disorders, is less prevalent in technologically complex societies. They compared four communities in the Blue Ridge Mountains. Two of them, Oakton and Rigby, were undergoing rapid social change and increasing technological complexity. Two others, Colvin and Needles, were static, simple societies. Sherman and Henry found a higher incidence of "psychopathy" in the simple societies. The people of Colvin and Needles "accepted sexual indulgence, stealing and lying; they had slight guilt feelings and shallow emotional relations. In general, they revealed a stunted emotional development."[108]

Most social scientists believe, however, that the stresses of modern society disrupt the family and thereby promote psychopathy. Sherman and Henry concentrated on the investigation of other types of mental disorder, and their finding pertaining to psychopathy has not been confirmed.[109]

Other anthropologists have investigated issues which indirectly relate to psychopathic causation. One important study analyzed the connection between guilt and cultural methods of socialization. In 1953 John Whiting and Irwin Child compared the child training patterns of a number of cultures, relating nurturance and discipline to guilt. For their study, they measured guilt in terms of the individual's feelings of responsibility for the sicknesses which befell him. A "guilty" culture was one in which invalids blamed themselves for their illnesses.

After computing correlations, the anthropologists concluded that cultures which punish by withdrawal of love create significantly more guilt than those which punish by physical means (although the amount of initial "nurturance" did not correlate with guilt).[110]

The work of Whiting and Child adds substances to the belief that the "socialization anxiety" created by withdrawal of love leads to the internalization of guilt. Psychological research has shown that psychopaths, lacking the reward of love, do not internalize social restrictions. The anthropological findings tend to show that cultural patterns may furrow the ground for the growth of psychopathy.

Another cultural study, Cora DuBois' analysis of the Alorese, produced some suggestive evidence concerning the relation between methods of socialization and psychopathic traits. The Alorese are reared in a changing, inconsistent, rejective atmosphere. Two weeks after birth, the Alorese mother returns to work in the fields. Her baby is left to the sporadic care of other children. Parents tease, ridicule, and deceive their children, and the infants have little opportunity for continuous identification with an adult.

Such child training, in DuBois' view, leads to an adult personality characterized by shallow guilt feelings, fearfulness, temper tantrums, a vague self-image, competitiveness, power seeking, and ambivalence. Although they have a subconscious desire for dependency, the Alorese maintain only tenuous, hostile relations with others.[111] Thus in many respects, the typical Alorese resembles what we call the psychopathic personality. Although they are not completely denied love, their identification with others is hampered and they do not have the opportunity for developing internalized social standards.

Anthropologists and sociologists use techniques which should be applied to the study of psychopathy. Such problems as the internalization of guilt, the effects of culture on psychopathy, the relation between social change and personality, and the impact of crises on character demand deeper examination than they have yet received.

Before the process by which a baby develops into a psychopath can be fully understood, all the varied resources of psychological, social, and medical science must be utilized.

NOTES

1. PARTRIDGE, G. E. A Study of 50 Cases of Psychopathic Personality. *American Journal of Psychiatry,* 7:953-973, 1928.

2. CRUZ, J. Estudio de Las Personalidades Psicopaticas en Nuestra Criminalidad. *Arch. Crim. Neuropsiquiatry,* 3:38-50, 1939.

3. GOTTLIEB, J. S., ASHLEY, M. C., AND KNOTT, J. R. Primary Behavior Disorders and the Psychopathic Personality. *Archives of Neurology and Psychiatry,* 56:381-400, 1946.

4. MOHR, PETER. Die Forensische Bedeutung der Psychopathen. *Schweiz Arch. Neurol Psychiat.,* 60:244-268, 1947.

5. See B. BERLIT: Statistical Study of Hereditary Taint in a Selected

THE CAUSES OF PSYCHOPATHY 75

Group: Siblings and Parents of 362 Officers and Inmates of a Hospital in
Saxony. *A. Ges. Neurol. Psychiat.,* 52, 1935.

6. Mental Deficiency Committee of Royal Medico-Psychological Association Report. *Journal of Mental Science,* 82:247-257 (May, 1937).

7. KALLMAN, FRANZ J. *The Genetics of Schizophrenia.* New York, J.
J. Augustin, 1939, 214-225.

8. Although the research of both Lange and Rosanoff dealt with delinquents in general, their findings bear on the problem of psychopathy. Some
psychopaths were presumably included in their samples.

9. LANGE, JOHANNES. *Crime and Destiny.* New York, C. Boni, 1930.

10. ROSANOFF, A. J. The Etiology of Child Behavior Difficulties. *Psychiatric Monographs,* 1, 1943.

11. Lange used physical resemblance, photographs, and fingerprints as
his criterion. Rosanoff did not state his standards.

12. Cited in L. WHEELAN: Aggressive Psychopathy in One of a Pair of
Uniovular Twins: a Clinical and Experimental Study. *British Journal of Delinquency,* 2:130-143, 1951.

13. Although Sheldon uses the terms "first and second order psychopathy,"
this category includes a variety of personality types.

14. HOOTON, ERNST. *Crime and the Man.* Cambridge, Harvard University Press, 1939.

15. SHELDON, WILLIAM H. *Varieties of Delinquent Youth.* New York,
Harper, 1949.

16. GLUECK, SHELDON, AND GLUECK, ELEANOR. *Unraveling Juvenile Delinquency.* Cambridge, Commonwealth Fund, 1950.

17. Currently, the Gluecks are relating body types to personality (as
ascertained by Rorschach tests and psychiatric interviews). In a forthcoming
publication, tentatively entitled "Physique and Delinquency," the Gluecks will
discuss the relation between body types and psychopathy.

18. CLECKLY, HERVEY. *The Mask of Sanity.* St. Louis, C. V. Mosley, 1941.

19. Inadequate diagnosis is one of the most critical defects in all research on the heredity of psychopathy. With few exceptions, the investigators
either gave no description of their cases, or defined psychopathy in vague
terms.

20. HENDERSON, DAVID. *Psychopathic States,* New York, W. W. Norton,
1939, p. 29.

21. FREEMAN, WALTER, AND WATTS, JAMES W. Prefrontal Lobotomy:
the Problem of Schizophrenia. *The American Journal of Psychiatry,* 6:742,
1945.

22. ALPERS, B. Hypothalamic Destruction. *Psychosomatic Medicine,* 2:286,
1944.

23. FULTON, J. E., AND INGRAHAM, F. D. Emotional Disturbances Following Experimental Lesions of the Base of the Brain. *Journal of Physiology,*
90, 1929.

24. Cited in W. N. EAST: Psychopathic Personality and Crime. *Journal of
Mental Science,* 91:426-466, 1945.

25. Henderson, *op. cit.* (note 20), p. 30.

26. BENDER, LAURETTA. Post-encephalitic Behavior Disorders in Childhood. In JOSEPHINE B. NEAL: *Encephalitis.* New York, Grune & Stratton, 1942.

27. Most observers would label such cases as either acting-out neurotics or as cultural deviants.

28. HILL, D. AND WATTERSON, D. Electro-encephalographic Studies of the Psychopathic Personality. *Journal of Neurology and Psychiatry,* 5:47-65, 1942.

29. BRADLEY, G. E.E.G. Patterns of Children with Behavior Disorders. *Connecticut State Medical Journal,* 6: 1942.

30. SILVERMAN, D. Clinical Studies of Criminal Psychopaths. *Archives of Neurology and Psychiatry,* 50:18, 1943. Silverman used extreme anti-social behavior as the criterion for his selection of psychopaths.

31. SILVERMAN, D. The Electroencephalogram of Criminals. *Archives of Neurology and Psychiatry,* 52:38-42, 1944.

32. SESSIONS-HODGES, R. The Impulsive Psychopath: A Clinical and Electro-physiological Study. *Journal of Mental Science,* 91:482-476, 1945. Sessions-Hodges used extreme anti-social behavior as the criterion for his selection of psychopaths.

33. Gottlieb, *op. cit.* (note 3). Their standard of selection was not reported.

34. SIMMONS, D. J., AND ROCKWELL, F. The Electroencephalogram and personality Organization in the Obsessive-Compulsive Reactions. *Archives of Neurology and Psychiatry,* 57:71-77, 1947. They used extreme anti-social behavior as the criterion for selection of psychopaths.

35. GIBBS, F. A., AND LENNOX, W. G. Classification of Epileptic Patients and Control Subjects. *Archives of Neurology and Psychiatry,* 50:111, 1943.

36. See also D. STAFFORD-CLARK AND OTHERS: The Psychopath in Prison: a Preliminary Report of a Cooperative Research. *British Journal of Delinquency,* 2:117-129, 1951. Also DENNIS HILL: E.E.G. in Episodic Psychotic and Psychopathic Behavior. *E.E.G. Clinical Neurophysiology,* 4:419-442, 1952.

37. SIMMONS, D. J., AND DIETHELM, O. Electroencephalographic Studies of Psychopathic Personalities. *Archives of Neurology and Psychiatry,* 55, 1946. Selection based on "unsatisfactory functioning of self-reliance or adjustment to the group in which they live." "Psychopathic" cases were divided into the "neurotic type," the "cyclothymic type," those with "poor ethics," "immature," and "inadequate psychopaths."

38. SIMON, B., O'LEARY, J. L., AND RYAN, J. J. Cerebral Dysrhythmia and Psychopathic Personalities: a Study of Ninety-Six Consecutive Cases in a Military Hospital. *Archives of Neurology and Psychiatry,* 56:677-685, 1946. Selection based on extreme anti-social behavior. The team did, however, find a higher proportion of F-2 and S-2 waves in the psychopathic cases.

39. GREENBLATT, MILTON. Electro-encephalographic Studies of Homicidal Psychopaths. In P. SOROKIN: *Explorations in Love and Altruistic Behavior.* Boston, Beacon Press, 1950. His standard for selection was not reported.

40. Ostrow, M., and Ostrow, M. Bilaterally Synchronous Paroxysmal Slow Activity in the Encephalograms of Non-Epileptics. *Journal of Nervous and Mental Disease,* 103:346-358, 1946.

41. The Ostrows also noted an exceptionally high proportion of slow paroxysmal waves (especially indicative of sub-cortical disfunction).

42. Silverman, *op. cit.* (note 30). Silverman used extreme anti-social behavior as his criterion for selection of psychopaths.

43. Sessions-Hodges, *op. cit.* (note 32). His standard for selection was not reported.

44. Strafford-Clark, D., Pond, D., and Lovett, J. S. The Psychopath in Prison: A Preliminary Report of Cooperative Research. *British Journal of Delinquency,* 2:117-129, 1951.

45. Simmons and Diethelm, *op. cit.* (note 37), p. 625.

46. Lindner, Robert. Experimental Studies in Constitutional Psychopathic Inferiority. Part I, *Journal of Criminal Psychopathology,* 3:252-276, 1943. Part II, *Journal of Criminal Psychopathology,* 4:484-500, 1943.

47. Lindner's test could be used as a diagnostic measure. Lindner administered it to 25 prisoners whom the prison psychiatrists had independently diagnosed—as psychopathic or non-psychopathic. The judgments agreed 96 per cent.

48. Silverman, *op. cit.* (note 30).

49. Gottlieb, *op. cit.* (note 3).

50. Strafford-Clark, *op. cit.* (note 44).

51. Shotwell, A.M. A Study of Psychopathic Delinquency. *American Journal of Mental Deficiency,* 51, 1946. Shotwell selected his cases on the basis of severe anti-social behavior.

52. Puntigam, F. Verursacht die Encephalitis Post Vaccinationem Bei Jugendlichen Kriminogene Persönlichkeits-veränderung? *Öst . Z . Kinderheilk Kinderfürsorge,* 4:2, 1950.

53. See R. A. Leonardo: Criminal Psychopaths and the Electro-encephalogram. *Medical World,* 56:101-104, 1947.

54. Silverman, D. E.E.G. and the Treatment of Criminal Psychopaths. *Journal of Criminal Psychopathology,* 5: 1944.

Walker, C. and Kirkpatric, B. Dilantin Treatment for Behavior Problem Children with Abnormal E.E.G. *American Journal of Psychiatry,* 103, 1947.

55. See chapter on treatment.

56. See Henderson (note 20), and Sessions-Hodges (note 43).

J. J. Michaels, the Boston psychiatrist, has found a high incidence of eneuresis among psychopaths. This may be connected with neural damage. See his *Disorders of Character.* Springfield, C. C. Thomas, 1955.

57. See Sessions-Hodges (note 43).

58. Partridge, *op. cit.* (note 1).

59. Knight, Elizabeth M. A Descriptive Comparison of Markedly Aggressive and Submissive Children. Abstracted in *Smith College Studies in*

Social Work, Vol. 4, 1933. Knight did not distinguish the psychopath from the aggressive child. Her descriptions show that some of her cases were psychopaths.

60. FIELD, MINNA. Maternal Attitudes Found in 25 Cases of Children with Primary Behavior Disorder. *American Journal of Orthopsychiatry,* 10:293-311, 1940.

61. HALLER, B. L. Some Factors Related to the Adjustment of Psychopaths on Parole from a State Hospital. *Smith College Studies of Social Work,* Vol. 13, 1942. Haller selected his cases on the basis of severe anti-social behavior.

62. SZUREK, S. A. Notes on the Genesis of Psychopathic Personality. *Psychiatry,* 5, 1942.

63. HEAVER, W. L. A Study of 40 Male Psychopathic Personalities: Before, During, and After Hospitalization. *American Journal of Psychiatry,* 100, 1943.

64. GREENACRE, PHYLLIS. Conscience in the Psychopath. *American Journal of Orthopsychiatry,* 100, 1943.

65. A more recent study by Szurek and Johnson recognized this criticism. In an article published in 1952, they added that this familial background was found only in cases where there was "no generalized weakness of the superego." See A. M. JOHNSON, and S. A. SZUREK, The Genesis of Anti-social Acting-out in Children and Adults. *Psychoanalytic Quarterly,* 21:323-343, 1952.

66. Lindner's definition of psychopathy resembled the syndrome presented in the first chapter. Lindner's position on guilt, however, is not clear. He intimates that the psychopath may have deeply repressed guilt concerning his attacks on society (and, in a symbolic way, on his father). See *Rebel Without a Cause, op. cit.* (note 18 of chapter 1).

67. FRIEDLANDER, K. *The Psychoanalytic Approach to Juvenile Delinquency.* London; Kegan, Paul, Trench, Tribner, 1947.

68. RABINOVITCH, R. D. Round Table on Psychopathic Behavior in Children. *American Journal of Orthopsychiatry,* 22:2, 1952.

69. BOWLBY, JOHN. *Maternal Care and Mental Health.* Geneva, World Health Organization, 1952.

70. In 1948 Terry Rodgers studied fifty "psychopaths" at the Portsmouth Naval Prison. He loosely defined psychopathy in terms of behavior and found that 70% of his cases came from rejecting families, 96% from "abnormal" families. Rodgers felt that there was a close relation between neurosis and psychopathy: "Anxiety is the *vis a tergo* of each." See T. RODGERS: A Dynamic Study of the So-Called Psychopathic Personality. *Journal of Nervous and Mental Disease,* 107, 1948.

71. BENDER, LAURETTA. Psychopathic Behavior Disorders in Children. In ROBERT LINDNER AND ROBERT SELIGER, Eds., *Handbook of Correctional Psychology.* New York, Philosophical Library, 1947.

72. David Levy cites a few cases in which he believes overprotection resulted in psychopathy. From his brief descriptions of these children, it seems more probable that they are acting-out neurotics. Although uninhibited, they

felt guilt; although selfish, they formed affectional relations. See D. Levy, *Maternal Overprotection*, New York, Columbia University Press, 1943.

73. Statements by a mother that her child was unwelcome at birth were used in the selection of cases. See H. W. Newell, in *American Journal of Orthopsychiatry*, 4, 1934, and 6, 1936.

74. Levy, David. Primary Affect Hunger. *American Journal of Psychiatry*, 94, 1937.

75. Symonds, P. M. *The Psychology of Parent-Child Relations*. New York, D. Appleton-Century Co., 1939. In spite of Symond's careful tabulations, there were deficiencies in the study. Conversation with parents accounted for most of the data and, in all likelihood, rejectant parents would indicate negative personality traits of their offspring and acceptant parents would report more positive personality traits.

76. Burgum, Mildred. Constructive Values Associated with Rejection. *American Journal of Orthopsychiatry*, 10:319, 1940.

77. Wolberg, L. The Character Structure of the Rejected Child. *The Nervous Child*, 3:81, 1943-44, 2.

78. Baldwin, A. L., Kalhorn, J., and Breese, F. H. Patterns of Parental Behavior. *Psychological Monographs*, No. 3, 58:69, 1945.

79. Schactel, A. H., and Levi, M. B. Character Structure of Day Nursery Children as Seen Through the Rorschach. *American Journal of Orthopsychiatry*, 15, 1945, 2.

80. *Ibid*, p. 221. Some of the children, however, could maintain intimate relations with other people.

81. Sears, R., Maccoby, E., and Levin, H. *Patterns in Child Rearing*. Evanston; Row, Peterson, 1956.

82. In *Unraveling Juvenile Delinquency*, Sheldon and Eleanor Glueck found a much higher proportion of rejected children among the delinquents than among the non-delinquents. The Gluecks' work showed that a fairly large proportion of delinquents were rejected, yet only a minority (7.3%) became psychopathic. They found that 16.9% of fathers of delinquent boys rejected their sons, and 1% of the non-delinquents' mothers did so. Only 32.5% of the delinquents' fathers seemed emotionally attached to their boys, but 65.1% of the non-delinquents' fathers maintained close ties. 64.9% of the delinquents' mothers were emotionally attached to their children, though 89.8% of the non-delinquents' mothers had strong emotional ties (*op. cit.* [note 16] pp. 125-127).

83. Godlfarb, W. Psychological Privation in Infancy and Subsequent Adjustment. *American Journal of Orthopsychiatry*, 15, 1945.

84. *Ibid.*, p. 253.

85. Lowrey, L. G. Personality Distortion and Early Institutional Care. *American Journal of Orthopsychiatry*, 10, 1940, 3.

86. Freud, A. and Burlingham, D. *Infants Without Families*. New York, International Universities Press, 1944.

87. Bowlby, *op. cit.* (note 69).

88. *Ibid.* p. 4.

89. DAVIS, K. Extreme Social Isolation of a Child. *American Journal of Sociology*, 45, 1940.

90. Institutionalization does not appear prominently in the histories of psychopaths. Lauretta Bender, however, in her studies of psychopathic children at Bellevue Hospital, found that most of the children had undergone critical breaks from their families (*op. cit.*, note 26).

91. Possibly, entirely different factors can result in psychopathy. The psychopathic syndrome may be a "pheno-type," that is, a complex of symptoms (like fever) which can be caused by numerous factors. Nevertheless, it seems more likely that either severe rejection or rejection in combination with neural damage account for the phenomenon of psychopathy. Neither mild rejection nor brain damage alone seem to cause psychopathy.

92. Perhaps, as Maslow believes, the constant early frustration of the psychopath's need for love extinguishes the need.

93. The Laboratory of Human Development at Harvard has been studying the relationship between identification and guilt and between guilt and methods of discipline. Their evidence tends to confirm this hypothesis.

94. Recent experimental evidence tends to confirm this theory. Christopher Heinecke studied parental attitudes of a group of families. Then he watched the behavior of their children in doll-play. In the experiment, the doll violated a moral rule. Heinecke observed the children's reactions and later questioned them about their concepts of evil, confession, etc. He concluded that the children with the greatest guilt received the greatest "nurturance," and that their parents disciplined them primarily by withdrawal of "nuturance." Also, the children with the greatest guilt more often identified with the parent of like sex, more often identified with the adult role, and less often evidenced overt aggression. See C. HEINICKE: *Some Antecedents and Correlations of Guilt and Fear in Young Boys.* Harvard University Ph.D. dissertation, June, 1953.

95. See GORDON ALLPORT: *Becoming* (New Haven, Yale University Press, 1955) for a discussion of different "levels" of conscience.

96. See chapter 6: Milieu Therapy: an Evaluation.

97. Many observers believe that the psychopath uses aggressive behavior to get attention and recognition. In any case, all psychopaths are subject to aggressive explosions. While some can temporarily maintain a sociable exterior, frustration almost invariably produces an aggressive reaction.

98. GOUGH, H. G. A Sociological Theory of Psychopathy. *American Journal of Sociology*, 53, 1948.

99. Gough conceptualized the psychopath's weak conscience in similar terms. The psychopath has no early social interaction. He therefore never learns to take "the role of the other" and to evaluate his actions through the eyes of other people. Thus he never develops an image of the "generalized other," society.

100. It may be that all psychopaths have brain disorder. It could be this factor alone which makes a rejected child into a psychopath. The best research, however, has shown that only some psychopaths have neural disorder.

Perhaps better instruments and further investigation will uncover more widespread disfunction.

101. Probably the most critical test of its validity would be a combined neurological-environmental study. If psychopathy is caused both by severe rejection and by mild rejection plus neural damage, then all psychopaths who have been only mildly rejected should show signs of brain damage.

102. Freud and Burlingham, *op. cit.* (note 86).

103. PRITCHARD, R., AND ROSENZWEIG, S. The Effect of War Stress Upon Childhood and Youth. *Journal of Abnormal and Social Psychology*, 37, 1942.

104. Cited by Bowlby, *op. cit.* (note 69).

105. The upper class parents in the Fels research were primarily college teachers. The unique attitudes and superior education of this group may have affected their attitudes toward children and thus biased the Fels sample. Baldwin et al, *op. cit.* (note 78).

106. Sears et al, *op. cit.* (note 81).

107. Studies of psychopathy in relation to social class have not been made.

108. SHERMAN, M., AND HENRY, T. R. *The Hollow Folk*. New York, Thomas Y. Crowell, 1933.

109. There seems to be no theoretical reason why simple societies and psychopathy should be connected.

110. WHITING, J., AND CHILD, I. L. *Child Training and Personality: a Cross-Cultural Study*. New Haven, Yale University Press, 1953.

111. DuBois, C. *The People of Alor*. University of Minnesota Press, 1944.

5

The Treatment of Psychopathy

This disease is beyond my practice . . .
Doctor, in "Macbeth."
SHAKESPEARE

"AS A PROBATION OR PAROLE RISK the psychopath's chances of failure are 100 per cent," a psychologist recently said. He added gloomily, "There is no evidence to my knowledge that any psychopath has ever been cured by imprisonment—or by anything else."[1] Such pessimism is by no means unique; almost every prison administrator would agree. After reviewing his experiences and the conclusions of others, a prison psychiatrist observed: ". . . the disease is of lifelong duration in almost every case."[2] A psychotherapist who personally dealt with many psychopaths reached the typical conclusion: " 'We must learn to face the fact . . .' that psychopathy is untreatable."[3]

Prisons have done little to reform the criminal, be he non-psychopathic or psychopathic.[4] Yet incarceration has been society's major response to crime. In prison, the psychopaths lead most of the riots, pass most of the drugs, and indoctrinate most of the young newcomers.[5] The psychopaths commit the greatest number of prison offences[6] and spend the most time in solitary confinement.[7] In prison and out of prison, the psychopath contaminates society.

The well-publicized story of Earl Ward illustrates the effect of prison on the psychopath—and the effect of the psychopath in prison.

On Sunday evening, April 20, 1952, a young convict at the Jackson Prison shoved a knife into the stomach of a guard and forced him into a cell. The convict opened the doors of other prisoners in Jackson's block 15, its "hole." Picking up crowbars and knives, the men went on a rampage, beating all those who opposed them. Convicts smashed and burned furniture, started fires in the vocational shops, and flooded the cells.

Unable to stop the riot, the Jackson warden called in two hundred state troopers who subdued all the prisoners, except those in block 15. There, the toughest convicts locked themselves in, holding fifteen terrorized guards as hostages. The leader of the block: Earl Ward, psychopath.

Ward and his partner, "Crazy Jack" Hyatt, presented a list of demands to the prison authorities as their price for ending the battle. Mercilessly, they beat up those who wanted to surrender. One burglar, beaten with a black-jack and kicked in the head, was thrown into the prison yard.

After days of negotiation, the Governor consented to Ward's petition and the block surrendered.[8] The riot cost millions of dollars in physical damage. In human terms, the riot took a toll of fifteen wounded men, the nervous breakdown of a hostage, and one dead convict.

In childhood, Earl Ward hated his parents, fought with his teachers, and revolted against every form of authority. At fifteen, Earl tried to join the Army, but his father refused permission. Earl ran away from home, was arrested several times, and chose reform school rather than return to his parents.

Ward was sent from one school to another. Always, he fought, ran away, and caused "trouble." After each release Ward attacked his family or stole. Extensive analysis in a state hospital resulted in Ward's diagnosis as a psychopath.

During early adulthood Ward posed as a doctor, stole drugs, and performed illegal abortions. In 1949 a charge of burglary sent him to Jackson Prison. Jackson's administrators, intimidated by hints of past murders and anxious to rid themselves of a potential menace, transferred Ward to smaller Marquette. There Ward joined a group planning to kidnap the Governor when he visited the prison. The plot failed; but Ward's part in it (plus a death warning to a Marquette official) brought Ward's return to Jackson's maximum security section. The official whom Ward threatened to kill said: "In my fifteen years in this business I have heard many threats. This one, however, I take as no idle jest."[9]

Back at Jackson, Ward threatened to kill a guard who had searched his cell. Everyone in the prison feared Ward. Yet the disciplinary committee was impressed by his "sincerity" and "understanding." Though he appeared before them three times in one year, Ward's demeanor could be convincingly contrite.

During the 1952 riot, Ward asumed leadership: "They had no

more idea what the hell they wanted than flying in the air. That's why I took control."[10] He conducted negotiations skillfully, won all his demands, and, after surrendering, was put on trial.

The Jackson riot brought to public attention many of the inadequacies of the American prison system. For a time, the publicity given Ward's case dramatically pinpointed the psychopath's menace to society. Yet memories are short, and there are many Wards in prisons from Sing Sing to Alcatraz.

Though tempted to say—like the doctor in *Macbeth*—"This disease is beyond my practice," a few intrepid therapists have tried to cure the psychopath. Their experiments have approached the problem with a variety of techniques: group therapy, prison counseling, psychodrama, psychoanalysis, drugs, electro-shock, and even lobotomy.

Some of these experiments have required courage not usually demanded of the therapist. The psychopath is like a chow dog who may turn and bite the hand that pats him. The psychopath's hard emotional shell, his disturbing aggression, and his complete irresponsibility make therapy a thankless task. Nevertheless, a few determined men have accepted the challenge which society has long ignored.

I. The Treatment of Adult Psychopathy

Institutionalization has failed to cure the psychopath. Few objective studies have been made, but those few indicate that the chances of success are slim.

From Switzerland, Peter Mohr reported that the well-equipped Königsfelden asylum failed to cure most "psychopaths." Although Königsfelden was ostensibly an asylum for psychopaths, it treated many cases of sex deviance, neurotic criminalism, and other types of psychiatric disorder. Only 40 per cent of the patients had not committed a crime within two years of release.[11]

American institutions have had no greater success.[12] The most optimistic estimate, by W. L. Heaver, places the proportion of success with psychopaths treated in a hospital at 40 per cent.[13] Other follow-up studies have shown more disappointing rates of reformation. B. L. Haller, investigating 52 psychopaths six months after their release from a mental hospital, found that only 13 per cent had made a "satisfactory adjustment."[14]

Punishment seems useless. A British research team found, in 1951, that the average psychopathic convict had already served seven sentences: twice the number of convictions of the ordinary British criminal.[15] In other words, double the usual punishment had not deterred these psychopaths.[16]

Isolation offers but limited protection to society. Under our contemporary system of justice, the imprisoned psychopath will some day be set free to continue his depradations, and new generations of psychopaths constantly appear. Society's best hope for protection lies not in imprisonment, but rather in curing the disorder.

Some therapists believe that this cure might be effected within the prison, but only if special techniques are used. Group therapy has often been advocated as a treatment for psychopathy. During the last war, the Army met the costly problem of criminality by establishing "rehabilitation centers." According to Army claims, these institutions had amazing success, particularly with their group therapy programs. Imprisoned soldiers (30 per cent of them psychopaths) participated in discussions of alcoholism, personality development, relations to authority, and "levels of loyalty."[17] The leader maintained a permissive, non-authoritarian attitude.

The convict-soldiers were divided into separate groups according to personality traits. The psychopaths were placed in the "aggressive" section. During typical sessions in this group, the leader tried to get the men to identify with him as a friendly figure, and with his goals as both reasonable and right. This approach—and the leader's skillful way of deflecting hostile attacks—is illustrated in the following exchange:[18]

One soldier grumbled, "I don't like the way Sergeant . . . treated K." Approving comments swept through the group.

"The Sergeant is always doing things to K," the first soldier continued. "They are all the same, making us unhappy." The other group members nodded in agreement.

The leader, who had kept quiet until then, asked: "How do you like me?"

"You are like all the rest. I hate you too!" said the soldier. The remark antagonized the group. They began to shift their allegiance to the leader:

"He never done anything to us."

"He is our friend."

The first soldier answered, "You're just hand-shaking."

Gradually, with group support, the leader questioned the soldier. Why did he feel the way he did?

Eventually, the soldier concluded that he might have transplanted his attitude toward his father to officers. With this insight, the soldier began to form different, warmer relations with the leader.

Supervisors of the group therapy program believed that it held unusual promise in the treatment of psychopaths: reportedly, most psychopaths achieved some form of identification with the leader. Unfortunately, no study assessed the long-term effects of this method on the psychopathic personality.[19]

After the war, other institutions initiated group treatment. Chillicothe Reformatory set up a segregated unit for habitual offenders, a unit which soon became known as "Little Alcatraz." Inmates were forbidden visitors, movies, and trips to the canteen. Stern punishment kept the segregated block under control.

Treatment consisted in vocational classes, occasional well-disciplined discussion groups, and brief conferences with a psychologist. An official committee reviewed each man's progress periodically, giving him greater privileges if his behavior merited them. Chillicothe officials called their system "demonstro-therapy" because of its emphasis on achievement.[20]

According to prison diagnosis, only 12 per cent of the "Little Alcatraz" convicts were "fully developed, mature psychopathic personalities."[21] Probably the proportion of psychopathy was higher. Most of the habitual offenders were described as egocentric, unable to learn from experience, highly aggressive, and unable to form close ties.

Chillicothe officials felt enthusiastic about their "demonstro-therapy." Tests showed some gains in the convicts' school achievement, personality adjustment, and a marked improvement in their behavior within the prison.[22] Since no control group was established, we have no way of knowing whether such changes may have been due to chance.

San Quentin Prison, too, has utilized group methods in attempting to curb psychopathy. In addition to regular group discussions in a permissive atmosphere, the prison psychologists used psycho-drama.[23] Small groups of volunteers met several times a week to act out their problems and their pasts in spontaneous plays. After some initial shyness, the men participated in role-playing with enthusiasm. The story of one psychopathic convict demonstrates the method:

"B. E.," a 21-year-old burglar, had spent his childhood in foster homes. As a boy, he wandered from job to job, farm to farm. During the war, he joined the Navy. Because of drinking sprees, extensive

A.W.O.L., and gambling, B. E. spent 18 months in a Navy prison. "The Navy," he later complained, "was mean to me."

Following a series of burglaries, he landed in San Quentin Prison. In regular group therapy, the young convict remained aloof. In psycho-drama, however, he slowly dropped his shell of emotional hardness. After first observing the group for several weeks, he suddenly volunteered to re-enact his belligerence toward the Navy and his attempted escape from prison. His attitude became more cooperative. He gradually admitted the futility of his conduct, and later he volunteered to take the part of obnoxious, aggressive people in other plays. During the sessions, B. E. formed a "big-brotherly" attachment to another convict. By the end of treatment, the psychologist noticed definite changes in B. E.'s personality: " . . . he had a sincere belief concerning the futility of his conduct. The dramatizations afforded an abreaction of any doubt."[24]

Unfortunately, San Quentin, like the Army and Chillicothe, has made no systematic study of the treatment's effect on psychopaths.[25] Harrison Gough, nevertheless, believes that psycho-drama is uniquely beneficial for the psychopath. Because the psychopath is seriously deficient in his ability to relate to other people, role-playing might help in showing him the feeling of others. Although in the last few years a number of prisons have experimented with group treatment of psychopathy, none has made a complete evaluation of its impact.[26]

The effects of individual counseling have, however, been more thoroughly analyzed, and the results have not been as discouraging as many social scientists believe.

Harry R. Lipton, a prison psychotherapist, noted remarkable improvement in a psychopath who received only sporadic counseling from a chaplain and a psychiatrist. Lipton's case underwent the typically harsh treatment in childhood that seems conducive to psychopathy. Raised by a brutal uncle, he began his asocial career at the age of nine. Many crimes followed: burglaries at thirteen, manslaughter at nineteen, robbery at twenty, assault and robbery at twenty-five. Society retaliated with reform school and prison terms. In prison, the cynical young man bragged, fought, and led violent disorders. Psychological examinations uncovered the psychopathic syndrome and an aggressive father-hatred.

Equipped with this information, the prison psychiatrist and the chaplain began patient counseling of the convict. After seven years, the man's behavior radically changed. He became editor of the paper, sponsored better inmate-guard relations, and established strong ties with his mentors. In 1944, after his release from prison, he began a successful career as copy writer for an advertising company.[27]

Louis Weber, also, developed rapport with a psychopath. "B. T.," Weber's patient, had witnessed his father's suicide. At eight, he began stealing from his grandmother, who had taken care of the abandoned child. He stole throughout adolescence, but still he graduated from high school. During service with the Navy, B. T. rolled drunks, picked up homosexuals, and smoked "reefers." Following his discharge, B. T. passed from job to job, forging checks and staying with relatives until he stole from them. Once, after robbing his grandmother, he borrowed $300 from her and skipped town. His mother's request brought him to jail.

After setting fire to his cell, he was transferred to a state hospital for observation. There, psychologist Weber began his counseling, but not soon enough to prevent B. T.'s escape. B. T. stole a horse, soon abandoning it for a stolen airplane. Although he had not studied flying, B. T. somehow got the plane off the ground and later landed it.

Returned to the State Hospital, B. T. boasted of his exploits, while Weber tried to reach him through counseling interviews. B. T. turned every friendly overture to his own advantage. When the psychologist— upon the patient's request—gave him a model airplane kit, B. T. secretly poured the kit's glue into "cokes" to make his own bootlegged liquor. Gradually, however, Weber made progress with the case. Under sodium amytal B. T. spoke about hatred of his parents and shock over his father's suicide.

After release from the prison hospital as legally "sane," B. T. went to the counselor's home three times each week. With the counselor's urging, the patient went to work and began repaying the airplane damage. Although he lost his first job, B. T. did well as a clerk in a grocery store.

The months passed and Weber noted an increasing attachment. The patient accepted almost all suggestions. He joined the Y.M.C.A., and signed up with the Naval Reserve. Worried because of his record, B. T. asked his counselor whether he should inform the grocery store about his escapades. Weber agreed that he should. The store owner already knew about them, B. T. discovered; but B. T.'s concern over the matter was remarkable because of his former absence of remorse.

The interviews tapered off as B. T. assumed more control over his life. Suddenly, the interviews stopped altogether. B. T. lost his job and left without a word—for California.

Did the long counseling process fail completely? Probably not. B. T.'s mother reported that the young man was leading a normal, successful life in California and, for a year, had not gotten into trouble. The psychologist cautiously assessed the result: "Although [I] would hesitate to conclude that there was definite and lasting improvement, it does appear that some improvement took place."[28]

The psychopath's disorder, Robert Lindner felt, lies too deep for ordinary methods to affect it. In an attempt to cure psychopathy, Lindner tried the unusual instrument of hypno-analysis. After an hypnotic trance had been induced, Lindner used free association and dream analysis, supplementing these psychoanalytic techniques with hypnotic suggestion.

In *Rebel Without A Cause,* Lindner reported his experience with criminal psychopaths. He reproduced tape-recorded transcripts of his interviews with one patient. Harold, the psychopathic subject, was a federal convict boasting a long court record. In addition, he had an eye disability approaching blindness.

Harold first came to Lindner's office for treatment of his blindness. Medical tests indicated a psychological, rather than organic, cause. Slowly, Lindner led the patient into discussion of his anti-social behavior. Harold agreed to undergo hypno-analytic treatments, ostensibly for his blindness.

During the first hours, Harold evidenced stubborn resistance: "I feel as if I am in a daze or up against a big cliff. It seems somehow as if my path is blocked."[29] Gradually the convict unveiled a picture of his earlier years: the harsh authority of his father, his sexual attachment to his mother, and lurid erotic experiences. In talking of "Perry," his homosexual friend in the prison, Harold showed the beginnings of an attachment to his therapist: "He is the first one besides you who ever took any interest in me."[30]

As the therapy progressed, Harold's hatred of his father emerged. The boy's first thefts began with the stealing of his father's pen-knife and razor. This act he committed in reaction to the father's threat of castration: "My sister was a tomboy and he would say things about cutting off my penis and giving it to her."[31]

Conflict with the father began because of intense jealousy: "Well— I-I-ever since I can remember—because—these things—my mother . . . Well, because ever since I can remember I wanted to possess— my mother—more than anyone else . . ."[32] This maternal attachment and the resultant father-hatred culminated in the attempted murder of a criminal who had jokingly taunted Harold about his love for the mother.

Under deep hypnosis, Harold recalled watching his mother and father having intercourse. Lindner believed that Harold associated the traumatic experience with an early movie in which his eyes had been blinded by the movie projector. The lustful glint in his father's eyes became attached to the momentary experience of blindness. Harold had "seen things that were forbidden" and had permanently blinded himself as punishment.

By the end of therapy, Harold accepted the connection between his blindness and the early traumatic experience. Furthermore, according to Lindner, Harold recognized that his criminality was an attempt to prove his manliness. Both were manifestations of his hatred for his father: "He was stronger than me, I was afraid of him." Lindner believed that the father's brutality caused distrust in Harold and a blind drive to express his aggressive feelings.

Although Lindner did not report on Harold's life after termination of hypno-therapy, he felt that the psychopath's new insight caused a startling reorientation of character. Realizing that his clashes with the law came from father-hatred, Harold was better able to control his hostile urges. Harold's highly repressed "guilt" about incestuous desires—perhaps existent in all psychopaths—became conscious.[33] Lindner reported success with the method in 7 other cases of psychopathy. Hypno-therapy seems to provide the patient with an opportunity for working out youthful hatreds and for gaining deeper insight into behavior.

Terry Rodgers, a Naval psychologist, found that hypno-therapy improved a passive, emotionally-starved Marine in a mental hospital. The Marine gained insight, and many of his painful symptoms disappeared. Although Rodger's patient was not a psychopath (as Lindner's may not have been), his family had been highly rejectant. Rodgers believes that hypno-therapy can be particularly valuable for those who have been raised in a loveless environment.[34] Possibly it breaks through the hostile, suspicious barriers which ordinarily make relationships so difficult. Hypno-therapy, as yet scarcely tested, may prove to be one of the most valuable instruments for the treatment of psychopathy.

Psychoanalysis, unsupplemented by hypnosis, has also been used with psychopaths. The earliest experiments had dismal outcomes. In 1924 Mary O'Malley reviewed the reports on psychoanalysis and concluded: "Psychoanalysis as a therapeutic measure for the psychopathic personality . . . has proven a failure . . . "[35]

In Germany, only 1 of 23 psychopaths treated at the Berlin Psychoanalytic Institute "improved greatly." Eighteen patients had discontinued treatment, and 4 had shown no improvements under analysis.[36]

In 1948 Walter Bromberg psychoanalyzed a psychopath in a Naval prison. Bromberg's 19-year-old patient had been raised by his grandmother. His parents were divorced and his father, a criminal alcoholic, persistently beat the boy. The patient's record of fights, knifings, and riot leadership within the prison made him a dangerous challenge.

In the first analytic sessions (which the prisoner was forced to attend) the boy refused to talk with his analyst. Once the psychopath drew a knife on Bromberg. Eventually, however, the boy's extreme resistance gave way under the therapist's patient prodding. The boy related the story of his love-impoverished life. His first dreams dealt with killing: killing guards, killing convicts, and killing his therapist. Later the theme shifted to fear of the analyst.

Bromberg's non-demanding friendliness, coupled with firm consistency, impressed the convict—and partial identification took place. Unfortunately the analysis ended abruptly when Bromberg returned to civilian life.[37]

Melitta Schmideberg reported a high degree of success in her use of psychoanalysis with psychopathic personalities. Schmideberg analyzed 11 major criminals: "habitual, hardened, callous" offenders.[38] In addition to their anti-social attitudes, most of her patients had meager guilt feelings and impoverished relational abilities. Schmideberg diagnosed the majority as true psychopaths.

Surprisingly, Schmideberg reported substantial improvement in every case. Two of her cases illustrate the startling transformations:

One man, an American "tough guy," had committed thirty-two

armed hold-ups. "He claimed that there is no crime that he did not commit with the exception of murder, counterfeiting, and cheating at cards." He had never held a job, earning money instead through constant criminal activity. One of the patient's favorite techniques was luring homosexuals to his room and, while the victims slept, smashing them over the head with a bottle and stealing their money.

Immigrant parents had deserted the patient in early childhood. At thirteen, convicted for twenty minor offenses, he entered a reformatory. After discharge he lived the life of a vagrant gangster. At twenty-one, with a long record of robberies, he was sentenced to prison.

Paroled from prison 6½ years later, the patient was sent to Schmideberg for analysis. With patience, with repeated demonstrations of her confidence in him, and with permissive acceptance, Schmideberg slowly established rapport. The treatment, more than 60 sessions, stretched over a long period.

As therapy progressed, the man disclosed profound feelings of inferiority and rejection. The causes of his behavior, Schmideberg reported, became clear to him. By the end of treatment, his personality had undergone a striking change. Perhaps most importantly, his ability to form emotional relations developed to a mature level. The analyst's last check on him showed that he had married, had children, and had turned into a "settled, contented, good father and husband."[39]

Another of Schmideberg's patients, a middle-aged English woman, had served fifteen sentences for misrepresentation and theft. Her father, a clergyman, was also an alcoholic. Her relatives protected their social prestige by paying five thousand pounds to cover the woman's crimes. In her twenties several psychiatrists had examined her. Finding her a psychopath, each refused to treat her.

She married an irresponsible man and gave birth to two children. Abortions prevented the birth of others who had been sired by lovers.

Released from one of her many prison sojourns, the patient went to the Institute for the Scientific Treatment of Delinquency. Schmideberg accepted the case.

At first, therapy achieved nothing. The patient continued to steal and returned to prison. Undiscouraged, Schmideberg visited her in prison. Assured of the analyst's support, the patient gained new emotional security.

Again paroled, she showed improvement. Suddenly however, she renewed her thieving. Only later did the analyst discover the reason for the relapse: blackmail. A former lover had been extorting from the woman because she had killed their illegitimate baby years before. Again the analyst came to her aid and saved her from a return to prison.

Prolonged therapy apparently developed new values and inner stability. The therapist's last examination showed that the woman had adjusted to society and its demands.[40]

One of Schmideberg's therapeutic problems was getting the psychopaths "to endure kindness."[41] Suspicious of all human beings, and inexperienced in maintaining emotional relations, the psychopaths rejected friendship. Only through persistent permissiveness could the therapist develop the patients' trust. Love, permissiveness, loyalty, and great patience seemed to ameliorate the symptoms of psychopathy. Schmideberg commented: " 'Standing by,' showing forebearance again and again helps the patient gradually to acquire the love and security he missed in childhood, and enables him to gain a social attitude by identification."[42]

Fortunately, the techniques used by Schmideberg are not exclusively the prerogative of psychoanalysis. Love, patience, and permissiveness can be used by any therapist who treats psychopathy and, if Schmideberg's cases are any indication, they can be used successfully.

Nevertheless, the transformations through psychoanalysis, reported by Schmideberg, and through hypnoanalysis, reported by Lindner, are exceptional.[43] Other therapists have experienced more failures than successes. Even when there has been improvement, as psychoanalyst Phillis Greenacre points out, success may be illusory: "(Psychopaths) very often . . . make quick dramatic improvements which are soon revealed to be only 'skin deep' or to disappear as dramatically as they were instituted; it is then apparent that the fundamentally unsound organization of the personality of the psychopath has not been much influenced or even touched."[44] Thus the impact of therapy requires careful and complete study.

Because the psychopath's capacity for identification is so limited and his sense of responsibility so meager, psychotherapy has been difficult. Some instrument is needed for easing the psychopath's transition into therapy. Drugs, of one variety or another, have been used to wedge the psychopath's resistance.[45]

Carl Adatto, for one, found barbiturates helpful in establishing initial rapport. From the Mendocino State Hospital, Adatto selected

14 "psychopathic" inmates and subjected them to narco-analysis. He administered Pentothal Sodium intravenously and, while the patient relaxed, asked personal questions. Many of the patients had strong hatred for their fathers, but also unexpectedly strong attachments to their mothers:[46]

> "Tell me about your mother," the interviewer asked.
> "Mother? She could have every last cent I got!" the patient began to cry.
> "I had the best mother in the world. I would lay down and die for her; but she is gone, she is gone."

Because Adatto did not define what he meant by "psychopathy," the mother fixation of his patients may not be typical of the true psychopath.

George Train, a psychologist at Lewisburg Prison, also used Pentothal Sodium on convicts. Again the drug proved useful as an adjunct to psychotherapy. One of Train's psychopathic patients had a record of juvenile crimes, an unstable work history, and unsatisfactory emotional relationships. During a pentothal interview, he described the "primal scene" he had witnessed, interpreted as a chastisement of his mother, and remembered vividly. Train deduced that this memory resulted in antagonism toward the patient's father and all authority. Other interviews followed, and the therapy caused a slight improvement in the patient's behavior. He was sent to a mental hospital. Four months later he was reported as "adjusted satisfactorily."[47]

F. A. Freyhan, a hospital psychiatrist, used drugs as a therapeutic aid. Freyhan selected two "psychopaths" and gave them sodium amytal. One man did not change; the other showed a greater willingness to talk and a more friendly attitude. He became more accessible to psychotherapy.[48] Unfortunately, Freyhan did not record the eventual outcome of his therapeutic sessions.

In their search for a cure, some scientists used drugs alone. In general, these investigators believed in a constitutional cause of psychopathy, an organic condition which could be entirely corrected by physical means.

In 1944 Daniel Silverman studied the effects of a variety of drugs on 64 psychopathic inmates of a federal prison.[49] Some patients were given dilantin sodium, others took phenobarbital, benzedrine sulphate, or a combined dosage of amytal and benzedrine. A control group received placebos of sugar and water resembling the narcotic tablets. Silverman traced the E.E.G. patterns of the subjects before and after treatment. In addition, he secured reports from the prison officials concerning the men's institutional behavior.

Only dilantin sodium seemed to bring any improvement. Prisoners who had taken the drug became less antagonistic and more reliable. They reported a greater feeling of well-being and contentment. Their E.E.G. patterns normalized. The other drugs brought no behavioral improvement and little change in the E.E.G. tracings. Benzedrine sulphate actually caused more abnormality in the brain waves. The placebos induced a feeling of "well-being" in some of the prisoners.

Silverman did not follow the subsequent behavior of the men, nor did he measure the impact on basic personality structure.[50]

Dennis Hill, in 1947, found that amphetamine sulphate, too, improved the behavior of "psychopaths." Hill administered the drug to aggressive, "bad-tempered" patients. After taking the narcotic, the patients' personalities appeared "more integrated" and they had a "more mature expression of the primary appetitive drives."[51] The drug, Hill hypothesized, exerted an oxidating influence on the associational areas of the cerebral cortex. Unfortunately, Hill did not report what happened once the drug was removed.

Also in 1947, H. J. Shovron reported from England on the effects of benzedrine. Using three adult "psychopaths," Shovron found that the drug had only temporary usefulness. The patients' aggression lessoned for a period, but the drug's effect was short-lived.[52]

The results of narco-therapy are disappointing. For some patients, particularly those with an epileptic history, dilantin sodium and some barbiturates may have a temporarily soothing, euphoric effect. Possibly such drugs will prove a useful supplement to psycho-therapy. By calming the psychopath's aggression they should help to "lubricate" the therapeutic relationship, but science has yet to develop a miraculous pill which can transform the psychopath.

Electric shock and lobotomy, the "last resort" instruments of modern psychiatry, have been tried on psychopaths. The first and the only thorough measure of the impact of shock treatment on psychopaths was made in 1944 by Eugene Green, George Geil, and Daniel Silverman. These prison psychiatrists selected 24 psychopathic convicts and subjected them to electric shock.[53] Before the experiment, the researchers took E.E.G. tracings and compiled reports on the prisoners' behavior.

Six months after treatment, the psychiatrists found that most of the men had not noticeably changed. The behavior of 4 subjects improved, 7 others showed slight improvement, and 13 convicts were unchanged by the experiment. When questioned about their feelings, 6 convicts said they felt better, 2 felt worse.

Remeasurement of brain waves showed that the E.E.G. patterns of 2 men improved, but those of 6 others became more abnormal. Fortunately the latter eventually returned to their original patterns.

The research team attempted to assess the psychological effects of shock treatment. Eight men from the experimental group took the Wechsler-Bellevue intelligence test before and ten months after the shock treatment. Their I.Q. scores increased an average of 9.8 points. The mean score of a control group of 8 other convicts increased 4.2 points during the same period. The researchers admitted that the treated convicts, because of the attention given them, may have tried harder.

"Before and after" Rorschach tests of 4 of these psychopaths revealed that their productivity (the number of responses to the pictures) significantly increased. The mean number of answers of the treated group went up from 11.7 to 33.7; those of a control group of 4 convicts increased only slightly, from 11.7 to 12.0. Once again, the motivation rather than the treatment may account for the difference. The Rorschach protocols reflected no changes in the character of the psychopathic convicts.

In other experiments with shock treatment, diagnoses were confused and many varied disorders labeled "psychopathic."[54] The results, at first glance, appear slightly more impressive.

H. F. Darling found that shock treatment benefited 2 "psychopaths" and did not help another.[55] Golden found that 3 out of 4 "psychopaths" improved under shock treatment.[56] And Banay, the most optimistic researcher, reported "beneficial reactions" in all but 12 of 51 cases.[57]

Lobotomy, the incision of a small rotating blade into the prefrontal lobes, has been practiced in the attempt to cure psychopathy. In 1938 Walter Freeman and James Watts first tried this drastic technique on a case "which bears a family resemblance" to the psychopathic personality.[58] Following the operation, the patient, an adult criminal, seemed less aggressive.

In 1942 R. S. Banay and L. Davidoff subjected a middle-aged "sex psychopath" to lobotomy.[59] Afterwards, the patient seemed to gain insight, his sense of responsibility appeared to increase and, as far as the authors knew, he had "socially recovered." His eventual adjustment was not reported; nor was his personality thoroughly analyzed.

In 1949 a Swedish psychiatrist, Lennart Nilson, performed the operation on an anti-social patient with a long criminal record. The man, loosely tabbed a psychopath, seemed to improve, but no full study was made.[60]

The most enthusiastic advocates of lobotomy, H. F. Darling and J. W. Sandall, tried surgery on 18 severely anti-social inmates of a mental hospital. Seventeen of the patients "improved," and 9 were released from the hospital. The researchers believed that psychopathy —although triggered by environmental causes—resulted primarily from inherited weaknesses. Only a change in organic structure, they believed, could cure the psychopath. "If psychopathy were a deficiency in the social interaction of the individual," they reasoned, " . . . the great improvement following the operation would be an impossibility . . . Certainly, the environment of the patients in the series was not changed by means of a leucotome."[61]

Such reasoning, from "cure" to cause, is dubious. Many types of disorders, both functional and organic, respond to lobotomy.

Experiments with lobotomy must be cautiously assessed. The label of "psychopathy," often abused, was particularly misused in these studies. Often the patient's only "psychopathic" trait was his anti-sociality. Furthermore, the ultimate effects of lobotomy were seldom examined.

The use of lobotomy with any patient is hazardous—and with psychopaths, particularly so. Lobotomy has been successful in decreasing the oppressive anxiety of some psychotics. But psychopaths have little or no anxiety. Indeed, one of the most important tasks of therapy is to increase their anxiety. Post-operative studies have found a striking increase of aggression in some patients, though in others aggression has decreased. For the psychopath—already an overly aggressive person—such unpredictability adds to the danger of lobotomy.

In summary, therapeutic experiments with the adult psychopath have shown:

> Incarceration in prisons or mental hospitals temporarily isolates psychopaths from the larger society. While we cannot be certain, it seems probable that imprisonment is even less effective in reforming these offenders than in reforming non-psychopathic delinquents.

The effects of "group therapy," whether in the form of discussion groups, "demonstro-therapy," or psychodrama, have not been conclusively ascertained. In some cases, such methods seem to make the psychopath better able to maintain affectional relations.

Psychotherapy has, in isolated cases, resulted in marked changes. Usually, however, even prolonged psychotherapy has not altered the psychopathic character.

Hypno-analysis, successful with a small number of cases, holds promise of usefulness. Its lasting effects on personality have not, however, been traced.

Certain drugs, particularly Pentothal Sodium and dilantin sodium, are potentially useful for easing the problems of individual counseling. They help to make the psychopath amenable to psychotherapy.

Drugs, unsupplemented by other treatment, have failed to bring lasting improvements in psychopaths.

The effects of electric shock treatment have not been fully measured. Tentatively, results indicate that shock does not alter the psychopath's personality structure.

The results of lobotomy on psychopaths are also unknown. Diagnoses have frequently been inexact, and subsequent behavior has not been thoroughly traced.

Unfortunately, many therapeutic experiments have commingled several disorders under the label "psychopathy." Disappointingly, too, few therapists incorporate personality analysis in their assessment of results. Without careful diagnosis and complete examination of personality changes, we cannot know what, if any, impact the methods have on psychopaths.

The prospect for successful treatment, while gloomy, is not altogether discouraging. Although inadequately assessed, psychotherapy seems to hold the most promise. In one of its forms, hypno-analysis, Robert Lindner found an effective means of treating several "psychopaths." Hypnosis apparently helped to establish rapport and to uncover repressed memories. The relationship itself offered the patients an opportunity for identification which they had lacked. Though few in number and questionable in diagnosis, Lindner's successes justify further trial of hypno-analysis in the treatment of psychopathy.

Psychotherapy, without resort to hypnosis, has at times been successful. If the resistance of the psychopath can be overcome, and if the therapist has great patience, an emotional bond can sometimes be made. Lipton, Weber, Schmideberg, and Bromberg have apparently utilized rapport for the inculcation of new values and a more acceptable "life style."

This process, however, is unpredictable. Many psychopaths seem incapable of establishing rapport. Moreover, psychotherapy requires an expenditure of energy and time which few psychologists can afford. Possibly such drugs as dilantin sodium, Pentothal Sodium, or sodium amytal could shorten the process of developing rapport. Here again, we need more experiments and thorough evaluation of results.

The adult psychopath is singularly resistant to treatment.[62] He lacks the desire for change and the anxiety over his condition which most therapists believe is the prerequisite for treatment. Most psychopaths see nothing wrong with themselves and, therefore, no reason to change.

Since rapport is basic to all psychotherapy, the psychopath's deficiencies in this area represent a serious handicap. Without experience in emotional relationships, the psychopath resists the complex patient-therapist bond.

Finally, the psychopath has little guilt. He feels no compunction about breaking appointments, about attacking the therapist (usually verbally, sometimes physically), or about stopping treatment altogether. These three traits—lack of anxiety, lack of "identifying ability," and lack of guilt—make the psychopath a poor prospect for successful therapy.

Thus psychotherapy offers a little hope, but no assurance, of success. Other approaches to the problem seem even less promising: incarceration alone, while temporarily protecting society, does not seem to change basic personality trends; organic treatment (with drugs, shock, or lobotomy) has shown few, if any, beneficial results.

In short, treatment of the adult psychopath, while not hopeless, is far from hopeful. Therefore, attention should be given to the prevention of adult psychopathy. Our best hope lies in the successful treatment of child psychopathy: in changing youths before they mature into hardened psychopaths.

II. The Treatment of Child Psychopathy

The child psychopath has the embryonic personality traits of the adult psychopath. His tantrums and delinquencies betray his aggressiveness. His truancies reflect his impulsivity. His cruelties to animals and children reveal his asociality. The child psychopath has little—if any—remorse for his diffuse, brutal, usually purposeless activities, and he seems unable to affiliate with other human beings.[63]

Many of the techniques used with adult psychopaths have been tried with the child. Most frequently, the juvenile psychopath has been incarcerated with other delinquents. Although we know that the usual reform school leaves few beneficial imprints on its charges,[64] there are unfortunately no studies specifically concerned with the adjustment of the psychopathic child.

Some social scientists, though not advocating the usual severity of the reform school, believe that the child psychopath must be treated in a disciplined environment.[65] Only strict regimentation and forced conformity, they contend, can inculcate values into the child psychopath. An experiment at the Hawthorne Cedar-Knolls School put this theory into practice.

The school officials decided that permissive methods would not help "Bernard," a highly aggressive boy. Immature, self-centered, and "affectless," Bernard had insulted his teachers, attacked other children, run away from home, gotten into "sex trouble," and frequently stole. Hawthorne Cedar-Knolls placed the boy under a special regime of authoritarian control and strict limitations. He was forced to conform to a routine. At all times, even when they punished him, the school officials tried to act without malice.

Bernard formed a limited attachment to a house mother, and his behavior became a little more moderate and self-controlled. He seemed to improve, but the change was not striking. After release, a follow-up report indicated that Bernard was "doing well" in the Army.[66]

In another study, B. M. Wolfe found that institutional conformity apparently had beneficial results with only a handful of psychopathic boys. Wolfe examined 16 psychopathic children who had been incarcerated in the children's group of a mental hospital. Their treatment consisted primarily in disciplined, patterned supervision. Of those cases which could be traced, 11 made an unsatisfactory adjustment, 3 made a "moderately satisfactory" adjustment, and only 2 seemed to have recovered—and on closer analysis, it was decided that these 2 boys were cases of "adolescent upset" rather than of true psychopathy.[67]

On the basis of admittedly slight evidence, it appears that forced conformity teaches the child psychopath little more than it does the adult psychopath. The cure, if there is one, probably lies elsewhere.

Hoping to find a surer solution to the psychopathic dilemma, some psychiatrists experimented with narcotics. Phenobarbital proved useless when tried with aggressive children in the 1940's.[68] Work with benze-drine sulphate, however, hinted at the exciting possibility that this drug might prove the answer to child psychopathy.

In 1941 K. K. Cutts and H. H. Jasper reported that benzedrine markedly improved 6 children who exhibited "behavior disorders." The boys apparently had epileptoid conditions, and the drug soothed and inhibited them. The narcotic did not seem to affect 6 other "asocial" boys.[69] In 1942 D. B. Lindsley and C. E. Henry administered benzedrine to aggressive children and noted beneficial effects on all.[70] In the same year, D. Davidoff and G. L. Goodstone used benzedrine and sodium amytal on psychopathic boys. They too found a startling increase in the children's behavioral control.[71]

Other experiments, however, dampened the initial enthusiasm for benzedrine as a cure for psychopathy. In one of these later studies, S. R. Korey selected 11 severely delinquent boys from the National Training School and gave them the drug. Of these boys 4 were neurotic; the other 7 psychopathic.[72] Benzedrine induced a feeling of well-being in all the boys, and the behavior of 2 of the psychopaths markedly improved. One other psychopath improved "moderately," another improved "subjectively," and 3 boys did not change. After the drug was removed, the "improved" boys reverted to their former states. None of the psychopaths changed permanently in personality structure.[73]

Benzedrine had even more disappointing results in cases treated by Lauretta Bender and Frances Cottington. These researchers had found that the drug made neurotics calmer, more secure, and more eager to learn. Yet, when the drug was given to 4 psychopathic children, an unfavorable reaction ensued.

Two of the children had been in foster homes. The other 2 had been severely rejected by their parents. All 4 had caused serious trouble in school. They were self-centered, quarrelsome, and apparently with-out affection.

The use of benzedrine on the 4 children increased their inner tension, instability, and excitability. The children gave way to disorganized fantasies and seemed baffled. Bender and Cottington believed that the narcotic made the psychopaths aware of emotions which they could not combat. As soon as the drug was withdrawn, its effects dis-appeared.[74]

Dilantin sodium may offer some hope in the treatment of child psychopathy. The drug has not been tried on known psychopaths, but it has been extensively used on aggressive children (some of whom may have been psychopaths). Lindsley and Henry found that the narcotic temporarily calmed behaviorally disturbed children.[75] In 1947 C. Walker and B. Kirkpatrick enthusiastically reported dramatic improvement in aggressive children who had undergone dilantin sodium treatment. Unfortunately, the improvement disappeared with removal of the drug.[76]

At least at the present time, there seems to be no "injection" which can cure child psychopathy. Drugs, though calming certain brain disturbances (like epilepsy), can hardly change the formative experiences of an individual. There is, however, reasonable hope that some drug (possibly dilantin) will prove useful in establishing therapeutic relations with psychopaths.

Patient therapists have attempted to bring forth less dramatic, but perhaps more permanent, changes through individual psychotherapy. Assuming that psychopathy is caused (at least primarily) by deficient affection, then emotional attachment should ameliorate the disorder. The psychotherapist tries to establish the rapport which the child psychopath does not have with his parents. If an attachment can be formed, the child identifies with the adult and begins to develop feelings of responsibility and internalized standards.

Dr. Stanley King's remarkable success with one case, as reported by Lipmann, testifies to the efficacy of individual therapy. Retiring from the Institute for Child Guidance, King and his wife decided to bring severely delinquent boys into their own home. One of these boys, a 14-year-old, had been rejected by his family and had been aggressively destructive for many years.

When the boy first came to the Kings' home he was defiant, abusive, and refused to speak with them. Although given his food with the family, he ate in a corner by himself. Primitive and uncontrolled, he frequently stole from the Kings. They never punished him, but instead tried to win him through friendliness and understanding.

Once Dr. King passed the boy on a street corner and heard him lying about his treatment in the foster home. The boy had described horrible beatings and deprivations, but King did not mention the incident.

After many months, the lad began eating with the Kings. Then one day he broke his silence by asking to drive to town with his foster father. From that time on, the boy eagerly sought the Kings' affection.

He soon recounted with bitterness his past life and his frustrations. Eventually, the boy followed Dr. King "like a shadow."

He continued to live with the family. His stealing, both at home and in the community, stopped. The Kings legally adopted him, and the boy went to college.[77]

Few psychopathic children can receive such encompassing treatment. Even within an institution, however, psychotherapy offers an opportunity for emotional attachment. Two cases reported from a New York school indicate the success in some cases with this technique.

One of the children, a 16-year-old girl, came from a disorganized, brutal home. Small and attractive, she had been the girl friend of a gangster. At the school, she was raucous, vulgar, and defiant. She had a long history of stealing, sex offenses, and other delinquencies. Not only did she seem guiltless about her past, she boasted of her "accomplishments."

E. A. Eisner, the school psychologist, selected the girl for psychotherapy and, much against her will, forced her to attend counseling interviews. Her dislike for treatment appeared in the first sessions:

> The girl entered the room and said, "Hello. You called for me? So???"
>
> "Yes," Eisner answered, "Yes, I did."
>
> "Have it your own way. Say, you know one of these days, you're gonna wise up."
>
> "Really?" Eisner said, "What'll happen then?"
>
> "Aw . . . skip it."
>
> As the therapist questioned the girl about her past, she grew more and more uncomfortable. "Jesus H! Will you lay off or do I just have to walk out? What did I ever do to you, I'd like to know."

The therapist's persistent and patient kindliness gradually broke through the girl's resistance. As the interviews progressed, she began to laugh at herself and her earlier antagonism.

She became attached to two boys within the school. Both were younger than she. One was babyish and dependent; the other acted older than his age. Although she had promised the therapist that she would "reform," she ran away from the school and lived with one of her two young "lovers."

After her recapture, continued therapy helped the girl realize that her relation to the two boys was a manifestation of her desire for security and love. The girl abandoned the younger boys, turning instead to an older staff member. She 'fell in love,' but this time she seemed truly concerned about the man's welfare.

In further interviews, she expressed antagonism toward her mother.

She seemed to gain security and insight. She gave up her superficial, sexually-tinged relations with men, and abandoned much of her anti-social behavior.[78]

Also at Hawthorne Cedar-Knolls, another case showed great progress under psychotherapy. "Robert," an 8-year-old boy, was an uncontrollable, aggressive delinquent.[79] In addition to school trouble, Robert had been involved in arson and stealing. He too had been rejected by his parents.

During his first months in school, Robert formed no close attachments. He tried to use adults for his own purposes, but he seemed unable to develop friendships with them. His behavior disturbed the whole institution. Once he almost blew up the gas tank of the school truck.

After a year within the school, Robert became friendly with a cottage "father." The counselor had long talks with the boy and maintained a consistently warm attitude. He "deprived" the child only sparingly. After two years the boy began to change. He became less irresponsible and aggressive. Near the end of treatment, Robert quipped, "Pop will make a man out of me if it kills us both."[80]

The most intensive form of psychotherapy, psychoanalysis, has been tried only on a few child psychopaths. Kate Friedlander found the treatment a useful, but imperfect, instrument. Over a two-year period, Friedlander psychoanalyzed an 8-year-old, "Billy," who was defiant, "vicious," and impulsive. The boy could stand no interference with his desires. He was a constant truant and stole purposelessly. Friedlander commented: "The most striking factor in this behavior was his absolute lack of feeling of guilt."

During the first therapeutic sessions, Billy set fire to curtains, destroyed toys, was constantly late, and refused to talk about himself. Later, he disclosed hatred for his mother who, in turn, hated the little boy. She wanted a girl, and Billy proved a serious disappointment to her. Underneath this hostility, Friedlander noted that the boy longed for his mother's love.

The analysis uncovered no signs of conscience. Billy's instinctive urges appeared very powerful, unmodified by either a strong ego or an independent superego. The "pleasure principle" dominated his behavior, and he gave full reign to "the onrush of demands arising in the id."

Although the first year of treatment disclosed the mechanisms of

Billy's character, it led to no improvement in his behavior. After 18 months, however, incipient signs of character change appeared. One day Billy remarked that he "should not have stayed out late the night before, as then he would not have to stay in today." This represented, for Billy, the first indication of developing foresight and superego control.

Billy's school behavior improved, his interest increased, and his truancy ended. His penchant for fighting decreased, and a positive relation began with a friend of the mother. Billy formed friendships with other children of his age, and he dropped his former bullying attitude. "He was still not a model boy when treatment ended," Friedlander admitted, "but he had succeeded in . . . developing an independent Super-Ego."[81]

S. A. Szurek, a San Francisco psychiatrist with long experience in the treatment of delinquency, found that psychoanalysis did not work with the child psychopaths handled in his clinic.[82] Because their relations with other people were characterized by "impulsive self-gratification," and their loyalties "showed a relatively poor integration," the psychopathic child was a poor therapeutic risk.[83] Moreover, Szurek believes the method is theoretically unsuited to the psychopath because while analysis aims at uncovering unconscious impulses, the psychopath already has insufficient inhibition. Szurek's criticism applies to conventional psychoanalysis, but Friedlander's long-term treatment—a process by which affectional relations are built—seems to create the necessary inhibitive qualities.[84]

Even less encouraging has been the work of Lauretta Bender. A psychiatrist at the Bellevue Hospital, Bender has faced hundreds of cases of the disorder and has tried a great many approaches in attempting to cure it. The children had such a pathogenic lack of love that therapy based on emotional attachment never reached them. "Once the defect is created," she felt forced to conclude, "it cannot be corrected.[85]

Hyman Lippman of the New York Institute for Child Guidance also found that psychotherapy failed to help many of the chronic delinquents whom he treated.[86] C. A. Whitaker, another psychiatrist with wide therapeutic experience, concurs that the disorder is virtually hopeless. Whitaker, using "forced psychotherapy" at Ormsby Village, found that only one of his psychopathic children recovered.[87]

Thus, the impact of psychotherapy on psychopaths remains uncertain. A minority of such children—possibly a distinct minority—benefit from the treatment.[88]

The Cambridge-Somerville experiment, a controlled study of delinquents, attempted a rigorous evaluation of individual counseling. Dr. Richard Clarke Cabot, the distinguished physician and social philosopher, initiated the experiment in 1935. He sought to test the premise that an intimate, friendly relationship could deflect a boy from anti-social behavior.

Cabot's original sample of 650 boys was divided into a control and an experimental group. Within each group were equal numbers of "pre-delinquent" and "normal" boys. The control group received only the usual community and school attention. The experimental group was given extensive community aid plus the advice and support of a special counselor. The experiment was to run over a 10-year period, the same counselors remaining with the boys throughout the project.

Cabot's plan, simple in origin but complex in fulfillment, met several obstacles. The war intervened. Counselors (and boys) were called into service. Even with counselor replacements, no boy was treated longer than eight years, and most boys received about five years of intermittent therapy.

The counseling itself was not uniform. Some counselors emphasized friendship and warmth; others leaned toward rather firm guidance of the child's behavior. Some counselors depended mainly on verbal advice; others adhered to modern case work techniques. All of the counselors, however, called upon community resources for aid: school tutoring, medical aid, camps, and settlement houses.

In evaluating the results of the treatment, varied methods were used: statistics of delinquency, personality tests, an impartial observer's rating of terminal adjustment, and analyses of case records. These measures pointed to a disillusioning conclusion: such treatment did not prevent delinquency. The treated boys and the control boys appeared before courts with approximately the same frequency.[89]

Gordon Allport noticed a hopeful trend in the statistics. At the end of treatment, the treated boys committed less serious crimes and appeared less often in Massachusetts correctional institutions. He hypothesized that the treatment—although ineffective in preventing delinquency—may have had a latent effect after the boys' first brush with the law. "The boy must learn, in part, from hard experience. *He then learns more surely if he has had the benefit of friendly precept and example.*"[90]

Analysis of the case records by an independent observer, Dr. Helen Witmer, indicated that 20 per cent of the boys had received substantial benefits from the treatment. In another 42 per cent however, the counselor's work seemed "clearly ineffectual."

Witmer concluded that the home situation seemed the major determining factor for success or failure. Counseling could accomplish little when contravened by a rejecting, disrupted home. Moreover, the nature of the child's problems affected the outcome of treatment. The more emotionally disturbed the child, the less he appeared to benefit from treatment.

The research team did not make a specific evaluation of the project's effects on psychopathic children. They did, however, describe a group of "extremely maladjusted" boys—boys who had been rejected by their parents, who were "unable to form close relationships with anybody," and who derived very little benefit from the treatment. Some of these cases, they pointed out, closely resembled the psychopathic syndrome:

"Wilbur," a 10-year-old boy, was one of three illegitimate children. His mother and grandmother led promiscuous lives. The mother, a weak and indecisive person, cared little for Wilbur. His stepfather intensely disliked the boy. The grandmother continuously disparaged him. Only an aunt had the slightest affection for Wilbur, and it was to her the boy turned when "things got too bad elsewhere." Wilbur was a "sullen, moody boy, resentful of everybody." He was described as "having a shell around him that the counselors could not penetrate."[91]

"Tony," too, came from a disturbed family. His father, an egocentric man, felt no affection for Tony and deserted him whenever the boy got in trouble. The boy's mother, although fond of him, was apathetic and ineffectual. A description of Tony's character conveys his psychopathic traits:

> Temporarily he could adapt to any person or situation very well but, though jealous, he could not form a close relationship with anybody. He stole continuously, derived great pleasure from doing so, lied about it with no sense of guilt, and boasted of deeds that had escaped police attention. He was always demanding material evidence of people's affection for him.[92]

With boys like Wilbur and Tony, the counseling had little effect.

Although the counselors devoted a great deal of attention to them, they could not break through the boys' emotional indifference. "The whole personality was organized against interpersonal relationship; to have been beneficial the counselors would have had to effect a complete personality change in these boys," Witmer concluded.[93]

As Witmer observed, the "cure" of psychopathy requires complete transformation of the child's personality. Some therapists believe that the best way of accomplishing this radical change is through mobilizing the child's total environment for therapeutic purposes. A transformation of personality, they believe, demands a reorientation of environment. Every part of the child's life, from breakfast to bedtime, must be geared to therapeutic purposes. Increasingly, during the last 25 years, social scientists have looked to such "total push" or "milieu" therapy for the cure of a variety of emotional disorders and social maladjustments.[94]

The story of milieu therapy is intimately linked with the life and work of the Viennese psychoanalyst, August Aichhorn. Born of an unexceptional family in 1878, Aichhorn's background held no hint of his future destiny. Conventional training led Aichhorn into the comfortable life of a Victorian educator. In 1907, however, the young teacher fought the establishment of military homes for orphaned and maladjusted boys by organizing his own homes for the children.

The end of the war, in 1918, with Austria's defeat, left the nation with a mass of disillusioned, rebellious youth. To meet the surge of crime, Aichhorn founded, in Oberhollabrunn, a home for delinquents —a home that was to become so famous that it was praised even in the English Parliament.

Impressed with Freudianism, Aichhorn applied psychoanalytic methods with success to the problem of delinquency. His techniques, unusual even in the experimenting atmosphere of the twenties, won him the acclaim of the world of psychology. Throughout Vienna, Aichhorn founded child guidance clinics. He expanded his work to the whole range of childhood maladjustment.

After Austria's liberation ended Nazism (which Aichhorn, although Jewish, somehow survived), he was elected President of the Viennese Psychoanalytic Society. He wrote a book, *Wayward Youth,* and many books have been written about him.

Two distinct types of children came under Aichhorn's care. One group consisted of boys whose dissocial behavior covered an under-

lying neurosis. With them, Aichhorn offered approval only in reward for achievement, as "payment" for increasing socialization.
Many of these children had already been overindulged; others had
been neglected. They required not more indulgence, but more control.

Aichhorn's other group of children concerns us more: his dissocial
boys, without neurosis, who were in constant conflict with their environment. These boys, many of whom were undoubtedly psychopathic,
satisfied their impulses with indiscriminate, aggressive abandon. They
had not developed sturdy superegos or consciences.

With this second group, all of whom "had been brought up without
affection and had suffered unreasonable severity and brutality,"[95]
Aichhorn aimed at satisfying their frustrated desires for love:

> First we had to compensate for this great lack of love and then gradually
> and with great caution begin to make demands upon the children. Severity
> would have failed completely. Our treatment of this group could be charac-
> terized thus: a consistently friendly attitude, wholesome occupation, plenty
> of play to prevent aggression, and repeated talks with individual members.[96]

This brief description conveys neither the flavor nor the hazards
of such therapy. The first meeting, Aichhorn believed, set the tone
of treatment. The interviewer could not be too harsh and thereby
antagonize the boy. Nor could he be too loving, for then the child
would think him weak. "Our motto was: as far as possible, let the
boys alone."[97]

The attempt to build an affiliative relation had to be undertaken
with great caution. Aichhorn insisted upon a permissive attitude, an
avoidance of any belligerence even in response to aggressive attacks.
A colleague described an incident of exaggerated aggression, showing
the reaction of one boy to this permissiveness:

> In the presence of Aichhorn one of the boys attacked another with a
> large bread-knife, screaming that he meant to kill him. Aichhorn, noticing
> the exaggeration, did not look around and did not move. The boy, unable
> to impress his leader, threw the knife on the floor in despair and started
> to cry bitterly. For days afterwards he was quiet and amenable to discussion.[98]

Most of the anti-social boys went through the same metamorphosis:
". . . the boys responded to this [permissiveness] with an increased
feeling of their own power which found its expression in greater and
more frequent acts of aggression; these later gave way to tears of rage,
then to a period of sensitivity, and finally to acceptable behavior."[99]

The lack of punishment contradicted the boys' past experience; it
was something entirely new in their lives. Unsure of the new environ-

ment, perhaps believing they had not been "bad enough," the boys
tested the staff with increased aggression. Sudden, sometimes dramatic,
insight allowed the boys to perceive the almost boundless permissiveness of the staff. The shock of finding that some adults could be
kind and understanding opened new emotional possibilities to the boys.

Only an emotional crisis, Aichhorn believed, broke the boys' defenses
against interpersonal relations. Sometimes the staff deliberately pro-
moted such crises:

An aggressive, delinquent boy, whom Aichhorn knew to be "guiltless," operated the school tobacco shop. Noticing a discrepancy in
the canteen books, Aichhorn decided to use the situation as a means
for instilling a sense of guilt and anxiety in the culprit. He invited the
boy to his office and casually asked: 'How much do you take in each
week?" The boy stated a figure. "Does the money always come out
right?"

A hesitating, "Yes," in answer.

"When do you have the most of your trade? In the morning?"

The boy became increasingly restless, but Aichhorn ignored it. Put-
tering around his office, straightening books, Aichhorn returned again
and again to the topic. Suddenly Aichhorn said, "Well, when we get
through here I'll go and take a look at your cash."

The boy dropped the book he had been taking down from a shelf.
"What's the matter?"

"Nothing!"

"What's wrong with your cash?"

The boy, overcome with fright, stammered as he stated the missing
sum. Aichhorn said nothing, but handed him the cash.

The boy left the room. Ten minutes later he returned and sobbed,
"Let them lock me up. I don't deserve your help—I'll only steal again."
The boy poured out his story to Aichhorn.

Eventually the money was repaid. The crisis, Aichhorn believed,
induced a feeling of guilt which the boy had not known before. After
the incident, Aichhorn reported that the boy was "cured."

Aichhorn based his therapy on affection: "We must make good
the love of which he has been deprived." Once rapport had been
solidly established, the staff increased their demands upon the boys.
They criticized and imposed social controls. Using the affectional
bonds, they apparently brought the boys to a new sense of social responsibility. Aichhorn reported that his aggressive boys acquired new

tolerance for frustration and new consciences. All of the boys, he reported, subsequently became adjusted to society.

Aichhorn's report of success intrigued the scientific world. Yet few dared to copy him. In the 1920's, the method was revolutionary—and even today, few training schools have adopted "milieu therapy."[100]

During the 1930's, Hawthorne Cedar-Knolls based its treatment on Aichhorn's precepts. A research team traced the lives of 81 girls who lived at the school. The report constitutes one of the few evaluations of milieu therapy's impact.

Many types of delinquent girls went through the institution, but one group stood out from the others. Although school therapists did not use the concept of psychopathy, these girls closely resembled the syndrome:

> Early in the work a group of girls was recognized who were asocial but not obviously neurotic. . . . Later it became clear that the feature common to them was an inability to make a real transference to any member of the staff. . . . They acted largely, some of them seemingly exclusively, on impulse and apparently had little or no neurotic or real conflict or sense of guilt. . . . This type of delinquent is readily recognized by the living out of wishes without thought of consequence or regret, and with no real understanding of the 'why not.'[101]

These girls did not respond to the Aichhorn approach. Therapy did not change their seriously disordered personalities.[102]

Within the last two decades, such schools as Detroit's Pioneer House, Chicago's Orthogenic School, and New York's Wiltwyck have used milieu therapy on young psychopathic children.

Founded in 1946, Fritz Redl's Pioneer House exemplified this approach to the problem. The school treated a small group of severely disturbed children. Although Redl never specifically labeled the boys "psychopathic," that diagnosis seems apt. The children were filled with hate, "whirlpools and rivers and oceans of it." They failed to control their aggression and to postpone their demands for immediate gratification. The "children who hate" could not "establish adequate relations to future experience" nor could they plan their lives with foresight.[103]

Redl described the children as "Untaxed by guilt, embarrassment, or shame . . . impulse freedom is guaranteed."[104] The children—have "only a dim, if even existent insight into their own responsibility for what happens to them and the weakest possible resistance in the face of temptation."[104] Typically, the boys had "extremely weak, distorted and confused wishes for object relations with adults. . . ."[105]

Because the Pioneer House children lacked the initial ability of establishing rapport, had insufficient inhibitions, and were retarded in communicative abilities, Redl rejected the psychiatric interview as the sole treatment procedure. He also abandoned the usual methods of education because the children lacked the necessary prerequisites: a high frustration tolerance, sublimative ability, and a capacity for controlling their destructive impulses.

Rather than employ the usual "reformative" methods, Pioneer House attempted to establish an encompassing atmosphere which, in its smallest detail, aimed at the improvement of the youngsters. Every ball game, every meal, every temper tantrum was handled with an eye to the child's treatment. Each individual, from the director to the cook, participated in the program. Even the house itself, its design, furnishings, and upkeep formed an integral part of therapy.

Like Aichhorn, Redl believed that affection is the indispensable center of all treatment: "The children must get plenty of love and affection whether they deserve it or not; they must be assured the basic quota of happy recreational experiences whether they seem to 'have it coming' or not."[106]

The Pioneer House program had many goals: "impulse drainage," cultivation of new interests, increasing the child's ability to tolerate frustration. Although the staff allowed wide leeway for regression, they continually tried to develop the child's ability to use inner resources for satisfaction. The recreational activities attempted to inculcate "depersonalized controls," controls which sprang from the "rules of the game." Accepting primitive group codes was an important step toward the acceptance of more important standards.

Controlling the boys' bellicosity was, of course, an ever-present problem. Sometimes the staff ignored belligerence. More often humor, regrouping, or reminding the child of possible results served to inhibit aggression. More rarely, the staff removed a child from the group until he had been calmed, or physically restrained him. At all times, the staff carried out discipline without malice.

The staff utilized Aichhorn's method of precipitating an emotional crisis. Such dramatic displays were followed by therapeutic interviews: The "rub-in" interview brought out certain aspects of reality which the child had ignored (e.g., the reaction of neighbors to back yard cursing); the "guilt-squeeze" interview attempted to "bring to the surface," or instill, feelings of guilt. Other interviews—"expressional," "counter-distortional," or "group"—allowed the children to experience a catharsis and then countered their alibis and hostility with facts.

The "interpretational' interview aimed at making the child aware of his motives. This technique was used when one boy, who was disliked and baited by the others, wished to take a knife along on one of the school outings. David Wineman, one of the school directors, said: "Look, you know darn well you don't want that knife. You're just going to get all the guys against you and that's what you want so you can keep up your complaint to me that they are mean to you. Now look how you're starting the whole thing yourself and then you are going to say that the other guys are picking on you . . ."[107] The boy left the knife at home.

The withdrawal of community financial support forced the closing of Pioneer House before an adequate assessment of the treatment could be made. All but one of the boys went to foster homes and post-treatment adjustment has not been reported. Nevertheless, Redl believed the therapy made significant gains in certain important areas. The children seemed better able to communicate verbally, to accept frustration realistically, and to modify their behavior in accord with the *esprit de corps* of Pioneer House. Their aggressive and destructive actions decreased. They became more "sensitive" to social values, and they accepted school rules and routines without rebellion. Furthermore, the children seemed more responsive to the affection of adults.

If the treatment had continued—if the community had responded to the school's need for money—the children might have been transformed. But no money came: "Thus our 'children who hate' went back into the limbo of 'the children that nobody wants.' "[108]

More fortunate financially has been the Orthogenic School in Chicago. With Bruno Bettleheim as director, the school treats many varieties of emotionally disturbed boys and girls. Bettleheim believes that this melting pot of maladjustment has therapeutic value. The withdrawn child, for example, sees a good deal of aggressive behavior and may seek to try such freedom. The psychopathic child, in turn, may be influenced by his more inhibited comrades.

Bettleheim's therapy calls for an environment in which the child is constantly under treatment. The school draws heavily upon Freud and Dewey, but like all such ventures, develops its own philosophy. The staff is highly permissive of deviant behavior and attempts to satisfy generously the infantile needs of their charges, thereby inducing a "positive relation to the adults who provide for his well being." Each part of the child's life is made as non-threatening, as pleasurable, as possible.

The school maintains its own classrooms, but the stringency and competition of the public school are not to be found. Children are free to leave class at any time, or not to attend at all.

Food, the "great socializer," plays a major role in Orthogenic's therapy. Extra servings are always available at meals, and an unlocked candy and cake chest lures hungry children between times. Bedtime, with its transition into the unreal state of nightmares, is made palatable with snacks, teddy bears, and counselor encouragement. Again in the morning, food greets some children as they reach from the covers, testing the advisability of starting a new day.

The bathroom, too, is a part of the treatment program. Bath-taking, abetted by counselor washdowns and a flotilla of toy boats, becomes an adventure rather than a threat.

Recognizing that most emotional disturbances originate in the home, the school avoids pseudo-parental relationships. Treatment begins with the "simplest and not the most complex relationship." The newcomer is offered casual acquaintanceship, friendship, and care—but not overwhelming love. In time, most children select a mentor. A "love-relationship" occurs, but only after the child's "own experiences have taught him to want such a relationship, after his adjustment has made him ready for it, after he has slowly convinced himself that he can handle it successfully."[109]

Once friendly intimacy is established, the child is (figuratively) urged "to change his personality at least in part in the image of the person or persons who are now so important to him. He identifies with them, as we say, and this identification is often the starting point for the organization of his personality."[110]

Bettleheim noted three stages in the development of the school's aggressive children, some of whom seemed psychopathic. At first, "their controlling institutions were so underdeveloped that they could neither restrict the socially unacceptable tendencies pressing for release, nor postpone the gratification of those needs which were legitimate."[111] Then, as the bond between the child and the counselor matured, the child felt anxiety if he violated (or wished to violate) the adult's values. In order for the anxiety to operate during this stage, the counselor had to be near the boy. In the third stage, the superego seemed to gain strength and the counselor's physical presence was no longer required.

The child often used illness or injury to bolster his inner controls. One child, with a serious cold, stood in front of an open window. He contracted pneumonia, thus (Bettleheim believes) stopping himself from escaping from the school. Another boy had a cast on his broken arm. He thrust the cast through a window and severely lacerated himself. Bettleheim viewed this as the child's attempt to overcome the desire to hit another boy.[112]

The impact of Orthogenic treatment on child personality has never been objectively evaluated. Milieu therapy, however, seems promising for the treatment of psychopathy: Bettleheim, like Aichhorn and Redl, has enthusiastically reported striking behavioral changes in the children. Yet Hawthorne Cedar-Knolls reported almost total failure in its treatment of psychopathic girls.

Each of the four schools embellished the basic philosophy with its own improvisations. These slight variations may explain the differing results. Unfortunately, none of the schools thoroughly traced the effects of its approach on the children's personality.

In summary, the last decades of research into the treatment of child psychopathy have tentatively demonstrated:

Except in unusual cases, forced institutional conformity does not improve the child psychopath.

Narco-therapy in some experiments brought temporary relief of symptoms, but in other experiments drugs aggravated the disorder.

Psychotherapy can be useful in the treatment of child psychopathy. Some therapists have been successful, but more therapists report almost total failure.

Milieu therapy has changed the behavior of some psychopaths. Three schools have reported at least temporary success with the method. One school reported complete failure. The treatment's effectiveness in reorganizing the personality has not been ascertained.

The preponderance of evidence, admittedly inadequate and partly contradictory, indicates that milieu therapy offers the most promising answer to the disorder. Milieu therapy, of all the varied approaches, apparently has achieved the most substantial changes in behavior. Certainly it deserves further analysis.

What, if any, are the changes in personality brought about by a "therapeutic environment"? The next chapter, set in the context of the Wiltwyck School, attempts to answer this question.

The Wiltwyck School closely resembles the other representatives of milieu therapy. The institution emphasizes close counselor-child attachments, and a non-punitive, permissive atmosphere is always maintained. Every situation in the child's life is incorporated, at least theoretically, into the therapeutic program. Perhaps more than the other schools, Wiltwyck integrates psychotherapy with its program. The school's attempt to impress the child with the realistic consequences of his behavior is an important, although not unique, feature of the treatment.

Advocates of milieu therapy believe that a reorientation of the child's total environment will transform personality. The evaluation of Wiltwyck's effect on the psychopathic child, and on other types of disordered children, will furnish, we hope, an objective test of this challenging theory.

NOTES

1. McCann, Willis H. The Psychopath and the psychoneurotic in Relation to Crime and Delinquency. *Journal of Clinical and Experimental Psychopathology,* 9:551, 1948.

2. Darling, H. F. Definition of Psychopathic Personality. *Journal of Nervous and Mental Disease,* 101:125, 1945.

3. Lindner, Robert. Therapy. In V. C. Branham and S. B. Kutash: *Encyclopedia of Criminology.* New York, Philosophical Library, 1949, p. 491 (a reference to J. Chornyak: Some Remarks on the Diagnosis of the Psychopathic Delinquent. *American Journal of Psychiatry,* 97:1326-1340, 1941).

4. Sheldon and Eleanor Glueck found that 80% of parolee convicts commit at least one other offense within five years of their release.

5. Corsini, Raymond. Criminal Psychology. In *Encyclopedia of Criminology, op. cit.* (note 3).

6. Lindner, Robert. Experimental Studies in Constitutional Psychopathic Inferiority, Part II. *Journal of Criminal Psychopathology,* 4:484-500, 1943.

7. Stafford-Clark, D., Pond, Desmond, and Doust, Lovett. The Psychopath in Prison: a Preliminary Report of a Cooperative Research. *British Journal of Delinquency,* 2, 117-129, 1951.

8. The state later revoked the agreement.

9. Martin, John Bartlow. *Break Down the Walls.* New York, Ballantine Books, 1951, p. 78.

10. *Ibid.* p. 83.

11. Mohr, Peter. Die Forensische Bedetung der Psychopathen. *Schweiz Arch. Neurol. Psychiat.,* 60, 1947.

12. Mohr and Heaver found a higher proportion of cures in "psychopaths" than did the Gluecks with non-psychopaths. The Gluecks, however, used more rigorous methods and traced even unreported crimes. In all probability, use of the Gluecks' methods would have further decreased the small proportion of success found by Mohr and Heaver.

13. HEAVER, W. L. A Study of Forty Male Psychopathic Personalities, Before, During and After Hospitalization. *American Journal of Psychiatry,* 100:342-346, 1943. Heaver based diagnosis on five major traits: lack of concern for others, impulsivity, inability to learn from experience, instability, and emotional immaturity.

14. HALLER, B. L. Some Factors Related to the Adjustment of Psychopaths on Parole from a State Hospital. *Smith College Studies in Social Work,* 13:193-194 (abstract), 1942. Selection based on severe anti-social behavior.

15. Stafford-Clark et al., *op. cit.* (note 7).

16. CASON, H. and PESCOR, M. J. A Statistical Study of 500 Psychopathic Prisoners. *Public Health Reports,* Washington, 61:557-574, 1946. They found that 62% of a group of "psychopaths" had no record 19 months after release from prison.

17. "Levels of loyalty" meant, in essence, explaining to the soldier why he should obey his officers.

18. ABRAHAMS, JOSEPH AND McCORKLE, LLOYD. Group Psychotherapy at an Army Rehabilitation Center. *Diseases of the Nervous System,* 8:50-62, 1947.

19. After a brief three months' study, the Army concluded that 78% had adjusted to military life. No evaluation was made of the specific adjustment of psychopaths.

20. GLASER, EDWARD AND CHILES, DANIEL. An Experiment in the Treatment of Youthful Habitual Offenders at the Federal Reformatory, Chillicothe. *Journal of Criminal Psychopathology,* July 1948, 376-425.

21. The major criterion for diagnoses of psychopathy was non-responsiveness to treatment.

22. Paper and pencil tests like the Bell Adjustment Inventory were used.

23. CORSINI, RAYMOND. The Method of Psycho-drama in Prison. *Group Psycho-therapy,* 3:321-326, 1951.

24. LASSNER, RUDOLPH. Psycho-Drama in Prison. *Group Psychotherapy,* 3:77-91, 1950.

25. Seventy-two percent of the convicts who had participated in the program (and were willing to report their feelings) said that they had benefited from the sessions. They rated a "gain in insight" as the most important result.

26. See PLOWITZ, PAUL. Psychiatric Service and Group Therapy in the Rehabilitation of Offenders. *Journal of Correctional Education,* 2:78-80, 1950.

27. LIPTON, HARRY. The Psychopath. *Journal of Criminal Law, Criminology, and Police Science,* 40:584-596, 1950.

28. WEBER, LOUIS. Working With a Psychopath. *Journal of Abnormal and Social Psychology,* 47:713-721, 1952.

29. LINDNER, ROBERT. *Rebel Without a Cause.* New York, Grune & Stratton, 1944, p. 35.

30. *Ibid.* p. 63.

31. *Ibid.* p. 46.

32. *Ibid.* p. 283.

33. Because of this "guilt," it may be incorrect to call Harold a psychopath. Nevertheless, this anxiety was constricted to one area, incestuous desires, and it failed to exert any type of socialized control over Harold's behavior. It seems more akin to a fearfulness of fatherly retaliation than an internalized conscience. Possibly hypno-analysis might reveal this same type of incestuous anxiety in other psychopaths.

34. RODGERS, TERRY. Hypnotherapy and Character Neuroses. *Journal of Clinical Psychopathology,* 8:519-524, 1947.

35. Quoted in O'DONNEL, L. P. The Problems of Treating Psychopaths. *Psychiatric Quarterly,* 14(2):752, 1940.

36. Quoted in CURRAN, D. AND MALLINSON, P. Psychopathic Personality. *Journal of Mental Science,* 90:266-286, 1944.

37. BROMBERG, WALTER. Dynamic Aspects of Psychopathic Personality. *Psychoanalytic Quarterly,* 17:58-70, 1948.

38. SCHMIDEBERG, MELITTA. The Analytic Treatment of Major Criminals: Therapeutic Results and Technical Problems. Psychology and Treatment of Criminal Psychopaths. *International Journal of Psychoanalysis,* 30, 1949.

39. SCHMIDEBERG, MELITTA. In K. R. EISSLER: *Searchlights on Delinquency.* New York, International Universities Press, 1949, p. 175.

40,41. Schmideberg, *op. cit.* (note 38).

42. Schmideberg, in *Searchlights on Delinquency, op. cit.* (note 39), p. 187.

43. Benjamin Karpman, although a believer in the "noncurability" of psychopaths, has reported several cases of successful therapy. Karpman believes, however, that these patients were not "true" psychopaths. From his point of view, psychopathy is caused only by "idiopathic" (unknown, presumably constitutional) causes; if psychogenic causes can be found in the patient's past, Karpman maintains that he is not a psychopath.

See BENJAMIN KARPMAN: Autobiography of a Bandit. *Journal of Criminal Law, Criminology and Police Science,* 3:305-325, 1946.

One of Karpman's patients, Jerry Briggs, had most of the symptoms which other social scientists would diagnose as psychopathic. Karpman himself called Briggs a neurotic because of his intense mother hatred, a "psychogenic cause."

Briggs, a famous bandit, came from a vain, social-climbing family and was severely rejected by his eccentric, cigar-smoking mother. After an early crime, the boy was committed by his mother to reform school. Briggs had a long history of anti-social behavior: stealing, shoplifting, gun-running, gambling, and armed robbery.

Briggs was caught and sentenced to prison for stealing $130,000 from a mail truck. In prison, psychotherapy helped, and he made a good adjustment. Some years after release, however, Briggs committed suicide.

Therapy, while not lifting him to a "normal" level, at least inhibited his criminality.

44. GREENACRE, PHYLLIS. Problems of Patient-Therapist Relationship in the Treatment of Psychopaths. In ROBERT LINDNER and R. V. SELIGER, Eds.: *Handbook of Correctional Psychology.* New York, Philosophical Library, 1947, p. 378.

45. See E. DAVIDOFF and G. L. GOODSTONE: Amphatamine-Barbituate Therapy in Psychiatric Conditions. *Psychiatric Quarterly,* 16:541-548, 1942.

46. ADATTO, CARL. Observations on Criminal Patients During Narco-analysis. *Archives of Neurology and Psychiatry,* 62:82-92, 1949. Basis for selection of cases not reported.

47. TRAIN, GEORGE. Pentothal Sodium: An Aid to Penologic Psycho-therapy. In *Handbook of Correctional Psychiatry, op. cit.* (note 44), pp. 542-557. Basis for selection not stated.

48. FREYHAN, F. A. Psychopathology of Personality Functions in Psychopathic Personalities. *Psychiatric Quarterly,* 25:458-471, 1951. Basis for selection not stated.

49. SILVERMAN, DANIEL. E.E.G. and Treatment of Criminal Psychopaths. *Journal of Criminal Psychopathology,* 5:439-466, 1944. Diagnosis based on severe anti-social behavior.

50. One other experiment confirmed Silverman's findings that dilantin sodium benefits psychopaths. Only one patient, however, was given the drug, and he was later shown to be an epileptic. See BRILL and WALKER: Psychopathic Behavior with Latent Epilepsy. *Journal of Nervous and Mental Disease,* 101, 1945.

51. HILL, DENNIS. Amphetamine in Psychopathic States. *British Journal of Addiction,* 44:50-54, 1947. Diagnostic standard not stated.

52. SHOVRON, J. J. Benzedrine in Psychopathy and Behavior Disorders. *British Journal of Addiction,* 44:58-63, 1947. Diagnostic standard not stated.

53. GREEN, EUGENE; SILVERMAN, DANIEL; AND GEIL, GEORGE. Petit Mal Electro-Shock Therapy of Criminal Psychopaths. *Journal of Criminal Psychopathology,* 5(4):667-695, 1944 (April). Severe anti-social behavior was the major criterion of diagnosis.

54. Darling's cases included: a neurotic with an intense fear of smothering, a manic-depressive who had stolen a car and who drank heavily, and a paranoid who had attacked an attendant and planned an escape.

Golden's patients had great anxiety and marked depressive characteristics—traits which a true psychopath almost never has.

Banay's patients, although anti-social, apparently included both neurotics and psychotics. The twelve cases who did not respond to treatment were paranoids.

55. DARLING, H. F. Shock Treatment in Psychopathic Personality. *Journal of Nervous and Mental Disease,* 101:247-250, 1945.

56. Cited in J. ALMANSI and DAVID IMPASTATE: The Use of Electroshock Therapy in Correctional Institutions. In *Handbook of Correctional Psychology, op. cit.* (note 44), pp. 542-557.

57. *Ibid.*

58. Quoted in Lindner, *op. cit.* (note 3).

59. BANAY, R. S., AND DAVIDOFF, L. Apparent Recovery of a Sex Psychopath After Lobotomy. *Journal of Criminal Psychopathology,* 4, pp. 59-66, 1942.

60. NILSON, LENNART. Frontal Lobotomy in Sweden. *Nurs. Times* (London), 45:447-451, 1949.

61. DARLING, H. F., AND SANDALL, J. W. Treatment of the Psychopath. *Journal of Clinical and Experimental Psychopathology,* 13(3), 1953(Sept.).

62. The responsibility for therapeutic failure must be partially accepted by the therapists themselves. Treating psychopathy requires time and patience. Many therapists believe that their time could be better spent with more hopeful disorders, and some therapists, it must be admitted, feel threatened by the psychopath. His ingratitude, his deformed sense of responsibility, his aggression and impulsivity make the psychopath an unpleasant patient.

63. See LAURETTA BENDER: Psychopathic Behavior Disorders in Children. In *Handbook of Correctional Psychology, op. cit.* (note 44). The article contains a succinct description of the child psychopath.

64. See WILLIAM AND JOAN McCORD: Two Approaches to the Cure of Delinquents. *Journal of Criminal Law, Criminology, and Police Science,* 44(4), 1953(Nov.-Dec.).

65. See RALPH RABINOVITCH: A Differential Study of Psychopathic Behavior in Infants and Children. Round Table, *American Journal of Orthopsychiatry,* 21(2), 1951(April).

66. SLAWSON, JOHN. Treatment of Aggression in a Specialized Environment. *American Journal of Orthopsychiatry,* 13(3), 1943.

67. WOLFE, B. M. The Later Adjustment of Sixteen Children Diagnosed as Psychopathic Personality. *Smith College Studies in Social Work,* 13:156-157 (abstract), 1942.

68. See K. K. CUTTS and H. H. JASPER: Effects of Benzedrine Sulphate and Phenobarbital on Behavior Problem Children with Abnormal E.E.G.'s. *Archives of Neurology and Psychiatry,* 41:1138-1145, 1939. Also D. B. LINDSLEY and C. E. HENRY: The Effect of Drugs on Behavior and The E.E.G. of Children with Behavior Disorders. *Psychosomatic Medicine,* 4:140-149, 1943.

69. Cutts and Jasper, *op. cit.* (note 68).

70. Lindsley and Henry, *op. cit.* (note 68).

71. DAVIDOFF, D., AND GOODSTONE, G. L. Amphetamine-Barbiturate Therapy in Psychiatric Conditions. *Psychiatric Quarterly,* 16:541-548, 1942.

72. Case descriptions of the psychopathic boys pictured them as extremely aggressive, "lacking in good judgment," affectively superficial, and indifferent.

73. KOREY, S. R. The Effects of Benzedrine Sulfate on the Behavior of Psychopathic and Neurotic Juvenile Delinquents. *Psychiatric Quarterly,* 18:127-137, 1944.

74. BENDER, LAURETTA, AND COTTINGTON, FRANCES. The Use of Amphetamine Sulphate (Benzedrine) in Child Psychiatry. *American Journal of Psychiatry,* 99:116-121, 1942.

75. Lindsley and Henry, *op. cit.* (note 68).

76. WALKER, C., AND KIRKPATRICK, B. Dilantin Treatment for Behavior Problem Children with Abnormal E.E.G. *American Journal of Psychiatry,* 103:484-492, 1947(Jan.).

77. Cited in HYMAN LIPPMAN: Difficulties Encountered in the Psychiatric Treatment of Chronic Juvenile Delinquents. In *Searchlights on Delinquency, op. cit.* (note 39).

78. EISNER, E. A. Relationships Formed by a Sexually Delinquent Adolescent Girl. *American Journal of Orthopsychiatry,* 15:301-308, 1945.

79. Robert was diagnosed as a "primary" behavior disorder. His basic problem was uninhibited, aggressive behavior. The line between this diagnosis and psychopathy seems particularly vague in Robert's case, so the results of his treatment have relevance to the issue of psychopathic therapy.

80. Slawson, *op. cit.* (note 66).

81. FRIEDLANDER, KATE. *The Psycho-Analytical Approach to Juvenile Delinquency.* London: Kegan, Paul, 1947, p. 217.

82. Szurek found that the factor which best predicts therapeutic success is the presence or absence of parental affection in the patients' lives. Without previous warmth, therapy is difficult.

83. SZUREK, S. A. Some Impressions from Clinical Experience with Delinquents. In *Searchlights on Delinquency, op. cit.* (note 39).

84. Szurek believes that the psychopathic child can be cured only by furnishing him with warmth, security, firmness, and fairness. Friedlander's methods, although labeled "psychoanalysis," seem to meet these requirements —at least in Billy's case.

85. Bender, Lauretta, *op. cit.* (note 63).

86. Lippman, *op. cit.* (note 77).

87. WHITAKER, C. A. Ormsby Village: An Experiment with Forced Psychotherapy in the Rehabilitation of the Delinquent Adolescent. *Psychiatry,* 9:239-250, 1946.

88. One major therapeutic approach, non-directive counseling, has not been tried on psychopathic children. George D. Watt used the method on eleven delinquent boys at Utah State Industrial School. Evaluation indicated that seven of the boys had achieved at least two of the aims of the therapy: free expression and greater insight. Comparison with a control group showed that the eleven cases made statistically significant improvements on the MMPI (particularly on hypochondriasis, psychasthenia, and schizophrenia) and on the California Test of personality. Non-directive counseling, though useful for normal delinquents, does not seem applicable to psychopathy. Psychopaths lack the desire for change which seems prerequisite for successful non-directive therapy. See GEORGE WATT: An Evaluation of Non-Directive Counseling in the Treatment of Delinquents. *Journal of Educational Research,* 42:343-352, 1949.

89. POWERS, EDWIN, AND WITMER, HELEN. *An Experiment in the Prevention of Delinquency,* New York, Columbia Press, 1951.

90. *Ibid.,* p. xx. A second follow-up study is currently in progress.

91. *Ibid.,* p. 558.

92. *Ibid.,* p. 559.

93. *Ibid.*, p. 559.

94. "Milieu" therapy is not ordinary group therapy. Group treatment attempts to establish a new experience for the child; but the experience is not one which encompasses his entire life. Few attempts have been made to use group therapy with child psychopaths. Some of the more promising experiments with serious juvenile delinquents have involved "controlled activity groups," and discussion groups. See H. H. SHULMAN: Delinquency Treatment in the Controlled Activity Group. *American Sociological Review,* 10, 1945. Also CHARLES GERTSEN: Group Therapy with Institutionalized Delinquents. *Journal of Genetic Psychology,* 80, 1952. The effect of these experiments on the few child psychopaths included in their samples has not been evaluated.

95. AICHHORN, AUGUST. *Wayward Youth,* New York, Viking, 1935, p. 171.

96. *Ibid.*, p. 172.

97. *Ibid.*, p. 172.

98. Friedlander, *op. cit.* (note 81), p. 242.

99. Aichhorn, *op. cit.* (note 95), p. 178.

100. The Children's Village of Ska near Stockholm, in some ways similar to Aichhorn's school, consciously attempts to instill infantile attitudes in the children. Regression is encouraged. Children drink from bottles and become dependent upon the staff. The value of this method (it presumably allows more complete identification) has not been ascertained.

101. POWDERMAKER, FLORENCE; LEVIS, H. T., AND TOURAINE, G. Psychopathology and Treatment of Delinquent Girls. *American Journal of Orthopsychiatry,* 7:61, 1937.

102. Diagnoses are often retrospective judgments. Perhaps because rapport *was not* established, certain girls were later tabbed as "unable" to form a relation. There may well have been girls who, at the beginning of treatment, were truly psychopathic; but who, because they *did* form an attachment and *did* respond to treatment, were excluded from this group of "failures."

103. REDL, FRITZ, AND WINEMAN, DAVID. *Controls From Within: Techniques for the Treatment of the Aggressive Child.* Glencoe, Free Press, 1954, p. 24.

104. *Ibid.*, p. 19.

105. *Ibid.*, p. 24.

106. *Ibid.*, p. 61.

107. *Ibid.*, p. 179.

108. *Ibid.*, p. 315.

109. BETTLEHEIM, BRUNO. *Love Is Not Enough.* Glencoe, Free Press, 1950, p. 18.

110. *Ibid.*, p. 28.

111. *Ibid.*, p. 28.

112. BETTLEHEIM, BRUNO. Somatic Symptoms in Superego Formation. *American Journal of Orthopsychiatry,* 28(4):649, 1948.

6

Milieu Therapy: An Evaluation

> *Punishing teaches the child only how to punish . . .*
>
> ERNST PAPANEK.

An impressive array of evidence has shown that the adult psychopath fails to respond to present treatment. He has lost the malleability of childhood, and with it, the chance for developing a mature conscience.

The unique approach of Aichhorn, Bettleheim, and Redl, on the other hand, offers reasonable hope that the psychopathic child can be socialized. Unfortunately, their work has been hampered by lack of money, personnel, and public cooperation. In consequence, such experiments have been short-lived or confined primarily to atypical middle-class children whose families could afford the expensive process. Most importantly, milieu therapy has not been subjected to a careful, independent assessment of its effects. The treatment is unique, experimental, eminently promising—but not scientifically validated.

Thus, one of the more important problems of social science is the careful testing of the milieu therapy approach in the cure of psychopathy. New York's Wiltwyck School for Boys offers an unusual opportunity for evaluating the curative effect of a warm, permissive environment, where individual and group therapy combine their techniques.

Wiltwyck has overcome many of the limitations of other experiments. Private individuals and public agencies, attracted by Wiltwyck's philosophy, have assured relative financial security for the institution. Top-quality counselors, psychologists, and social workers flock to the school (resulting in an almost one-to-one boy-staff ratio) because of its excellent reputation. Though the process of self-criticism and correction continues, Wiltwyck has for several years brought its therapeutic theory into practical application.

I. AIMS

"Punishing teaches the child only how to punish; scolding teaches him how to scold. By showing him that we understand, we teach him to understand; by helping him, we teach him to help; by cooperating, we teach him how to cooperate."[1] These words sum up Wiltwyck's philosophy. They represent the accumulated wisdom of the small group who founded Wiltwyck and particularly of its director, Ernst Papanek.

As a young man, Papanek studied with Freud and served in the Austrian parliament. While directing education in Vienna, he played an important role in the encouragement of Aichhorn's experiments. After "Anschluss," Papanek migrated to France and established homes for refugee children. With the fall of France, Papanek helped the majority of his children escape to England before he himself was captured by the Germans. The daring (and compassion) of a Nazi guard provided for Papanek's escape to the United States. In America, Papanek headed a Brooklyn school for delinquents before going to Wiltwyck. Under his leadership, Wiltwyck changed from a small orphans' home into a brilliant experiment in the treatment of maladjusted children.

The experiment rests upon an axiom of permissiveness and unconditional love. The children are allowed to express their pent-up bitterness and antagonism as long as no irreparable damage is done. With no disciplinary cottages, corporal punishments, or harsh scoldings, Wiltwyck attempts only to impress upon the child the consequences of his acts. For example, an aggressive newcomer to Wiltwyck broke thirty-two windows in the school dining room. After waiting for the boy to quiet down, Papanek explained that some money would be deducted from the boy's weekly allowance to help pay for the damage. Three weeks later, the Director called the boy to his office and quietly reinstated the full allowance. Thus, Papanek soothed the boy's bitterness and taught him that authority can help an individual as well as hurt him.

Although Wiltwyck allows its boys to express themselves freely, social responsibility is not ignored. Wiltwyck's one hundred students are urged to participate in their community affairs. An elected student council, food committee, job committee, canteen committee, and sports committee cooperate with the staff in the discussion of common problems. Cottage living (with two counselors for every twelve boys), student government, and weekly assemblies give the boys a chance to work out tensions, air hostilities, and train themselves in democratic procedure. These are lessons they sorely need, for most of the boys have been judged incorrigibly delinquent by their parents and by their communities, and many have been previously rejected by other social agencies.

Individual, group, and art therapy supplement the counselors' efforts. Three psychologists and two psychiatrists work with the most serious cases. Two group therapists meet with other boys. Ten social workers introduce new children to Wiltwyck, hold weekly interviews with them, and ease their transitions back to city life.

During the winter, Wiltwyck's children (who range in age from 8 to 14 years) attend classes within the institution. Teachers, skilled in the instruction of emotionally maladjusted children, conduct the ungraded school. For those who need it, and many do, a special instructor provides remedial help in reading.

Wiltwyck's counselors, the great majority of whom are college graduates, participate in a continuing program of education through group therapy sessions and regular conferences. Each week the staff meets to discuss one of Wiltwyck's boys. Usually the case illustrates personality problems common to several children, thus serving as a basis for general assessment of treatment.

The pragmatist may well ask: "Does this expensive and encompassing program cause real changes in the boys' personalities?" Late in 1953 we attempted to answer this question by submitting 35 Wiltwyck children to a battery of personality tests and comparing the results to those of 35 boys at a typical public reformatory.[2]

The New England school believed that harsh discipline and hard work would reform its inmates.[3] The staff, most of whom had graduated from high school, lacked psychological training. Use of a silent disciplinary cottage and corporal punishment maintained order within the school. Though in contradiction to the Wiltwyck approach, the New England school was typical of American reformatories. The contrast offered an excellent opportunity for testing the relative efficacy of the two philosophies.

In an attempt to measure the children's basic drives, we used the Adult-Child Interaction Test, other projective personality tests, a values questionnaire, and a sociogram. The boys' responses were analyzed and computed according to months of residence within the schools. We discovered that Wiltwyck made important and desirable changes in its children; New England appeared to have little effect upon its inmates. As a result of the 1953 investigation we found:

The *anxiety* of the Wiltwyck boys significantly decreased the longer the boy was exposed to the school program. At the New England school, insecurity and inner conflict showed a slightly increasing trend.

Authoritarian tendencies among the Wiltwyck boys decreased significantly with length of residence. New England children showed no change.

At Wiltwyck, the school treatment, implemented by an interracial staff, effected a significant decrease in *prejudice*. In New England, prejudice increased with length of stay.

Neither group showed a significant decrease in *aggressiveness*.

More Wiltwyck children viewed the world as good than evil. In New England, the opposite was true.

Wiltwyck children were more satisfied with themselves than were New England children, and they possessed more affirmative ideals.

Wiltwyck children had a more loving ideal of parents and other adults. New England children more often viewed them as punitive.

Wiltwyck children had a greater interest in constructive activities and a better understanding of Christian teachings.

Wiltwyck children chose constructive student leaders. In New England, the leaders showed intense hostility and anxiety.

Wiltwyck children evidenced a much closer attachment to the staff than did New England children.

The 1953 study, while indicating the beneficial results of Wiltwyck's program, uncovered new and intriguing problems: *Do all types of children respond to Wiltwyck in the same manner? If they differ, in what ways does each respond? How does the treatment affect guilt, aggression, and withdrawal tendencies of the boys? Can Wiltwyck alter the child's view of authority?* And, most importantly: *Can Wiltwyck do anything for the psychopathic child?*

In June, 1954, we began to investigate these problems.

II. Methods

Between June and September 1954, the 107 children then at Wiltwyck were given a battery of projective tests and questionnaires. At the same time, Wiltwyck's counselors gave judgments on the boys' behavior in many areas.

As an additional method of evaluating treatment effects, those boys who had been in residence for less than nine months when first studied were retested in February, 1955. Thus, the changes in individual boys could be measured.

In the summer of 1954, Wiltwyck's population consisted primarily of Protestant, Negro boys. Their average age was 11 years; their median I.Q., 90. The boys had resided at Wiltwyck, on the average, for 10 months.*

A. *The Diagnostic Problem*

Before admittance, every Wiltwyck child undergoes a psychiatric investigation at either Kings County or Bellevue Hospital. Since we wished to analyze the school's impact on different character structures, we used these diagnoses as the foundation of our classifications: neurotic, borderline psychotic, behavior disorder, and psychopathic.

Psychological traits showed slight overlap among the four categories: [4]

Sixty-three per cent of the psychopaths and behavior disorders, but only 16 per cent of the psychotics and neurotics were described as "strongly aggressive."

Ninety per cent of the neurotics and psychotics, but only 30 per cent of the psychopaths and behavior disorders were described as "extremely anxious."

Sixty per cent of the psychopaths, but no neurotics, psychotics, or behavior disorders were described as "completely lacking in guilt feelings."

Forty-five per cent of the psychopaths, 10 per cent of the behavior disorders, and 2 per cent of the neurotics and psychotics were described as "highly impulsive."

Forty per cent of the psychopaths, 10 per cent of the behavior disorders, and 5 per cent of the neurotics and psychotics were described as "highly resentful of all authority."

Forty per cent of the psychopaths, 10 per cent of the behavior disorders, but no neurotic or psychotic children were described as "highly destructive."

Descriptive reports will perhaps clarify each of the syndromes.

The 23 withdrawn *neurotic* children felt intense anxiety, inner conflict, and suspicion. Seldom involved in serious delinquencies, these children appeared in court because of neglect, truancy, or bizarre school behavior. Although markedly disturbed, they did not exhibit the usual psychotic symptoms of hallucinations and autistic thinking. "Danny"[5] typified Wiltwyck's neurotic children:

Danny, a 12-year-old Negro boy, seemed continually preoccupied. His "dead pan" face hid intense anxiety and highly volatile emotions. He

---

*See Appendix A for a more complete breakdown.

appeared joyless and enveloped in protective armor. During the intake examination, the psychiatrist noted: "He has no zest or drive and tends to withdraw from all frustration. He is not, however, completely immune to emotional stimulation or incestual fantasies." Danny had not completely lost his powers of concentration, of social comprehension, or his ability to relate to other human beings.

Danny feared his father, though his father had deserted the family several years before. Danny was overly attached to his mother, a prostitute who brought paramours home for rendezvous in the same room with Danny and his brother.

Public agencies supported the family until they discovered the mother's behavior. Late in 1953 a petition of neglect was filed against the mother. Although Danny offered no special school problem and had never been involved in delinquent activities, the court felt that he would benefit from Wiltwyck's treatment.

In January, 1954, Danny entered the school. During his first month, the group counselor described him as "pleasant, quiet, and timid." He exhibited little aggressiveness, but seemed disturbed by sexual problems and compulsively lost his belongings. During his first weeks at Wiltwyck, Danny made no friends. At night, he repeated again and again: "I want to go home. I want to go to my mother."

Five months later, during the research interviews, Danny still showed a high level of anxiety, strong withdrawal tendencies, a confused self-perception, and an unclear concept of family life.

Wiltwyck's 6 *borderline psychotics,* too, showed signs of intense anxiety, confusion, and suspicion. In addition, they exhibited autistic thinking, hallucinations, and a strong urge to withdraw from reality. Intellectual abilities, social comprehension, and the capacity to respond to others had deteriorated. "Tommy" exemplified the common traits of this small group:

Tommy, an 11-year-old white boy, gave the impression of being an extremely polite, effeminate child. Before admittance, projective test results had shown that Tommy felt "completely rejected, not only by his family but by the whole world." Though intelligent, emotional disturbances blocked Tommy's performance. He was preoccupied with monsters and had auditory hallucinations. Voices threatened him as he listened to television or read a book. A hospital psychiatrist found a "paranoid quality to his thinking" and a "fluidity of identification." Sometimes he thought he was Roy Rogers, Superman, or Space Cadet.

Neurological examination showed a normal E.E.G. pattern and no evidence of organic damage. In January, 1954, a New York hospital diagnosed Tommy as schizophrenic but added: "He is in sufficient control of his own impulses to avoid aggressive behavior or running away. His hallucinations are usually benign, and are not far removed from the average boy's."

Tommy's mother has been in a mental hospital. Like Tommy, she had auditory hallucinations and "paranoid ideation." She refused to associate with people and talked only in whispers. Tommy's father, a dull and irresponsible man, minimized the boy's problems. He agreed to send Tommy to Wiltwyck after a court petition of neglect had been filed.

Although non-delinquent, Tommy became explosive and aggressive in public school. There, Tommy often threw temper tantrums, fell into foaming rages, and tore up his work. Apparent rejection by the teachers seemed to bring forth the outbursts.

During his first months at Wiltwyck, Tommy posted notes: "I'll come tonight . . . K."; "You will never be able to catch me. I'll steal everything from this group. . . . K." After a foray of stealing from the other boys, Tommy's aggression subsided. He was then placed under a Wiltwyck psychologist's care.

The majority of Wiltwyck's boys were diagnosed as *behavior disorders*. Sixty-three cases fitted this category of anxious, aggressive, resentful children who "acted out" their conflicts. The primary problem of these children stemmed from their uncontrolled aggressive behavior and their destructive reaction to frustration.

The behavior disorders usually appeared in court because of delinquency or school problem behavior. Two of these children suffered from organic brain damage; 5 seemed to have become delinquent as a response to their cultural background. The behavior of the vast majority, however, appeared to be the result of brutal, rejectant families and delinquent slum neighborhoods. Although they closely resembled the "average" delinquent, Wiltwyck's behavior disorders had a great many neurotic traits: nail biting, eneuresis, and anxiety. "Bobby" indicates the typical problems of the behavior disorders:

Bobby, a 10-year-old Negro child, eagerly sought attention from adults. Handsome and muscular, Bobby had no neurological defects, an average intelligence, and he talked easily. He was, however, very lonely and viewed the world as hostile and threatening.

During an examination at a New York hospital, the psychiatrist noted: "Bobby is anxiety ridden because of an effort to prevent hostile impulses from breaking through. He has found no satisfaction from his environment and has, consequently, withdrawn into himself."

Bobby, the youngest of three children, came from an unstable family. The father, a drunkard, physically abused the mother, rarely contributed to the support of his family, and deserted at frequent intervals. Since April, 1951, he has not returned. Bobby's mother is a catatonic schizophrenic and periodically under treatment in state hospitals. When home, she accused the children of poisoning her food and was extremely depressed. In July, 1951, she re-entered a mental hospital.

At that time, one of Bobby's sisters went to a foster home and the other, a severe behavior problem, was committed to a state institution. The court sent Bobby to live with his grandmother. During his stay there, Bobby began to steal, attacked other children in school, and assaulted his teacher with a knife. The school principal and Bobby's grandmother initiated the court proceedings which led Bobby to Wiltwyck.

During his first weeks at Wiltwyck, Bobby could find no friends. His counselor commented: "He's extremely nervous, wets his bed frequently, and has silly 'jags'." Bobby seemed to feel that no one liked him and that no one ever could.

Interviewed for the research after several months at Wiltwyck, Bobby appeared to repress strong aggressive instincts and to feel a pervading anxiety. He had an unclear perception of himself and his parents, but seemed to desire friendship with adults. He had not become adjusted to the Wiltwyck environment and could often be found crying piteously or raging bitterly over some imagined rejection.

Only 15 children appeared to be truly *psychopathic* personalities. Aggressive, asocial, highly impulsive children, they exhibited dangerous delinquent tendencies, extreme maladjustment in school, and severe temper tantrums.[6] Unlike the psychotic and neurotic children, they were not highly anxious, withdrawn, or introverted. Furthermore, among the psychopathic children there was a pronounced lack of guilt feelings. In every important respect, they presaged the behavior of that ultimate social enemy, the adult psychopath. "Paul" denoted the psychopathic syndrome:

Paul, a 10-year-old white boy, wore a mask of enmity, creased with scowls and frowns. Extreme aggressiveness and uncontrolled impulsivity, at the age of 3½, had brought Paul to the attention of a psychiatrist.

Since first treatment, Paul's aggression, hyperactivity, and destructiveness had increased. In public school, Paul attacked several children, set fire to the teacher, and ravaged the class room. After one year, the principal suspended him. Taught at home, Paul drove teacher after teacher from the house. To "have his way," he sometimes resorted to banging his head against the wall. A second psychiatrist concluded: "He has no ability for relating to either adults or children, no comprehension of the consequences of his acts, and no guilt concerning them."

Detailed and frequent neurological examinations have shown no defect or damage in the child's brain.

Paul's family lived in a slum area. His father openly rejected the child and had beaten him severely since infancy. His mother, a weak and ineffectual woman, had no control over the boy.

While stealing from a warehouse, Paul struck a watchman on the head, causing severe concussions. For this offense, the court remanded Paul to a public home in New York City.

At the home, Paul set fire to the furniture and curtains. He horrified the other children by killing goldfish with pins and pulling out their intestines. The children's home moved him to Wiltwyck in July, 1954.

During the research interview (a month after his arrival), Paul showed no guilt feelings, a hatred of his parents and other authority figures, and such intense hostility that the interview could not be completed. He left the room saying, "Get me out of this hole!"

Our interest focused upon the 15 psychopaths, those "rebels without a cause."

B. *The Measurement Problem*

The second major problem involved the choice of tests. Personality changes are notoriously difficult to measure. Moreover, we wanted to measure changes which, in many cases, had never before been tested.*

Before we could fully understand Wiltwyck's children, we had to tap three interconnected areas of their characters: their unconscious processes, their conscious values, and their actual behavior. By studying unconscious drives, we hoped to ascertain the changes in the underlying motivations of the child. By measuring conscious values, we wished to distinguish whatever changes there might be in social attitudes. By observational ratings, we sought to relate these inner dynamisms to the outer behavior of the child.

For the purpose of the Wiltwyck study, we developed several new psychological tests, established their reliability, and investigated their validity on non-delinquent children.†

As measures of the unconscious processes of the children (guilt, aggressive desires, withdrawal fantasies), we designed two picture tests (the "Rover" and the "Cartoons") and two sets of open-ended stories (the "Guilt Stories" and the "Authority Stories").

To measure conscious opinions (the child's view of himself and his environment), we used the direct question method. Some of these questions had been used in the 1953 study and had uncovered interesting differences between Wiltwyck and New England. In 1954 we added a series of questions concerning moral values, and a self-perception "check list."

---

*See Appendix C for a discussion of the usability of various tests in this research.

†See Appendix C for a full explanation of the procedures used in validating the tests and in establishing their reliability. Appendix B includes complete copies of all tests, except for the Rover test and the Cartoon test.

To measure the boys' behavior, we called upon Wiltwyck's counselors. They rated their boys on a variety of factors. In addition, the majority of the children participated in an experimental test of reactions to frustration. The following pages briefly describe the instruments we used.

1. *The Counselors' Ratings.* Wiltwyck's counselors see the boys from morning until night, day after day. They wake the child in the morning, eat, play and talk with him, and stay with him until he is in bed. Therefore, we asked the counselors to help us in analyzing the attitudes and behavior of their children.

From the counselors, we received 146 sets of ratings on 91 boys. Forty-five of the children were rated by two or more counselors. As many as five counselors (including special counselors) rated a few of the boys.

The counselors did not know our purpose or method of treating the data which they would furnish. They could thus be expected to judge the boys in as objective a manner as possible. The counselors judged each child in 18 areas:*

Hostility	Guilt
Destructiveness	Rapport (with the rater)
Anxiety	Self-perception
Impulsivity	Perception of the world
Narcissism	Perception of authority
Knowledge of the	Reaction to frustration
social code	Relation to other boys
Knowledge of the	Leadership
Wiltwyck code	Desire for recognition
Suggestibility	Mental pathology

Agreement on the ratings (when we received more than one for a child) varied according to the trait measured. The counselors agreed 70 per cent[7] or more in their ratings of hostility, destructiveness, impulsivity, knowledge of the social code, knowledge of the Wiltwyck code, relation to other boys, leadership, and suggestibility. Disagreement on internal characteristics (anxiety, narcissism, guilt, self-perception, perception of the world, perception of authority, and desire for recognition), however, was so great that these measures seemed relatively useless.[8]

Though helpful in measuring outer behavior, the ratings were far

---

*See Appendix A for rating forms.

from reliable in the assessment of inner personality. We used the counselors' ratings, where agreement was high, both in assessing the effects of Wiltwyck upon behavior and in validating our other instruments.

2. *The Rover Test* (a measure of aggressive and withdrawal tendencies). It can safely be said that the greatest problem of the psychopath, and indeed of most delinquents, lies in his frightening aggressiveness. The major problem of neurotics and psychotics is their exaggerated withdrawal from reality. One of our prime goals, therefore, was the reliable gauging of Wiltwyck's effect on aggressive and withdrawal tendencies.

In the 1953 study we had attempted to measure aggression through use of the Adult-Child Interaction Test and a word association test. These tests, however, did not seem to distinguish between healthy assertiveness and morbid aggression. Thus, we decided to develop a test which would distinguish between truly aggressive fantasies and normally assertive ones and would, at the same time, furnish some evidence concerning withdrawal tendencies.

From the "Blackie Test" we took the idea of using a dog, "Rover," as our central figure.[9] A dog seemed both appealing and non-threatening to boys. Children can identify easily with a dog, yet feel free to express violent aggressiveness, for a dog can do many things that a child would not dare.

Pictures of Rover in a variety of situations, all of them frustrating, composed the test. With each picture we asked, "What does Rover want to do?" Then we presented three possible alternatives in random order. One of these pictured Rover reacting with aggression (an actual attack), another showed him withdrawing from the threat, and the third offered a neutral (sometimes assertive) response. The boys' choices were recorded.

A typical situation showed Rover being scolded by his master. With each picture, a question was asked. For example:

Does Rover want to bite his master?
    (The aggressive choice)
Does Rover want to show how sad he feels?
    (The withdrawn choice: the picture shows Rover sulking in a corner)
Does Rover want to shake hands and make friends?
    (The neutral choice)

The other pictures depicted Rover reacting to the arrival of a new baby, meeting a stranger, seeing his ugly reflection in a mirror, being tempted by a forbidden cake, seeing his "girl" with another dog, being splashed by a passing car, hearing a frightening noise, being injured, having food stolen, finding his home occupied, and (particularly for the delinquents) the "frustration" of Rover seeing a policeman on his beat.

Before administering the test at Wiltwyck, the "Rover" was validated on 79 public school children. We will not discuss the details of this procedure:* It should be noted, however, that the test agreed surprisingly well with teachers' judgments concerning the aggressive and withdrawal fantasies of the public school children. In 94 per cent of the cases the Rover aggression score agreed with the teachers' judgments, while in 86 per cent of the cases the Rover agreed with the teachers' judgments of the children's withdrawal tendencies.

Each child's score on the Rover was easily computed. By adding the number of aggressive choices and the number of withdrawn choices, then dividing each by 12, the child was given a percentage score on aggression and one on withdrawal. For example, a child who responded with 4 aggressive choices, 3 withdrawn choices, and 5 neutral choices to the 12 situations was given a score of 33 per cent on aggression and 25 per cent on withdrawal.

A comparison of the public school students and the Wiltwyck boys shows that Wiltwyck's psychopaths and behavior disorders, upon entering the school, had a mean aggressive score of 33 per cent; public school children averaged 28 per cent; Wiltwyck's neurotics and psychotics averaged 17 per cent.

The Negro boys at Wiltwyck had a higher average on Rover aggression than did the white boys at Wiltwyck. With the greater frustration of Negroes in America, their greater aggression seems logical.

The effect of age on the Rover is not as clear. Among the public school children, there was no significant difference by age. At Wiltwyck, however, Rover aggression decreased with increasing age: boys 7 to 9 years old averaged 27 per cent while boys over 11 years averaged only 10 per cent.†

The intelligence of the Wiltwyck children did not seem to affect their scores. Boys with an I.Q. below 81 averaged 20 per cent while those with an I.Q. over 100 averaged 19 per cent.

As one would expect, Wiltwyck's neurotics and psychotics appeared

---

*See Appendix C for a more complete discussion of validity and reliability.
†See Appendix C for further information.

to have greater withdrawal tendencies. The neurotics and psychotics chose the withdrawn alternative in 26 per cent of the situations, behavior disorders and psychopaths chose 21 per cent withdrawn responses, and public school children chose 18 per cent. Neither age, intelligence nor race significantly affected the withdrawal scores.

With its reliability and its high agreement with independent judgments, the Rover seemed a good tool for measuring changes in the hostility and withdrawal tendencies of the Wiltwyck children.

3. *The Cartoon Test* (a measure of aggressive fantasy). Since aggression takes many forms, we decided to develop a second test of hostile desires. This second measure, we hoped, would confirm what results we might obtain from the Rover and also provide further information about aggressive fantasy.

Using comic books (with their wide appeal to children and often gory brutality) as our basis, we wished to find an objective measure of aggressive fantasies—fantasies which might be hidden from the counselors.

In the "Cartoon Test" we presented three comic book pictures on a panel. One showed the hero engaged in some aggressive action (kicking a villain in the face, shooting Indians, etc.). The other two illustrations depicted an exciting, but non-aggressive, scene (cowboys galloping across country, an airplane flying over mountains, etc.). The same colors were used in each of the three pictures and the same hero dominated each set.[10] With every panel we asked, "Which of the three pictures do you like best?" The responses were recorded and the score figured as the percentage of aggressive pictures chosen.

After a pre-test and item analysis, 10 panels were retained. A typical one included pictures of "American Man" kicking a man in the groin (the aggressive picture), "American Man" and his companion running down a deserted street, and "American Man" with his companion consulting a group of boys in an alley. Before giving the Cartoon Test to the Wiltwyck children, we presented the 10 panels to 30 school students in Massachusetts. Unlike the Rover, the Cartoon test results often did not agree with teachers' judgments. In 61 per cent of the cases, the Cartoon test agreed with the teachers' judgments.*

A comparison of the answers of the public school children to the Wiltwyck boys' responses turns up an anomalous difference: public

---

*See Appendix C for further discussion.

school children averaged 48 per cent aggressive choices, but Wiltwyck's psychopaths and behavior disorders (during their first months of residence) averaged only 32 per cent. Obviously, the test did not reflect the true differences in the aggressive behavior of the children; yet, it did reveal a rather unexpected contrast in their aggressive fantasies.

Because of the strange difference between delinquents and non-delinquents, we felt the Cartoon test might offer some interesting insights, and included it in the battery.

4. *The Internalized Guilt Stories* (a measure of conscience). If, as Shakespeare wrote, "Conscience doth make cowards of us all," it also makes society possible. The "socialization" of the average delinquent demands the reorientation of his conscience, the replacement of gang values with community values. But with the "lone wolf" psychopath, treatment must build a conscience out of nothing. Upon the success of this difficult task depends the safety of society and the future of the delinquent. Certainly the process deserves careful consideration in any therapeutic evaluation.

Important as it is, conscience eludes both definition and measurement. We thought of conscience as internalized feelings of guilt which prevent the violation of generally accepted rules of conduct. As a measure of these internalized guilt feelings, we constructed 10 stories, each ending with a question. Every story described a situation in which "Bob" had violated some standard of behavior in American society.[11] After presenting the story we asked, "How does Bob feel?"

A typical story read: "Bob and Jack fought one day. Bob pulled a knife and stabbed Jack. How does Bob feel?" The responses included such answers as:

"Bob felt grand. He hated Jack."
    (satisfaction)
"Bob was scared. Jack might get him."[12]
    (fear of punishment)
"Bob felt sorry. He had hurt Jack."
    (internalized guilt)

Some stories described Bob committing a minor "crime": stealing cake, telling his teacher he did not like her, tripping his counselor, stealing from a ten-cent store, and taking a friend's marbles. Other stories told of more serious violations: running into a boy with his bike, breaking the teeth of another child, setting a house on fire and killing a man, breaking a school's movie projector "out of spite," and stabbing another boy.

Usually the answers could immediately be categorized as showing fear, happiness, or guilt. When given ambiguous responses such as, "Bob felt bad," the interviewer had to question the child further. Almost invariably, the resulting explanation furnished a scorable response.

The purpose of the Guilt Stories was not the measurement of the unconscious guilt felt by neurotics, but rather the measurement of those feelings of social inhibition, of "socialized" guilt, which form the core of conscience. Did the stories accomplish this purpose? The question of their validity is complex. Briefly, the stories did correspond well to teachers' judgments of a pre-test group of public school children, and, at Wiltwyck, the stories successfully distinguished between those boys whom the counselors rated as having little control over their aggression and those who were rated as having adequate control.*

If the stories measured internalized guilt, as we hoped, one would expect non-delinquents to obtain significantly higher scores than delinquent children. This proved to be the case: *The thirty public school children who participated in the pre-test averaged 82 per cent "guilt" answers; the 107 Wiltwyck boys averaged 63 per cent.*[13]

Furthermore, *the neurotic and psychotic children* (who would be expected to have greater internalized guilt than either the behavior disorders or the psychopaths) *averaged 67 per cent. The behavior disorders averaged 54 per cent. The psychopaths* (notorious for their lack of internalized guilt) *averaged 46 per cent.*

There was no significant relationship between intelligence and guilt, either among public school children or Wiltwyck boys.

Relating age to guilt (at Wiltwyck) we found, surprisingly, that the proportion of answers showing internalized guilt does not significantly change between the ages of 8 and 13. Eight-year-old boys averaged 65 per cent; 13-year-olds averaged 60 per cent.* The figures hint that socialization, as reflected in guilt feelings, occurs at an early age. Contrary to popular opinion, maturing does not seem to increase the level of internalized guilt.

---

*See Appendix C for further information.

Because of the Calvinistic emphasis upon original sin and individual responsibility, one might expect Protestants to have greater internalized guilt. Our test gave no indication of such a trend. *Protestants and Roman Catholics showed an identical mean guilt score of 63 per cent.*

Lower-class Negro culture, with supposedly lax controls and greater family brutality than lower-class white society, might result in less internalized guilt among Negro delinquents. Such was not the case. *Mean scores of Negro boys (64 per cent) and of white boys (62 per cent) showed no substantial difference.*

Although we cannot positively assert that the 10 stories measure internalized guilt, we can say this much: the stories have acceptable reliability, fair agreement with certain types of independent judgments, and a "logical," if not provable, validity.*

5. *Authority Stories* (a measure of attitudes toward authority figures). One of the delinquent's most disturbing, although often justified, characteristics is his bitter attitude toward society and its representatives. The delinquent child at best suspects all authority; at worst, hates it. The psychopathic child, of course, refuses even to recognize authority, much less admire or obey it. To improve behavior, therapy must alter the delinquent's perception of authority. Thus, evaluating views of authority became one of our objectives.

In the 1953 comparison of Wiltwyck and New England, we used a test of authoritarianism based on the Berkeley research. This test measured a variety of "authoritarian" opinions and values. It was not intended as a test of the individual's attitude toward his own parents, teachers, or other immediate authority figures.

In 1954 we used unfinished stories as a measure of the child's view

---

*We used some of the guilt stories as still another measure of aggression. Since 8 of the 10 stories describe a situation in which "Bob' injures another individual, we believed that the child's feelings about the act might reveal some of his hostile feelings. Consequently, with the 8 aggressive stories, we totaled the proportion of answers in which the child said Bob felt "happy" in committing the injury. The use of the stories in this manner was not pretested, but a chi-square comparison of the counselor ratings of aggression and the proportion of "happy" answers showed: *boys judged as extremely hostile by the counselors showed significantly more aggression on the stories than those rated as non-hostile* (d.f. $= 1$, $X^2 = 4.06$). Although the stories differentiated the extremely aggressive child from the non-aggressive, they did not significantly distinguish the occasionally aggressive from the other two categories. Neither age, intelligence, nor race significantly affect the child's response to the 8 aggressive stories.

of authority in his *personal* environment—a method less apt to create anxiety than direct questioning. In each of 5 stories, "Bob" transgresses accepted behavior. At the end of the story, an authority figure (mother, father, teacher, policeman, or counselor) appears. The children were asked: "What does (the authority figure) do?" The stories were constructed so that the child was forced to describe the authority figure either as punishing Bob or as helping him. The proportions of punitive and supportive answers were computed as percentages.

A typical story read: "Bob came home very late one night. He had fallen down and hurt himself. What did his father do?" Typical answers were:

"He whipped Bob for being late."
(punitive)
"He took Bob to the hospital."
(supportive)
"His father was mad."
(punitive)
"If he was hurt bad, his father bandaged him."
(supportive)

The other 4 stories depicted Bob fighting and being hurt, failing to do his arithmetic, hitting a ball into another's yard and being unable to climb the wall, and running away from Wiltwyck and returning dirty and tired.

As a measure of validity, we compared the boys' answers to the stories with their counselors' ratings of behavior toward authority figures. The stories successfully distinguished between those who were hostile to authority and those who had a normal, responsive attitude toward authority.*

A further confirmation of the test's validity appeared when the responses of 30 non-delinquent school boys were compared with the Wiltwyck answers. The public school boys averaged 36 per cent punitive responses. In consonance with their disorder, the psychopathic children at Wiltwyck (at the beginning of treatment) revealed the most punitive view of authority: 56 per cent of their story answers described the authority figures as punitive. Behavior disorders responded with 41 per cent punitive answers; the neurotic and psychotic children, with 37.[14]

---

*See Appendix C for further information.

The child's ethnic group makes no marked difference in his view of authority: Negro boys averaged 36 per cent punitive answers; white boys at Wiltwyck averaged 39.

Religion has no effect: Catholic children responded with 36 per cent punitive endings; Protestants, with 38.

Intelligence makes little difference in the child's response: children with an I.Q. below 81 averaged 28 per cent punitive answers while those with an I.Q. over 100 averaged 35 per cent.

The age of the child, on the other hand, does seem to influence his view of authority: *with increasing age, the punitive attitude toward authority decreases.*[15] The youngest children responded with the highest proportion of punitive endings.

This result is particularly surprising in view of the proverbial "adolescent rebellion." One would expect the older children to see authority with jaundiced eye. Perhaps, however, the young child's lack of experience, his small size, and his defenselessness cause him to view adults as overwhelming and threatening. With increasing size and experience, Wiltwyck's older children may have learned to differentiate between adults who abuse their authority and those who use it helpfully. Knowing the brutal family experience of the Wiltwyck children, it seems remarkable that they have any view other than hostility.[16]

Despite the high correspondence between the counselors' judgments and the answers to the Authority Stories, we felt that use of both would do more than increase the reliability of one measure alone. The ratings contributed information concerning the boy's attitude within the school. The stories questioned not only the child's view of school authorities, but also his attitude toward his parents and other community representatives.

6. *Self-Perception Questionnaire.* Since the way a child looks at himself and his problems influences his reaction to treatment, we needed some measure of self-perception. In the 1953 study of Wiltwyck and New England, we used a series of direct questions to assess the self-concepts of the delinquent boys. Wiltwyck children revealed more positive personal goals than the New England boys. We believed that further use of the same questions would give an interesting measure of the various personality groups. In addition, we added a self-perception "check-list" to our personality inventory of 1954.

To test the child's perception of his own qualities, we asked, "What do people like best about you?" and, "What do people dislike most about you?" To measure the child's "ego-ideal"—the model he emulates—we asked, "If you could be anyone in the whole world, whom would you be?" "Whom do you admire most in the whole world?" and, "What is a good boy like?"*

An analysis of answers from boys who had recently arrived at Wiltwyck uncovered these interesting differences among various personality syndromes†:

No psychopathic child believed that others liked him for his inner qualities. (Proportions who responded with an inner quality when asked about what people liked about him: psychopaths, 0%; behavior disorders, 19%; neurotics and psychotics, 62%; P<.02.) [17]

No psychopathic child had a positive ideal of the "good boy." (Proportions of positive responses when asked the traits of a "good boy": psychopaths, 0%; behavior disorders, 25%; neurotics and psychotics, 37%; N.S.) [18]

More psychopathic boys and behavior disorders would like to be a power figure, "if they could be anyone." (Proportions of power figures: psychopaths, 50%; behavior disorders, 50%; neurotics and psychotics, 22%; P<.05.) [19]

More psychotic boys admired power figures above all others. (Proportions of power figures: psychopaths, 45%; behavior disorders, 36%; neurotics and psychotics, 16%; N.S.) [20]

More psychopathic boys and behavior disorders than neurotics and psychotics admired their parents most. (Proportions of parents: psychopaths, 16%; behavior disorders, 20%; neurotics and psychotics, 0%; P<.10.) [21]

With the self-perception "check-list," 20 personality labels were read to the child. With each, the interviewer asked: "Does this describe you? Are you (strong, bad, smart, kind, cruel, etc)?" We did not expect the children to give accurate descriptions of themselves. Rather, we expected to find the extent to which the child admitted having negative qualities and the degree to which he exhibited a differentiated, realistic self-concept.

We determined differentiation by the number of qualified answers the boy gave (e.g., "Sometimes I'm bad and get in trouble; other times I'm good, or try to be good.").

---

*See Appendix C for a discussion of the methods of scoring the responses to these questions and of the reliability of the scoring.

†(P < ___) signifies the level of statistical significance as ascertained by either Festinger's non-parametric formula for the difference between means, or as ascertained by the chi-square method (two-tailed probability) for the differences between proportions; N.S. signifies that differences were not statistically significant.

Psychopaths, behavior disorders, neurotics, and psychotics appeared equally able to admit negative traits in their own characters. (Proportions of negative qualities admitted: psychopaths, 15%; behavior disorders, 9%; neurotics and psychotics, 13%.)[22]

Psychopaths, behavior disorders, neurotics, and psychotics appeared equally able to differentiate descriptions of themselves. (Proportions of differentiated answers: psychopaths, 20%; behavior disorders, 18%; neurotics and psychotics, 20%.)[23]

Age affected the check-list in only one respect: Wiltwyck's older children had a significantly more differentiated (and presumably, more realistic) self-concept: children aged 7 to 9 averaged 5 per cent differentiated answers; children over eleven averaged 24 per cent.*

The direct questions and the check-list indicated a possible influence of intelligence on self-perception. Although none of the differences were significant, boys with higher intelligence tended to differentiate their answers more frequently on the check list, responded with more negative answers, and answered with more positive ideals to the description of the "good boy."*

Neither race nor religion significantly affected the self-perception results. In general, it seems that the more intelligent, older child possesses the most realistic self-concept.

We hoped that these measures would prove useful in assessing Wiltwyck's impact on the way the child thought of himself.

7. *"Perception of the Environment" Questionnaire.* Equally significant for therapeutic success is the way the child interprets the motives and values of those around him. To register these views, we again used a set of questions which had been tried out in the 1953 research. Two questions dealt with the child's immediate environment: "What do you like most about Wiltwyck?" and "What do you like least about Wiltwyck?" Three other questions concerned the child's view of his parental environment: "What are good parents like?" "What happens to a boy when he does something wrong?" and, "Is what happens right?"†

A comparison of the responses of various personality groups during early months of treatment revealed these differences:

Fewer psychopathic children liked Wiltwyck because of the school's constructive activities. (Proportions of constructive activities mentioned: psy-

---

*See Appendix C for further information.

†See Appendix C for a discussion of scoring and the reliability of scoring.

chopaths, 57%; behavior disorders, 92%; neurotics and psychotics, 85%; P<.02.)[24]

More behavior disorders and psychopaths disliked Wiltwyck for unrealistic reasons. (Proportions of unrealistic answers: psychopaths, 33%; behavior disorders, 61%; neurotics and psychotics, 12%; P<.02.)[25]

Fewer psychopaths viewed the "good parent" as loving. (Proportions of loving descriptions: psychopaths, 20%; behavior disorders, 50%; neurotics and psychotics; 40%; N.S.)[26]

More behavior disorders qualified their views concerning the "rightness" of punishment. (Proportions of qualification: psychopaths, 0%; behavior disorders, 15%; neurotics and psychotics, 0%; P<.05.)[27]

Age, race, religion, and intelligence did not significantly influence the child's response to the questions.

8. *Moral Code Questionnaire.* Increasing the child's knowledge of society's morality has long been a primary goal of many who work with anti-social children. Wiltwyck does not try to indoctrinate a strict morality. It does try to teach the child that society, for various legitimate reasons, limits the individual's actions.

We presented statements of "accepted" attitudes, 5 dealing with society in general and 7 dealing with a code particular to Wiltwyck. For each we asked: "Do you agree or disagree?" The statements of general morality were:

> Stealing is always wrong.
> You should always be kind.
> It is always wrong to kill.
> You should never tell a lie.
> You should always be generous.

The Wiltwyck code statements were:

> It is always wrong to run away from the school.
> You should always think of the good of the school.
> If you do something wrong, you should take the consequences.
> There is always someone at Wiltwyck who likes you.
> You should go to class whether you want to or not.
> If a boy can't go home, it's not his social worker's fault.
> Going home would not solve everything for a boy.

Before each series, we told the child, "Some people think these statements are right; other people think they are wrong. Whatever you think—that is the correct answer. There is no really right or wrong answer."

Although such questions would not measure the child's actual attitude (we hoped that other tests, like the guilt stories, would do that), they indicate whether the child, on a verbal level, is aware of what is expected and acceptable. This conscious knowledge has often been proposed as a panacea for delinquency.

We found, not too unexpectedly, that *even at the beginning of treatment Wiltwyck's boys agreed overwhelmingly with both society's and Wiltwyck's code.* Neurotics and psychotics agreed with 86 per cent of the statements; behavior disorders, with 90; and even psychopaths agreed with 85. The maladjustment of these children cannot, therefore, be ascribed to a lack of knowledge of society's norms. The delinquents already "know the difference between right and wrong."

Our study confirms others which have found increasing age accompanied by a decline in the acceptance of moral strictures.[28] Among the Wiltwyck boys, agreement with the moral statements declines, though non-significantly, both with increasing age and increasing intelligence.

The decline in such agreement found with increasing intelligence may be due to detection of possible exceptions to moral generalities.

Neither the child's race nor his religious training was significantly related to his knowledge of the acceptable moral code.

9. *A Test of Reactions to Frustration.* The ability to meet frustration with calm realism marks the socially mature child. The psychopathic child, faced with frustration, often gives reign to bitter fury. Neurotic and psychotic children, on the other hand, more often turn their aggression inward, burning out their rage in deeply repressed channels.

Wiltwyck's supportive environment might be expected to increase the child's ability to accept frustration realistically. To find out if it does, we asked the counselors to arrange a controlled test.

This test involved a substitute of house cleaning during a period when the boys expected to be able to play. The counselors observed the reaction of each boy and recorded this on a rating scale which ranged from withdrawal to extreme aggression. Because some of the counselors feared that the planned frustration might set back therapeutic advances, only 50 boys underwent the experience. The counselors rated the expected reaction of another 42 boys.[29]

In their initial response to the situation, the psychopathic or behavior disorder newcomers to Wiltwyck responded to the situation with either aggression or hyperactivity. The neurotics and psychotics responded either by accepting the situation realistically or by withdrawing from it.

10. *Summary*. This array of personality tests, questionnaires, and behavior ratings served as our tools in assessing Wiltwyck's effect on its severely maladjusted children. By bringing to bear so many different approaches—projective tests, open-ended stories, direct questions, an experimental situation, observational ratings—we hoped to measure every important aspect of the child's personality. With the psychopaths, we were naturally most interested in seeing changes the tests of aggression, guilt, views of authority, and reaction to frustration might reveal.

With the behavior disorders, the results of the treatment on aggression, guilt, and authority were extremely important. With the neurotics and psychotics, on the other hand, our interest focused on their responses to the tests of withdrawal fantasies and self-perception.

III. The Effects of Wiltwyck Treatment

By use of these tests and ratings, we hoped to discover the way boys with widely different problems respond to Wiltwyck's therapy. We divided the test results in terms of length of residence at the school. In 1953 we had used this method and obtained statistically significant results. In 1954 we further divided the results by use of the boys' intake diagnoses. Re-testing, eight months later, provided a second check on the boys who had been recent arrivals in 1954. For convenience, we shall refer to the initial, cross-sectional study as the "1954 Study," and the findings of the re-testing as the "1955 Study."

A perusal of the 1954 tests and ratings showed that, in general, sharp changes appeared between the eighth and ninth months in residence at Wiltwyck. Therefore, for analytic purposes, we used 0–8 months as our new-arrival group.

Wiltwyck's records showed that most boys were released after they had been in the school between 16 and 23 months (the average being 18 months). Therefore, we used 9–23 months as the category most indicative of the effects of treatment. Our three divisions according to length of treatment were: 0–8 months, 9–23 months, and over 23 months.

The boys who had been at Wiltwyck at least two years represented an atypical group. Some of them have no home in the city. More often, they present exceptional problems. One of these boys suffers from organic brain damage, consequent low intelligence, and pyromanic tendencies. His mother, a prostitute, rejects him and no foster family will accept him. He has lived at Wiltwyck for five years, but eventually the school will have to send him to another institution. Others present equally complex disorders.

This group of long-term residents showed intense hostility (on the Rover), troublesome aggressive behavior (judged by the counselors), great anxiety (judged by the counselors), and little guilt (on the stories). In only one area did they seem better adjusted than those children who had recently arrived at Wiltwyck: Counselors rated children who have lived at Wiltwyck for at least two years as having a more realistic self-concept (P <.05).

The chart below shows the number of boys (divided according to diagnoses and months at Wiltwyck) in each category:

Months	Psychopaths	Behavior Disorders	Neurotics	Psychotics
0-8	7	20	6	2
9-23	3	21	13	4
Over 23	5	22	4	0

To allow sufficient numbers for statistical analysis, we had to group some of the diagnostic categories. Because their test results were comparable and their symptoms were similar, we grouped the psychotics with the neurotics. When computing statistical significance, we grouped the psychopaths with the behavior disorders.[30]

A. *Findings of the 1954 Study*

1. A comparison of the 0–8 month category and the 9–23 month category showed that *the aggressive fantasies of the behavior disorders and psychopaths decreased*. The aggressive fantasies of psychotic and neurotic children showed no significant change.[31]

All three measures traced the same pattern of decreasing aggression among psychopaths and behavior disorders: on the Rover pictures, the proportion of hostile choices decreased markedly (P <.05); on the aggressive (guilt) stories, the proportion of answers signifying happiness also dropped significantly (P <.05); while the results of the Cartoon test, although showing no significant change, followed the same decreasing pattern.*

*See Appendix D for a more detailed analysis of the changes on specific tests and for tables tracing this change.

2. A comparison of the 0–8 month category with the 9–23 month category showed that *internalization of guilt in behavior disorders and psychopaths significantly increased* (P <.01). The percentage of guilty endings jumped from 50 to 76 per cent. Neurotics and psychotics, with greater initial guilt, had no significant increase.[32]

Most importantly, when analyzed separately, psychopaths showed a large increase in the internalization of guilt. Their proportion of guilty answers rose from 46 to 69 per cent.

Even the boys in residence between 9 and 23 months, however, have a lower degree of inner controls than the public school children (who had 82 per cent).

The single factor which may most directly affect internalization of guilt is the child's relation to the staff. The normal child internalizes his parents' standards through identification and fear of losing their love. Most of the Wiltwyck boys and all of the psychopathic boys have been emotionally and physically maltreated by their parents. Consequently, they have not feared the loss of (a non-existent) love, nor have they identified with their parents. At Wiltwyck, we can hypothesize, the boys come first to respect and later to love adults with whom they come in contact. Perhaps the support and understanding given by the staff results in close identification.

3. A comparison of the 0–8 month category and the 9–23 month category showed that *the tendency of behavior disorders and psychopaths to view authority figures as punitive and threatening decreased significantly* (P <.05). The proportion of answers (to the authority stories) which pictured authority figures as punishing significantly decreased from 45 to 26 per cent.

The answers of the neurotics and psychotics did not significantly change.

Psychopaths, taken alone, showed a decrease from 56 per cent punitive endings for boys in the 0–8 month group to 36 per cent in the 9–23 month group.

In order to accept the standards of society, the individual must learn to respect its representatives. Because counselors protect as well as restrict, Wiltwyck seems to teach the child to appreciate the beneficial role of some authority figures. By emphasizing "consequences," rather than arbitrary punishment, the school apparently inculcates a respect for legitimate authority.

4. A comparison of the 0–8 month category and the 9–23 month

category showed that *the tendency of neurotic and psychotic children to withdraw from a threatening or frustrating situation decreased significantly* (P <.05). For psychopaths and behavior disorders the proportion of withdrawn alternatives chosen on the Rover Test did not change.

Other evidence tends to support the Rover Test results. During the experimental frustration of the boys, the counselor reports showed a (non-significant) decrease in the neurotics and psychotics withdrawal reactions. In the 0–8 month category, 40 per cent of the neurotic boys reacted by withdrawing from the situation. After 9–23 months of treatment, only 11 per cent withdrew.

5. A comparison of the 0–8 month category and the 9–23 month category showed that *the proportion of neurotics and psychotics rated as "realistic" in their self-perception significantly increased* (P <.05).[33] The counselors did not note a corresponding difference in the psychopaths and behavior disorders.

6. A comparison of the 0–8 month category and the 9–23 month category showed that the *psychopaths' and behavior disorders' knowledge of Wiltwyck's code of behavior,* as measured by the counselors' ratings, *increased significantly* (P <.02).[34] Counselor ratings indicate that the proportion of neurotics and psychotics with "an adequate understanding" of Wiltwyck's code does not increase with length of stay.

This gain in understanding of the Wiltwyck code is expected. The ratings probably measure an important trend: the child's increasing ability to moderate his behavior to fit the Wiltwyck demands.

7. *Other trends.* On other tests, the children showed changes in their conscious values and behavior which did not quite attain the 5 per cent level of significance:

a) Comparison of the 0–8 month category with the 9–23 month category showed that the proportion of behavior disorders and psychopaths who "most admire" a positive ideal increased from 17 to 37 per cent.[35] On the same question, the proportion of behavior disorders and psychopaths answering with a power figure decreased from 32 to 11 per cent.[36]

b) A comparison of the 0–8 month category and the 9–23 month category showed that the proportion of psychopaths and behavior disorders who responded with a positive answer to "What are good boys like?" increased from 15 to 33 per cent.[37] Neurotics and psychotics in the 0–8 month category answered with a higher proportion (37 per cent) of positive responses. The proportion was the same for the 9–23 month category.

c) The situational test of the children's reactions to frustration failed to uncover statistically significant changes. Yet, comparison of the 0–8 month category with the 9–23 month category on ratings of frustration reaction showed a trend toward more realistic acceptance. The proportion of psychopaths and behavior disorders who accepted the situation realistically increased from 39 to 50 per cent; the percentage who withdrew from the frustration decreased from 15 to 5 per cent. The neurotics and psychotics, on the other hand, tended to increase their aggressive reactions to frustration.

8. *Comparison to Normal Children.* Comparison of the test results of the Wiltwyck boys to the results of the public school children upon whom the tests were validated shows the following differences:

PERCENTAGE SCORES

	Behavior Disorders and Psychopaths		Psychotics and Neurotics		Public School Children
	0-8 mo. (27 boys)	9-23 mo. (24 boys)	0-8 mo. (8 boys)	9-23 mo. (17 boys)	(30 to 79 boys)
Rover *Aggression*	33	15†	17	19	28
Rover *Withdrawal*	20	20	26	12†	18
Cartoon *Aggression*	32	29	34	36	48
Internalized *Guilt*	50	76†	67	71	82
Punitiveness on *Authority* Stories	45	26†	38	32	36
Negative *Self-Perception*	10	11	13	11	17
Differentiated *Self-Perception*	17	20	20	28	37

†P<.05 in comparison between 0-8 mo. and 9-23 mo. categories.

During the first eight months at Wiltwyck, the behavior disorders and psychopaths had more aggressive fantasies on the Rover, more hostile views toward authority, and less guilt than did the normal children. Yet, after the boys had been at Wiltwyck for at least nine months, they had less aggressive fantasies, a less punitive view of authority, and almost as much guilt.

During the first eight months at Wiltwyck, the neurotics and psychotics had more withdrawal fantasies on the Rover than did the normal children. Those children who had been at Wiltwyck for at least nine months, however, had fewer withdrawal fantasies than normal children.

B. *Findings of the 1955 Study*

Up to this point, we have discussed the effects of Wiltwyck treatment on 107 boys. After dividing the boys into months of residence and diagnoses, significant differences appeared. The children who had lived at Wiltwyck between nine months and two years evidenced more guilt, more friendly acceptance of authority figures, less withdrawal, and less aggression than boys who had lived at the school for less than nine months.

The cross-sectional method used in the 1954 study assumed that the 0–8 month category and the 9–23 month category were matched. We tested this assumption by use of the longitudinal approach.

Our attention shifted from the 107 boys to 25 boys who were first tested in June, 1954, and retested in February, 1955. In June, 1954, the 25 children had been recent arrivals at Wiltwyck. A few were interviewed on the day they arrived, the majority had lived in the school for three months, and some had resided at Wiltwyck for as long as eight months.[38]

In late February, 1955, the boys were re-interviewed and re-rated by their counselors. Once again they took the Rover Test, furnished endings to the Guilt and Authority Stories, and answered the questionnaire. Eight months had elapsed between the two testings. By 1955 the average length of residence for the 25 children was just under one year.

Six of the 25 boys were psychopathic personalities, 13 were behavior disorders, 5 were neurotic, and 1 was a borderline psychotic.

Comparison of the 1954 test results with those of 1955 uncovered these significant changes in the 25 boys.[39]

1. *Aggressive fantasies of the psychopaths and behavior disorders decreased significantly.* On the Rover pictures, they made significantly fewer aggressive choices, decreasing from 35 per cent in 1954 to 15 in 1955 (P <.01).

The 6 psychopaths, taken alone, decreased from 33 to 11 per cent aggressive choices.

In their answers to the aggressive (Guilt) stories, the behavior disorders and psychopaths responded with significantly fewer hostile endings, decreasing from 37 per cent in 1954 to 16 in 1955 (P <.01).

The mean of the six psychopaths decreased from 35 to 15 per cent.

On the Cartoons, the aggressive choices decreased from 27 to 21 per cent, but this decrease is not statistically significant.

Thus, all three tests exhibited the same trend of decreasing aggressive fantasies. Was the change in the psychopaths and behavior disorders reflected in their behavior? The answer is not completely clear. In 1955 the counselors once again rated the boys' behavior and personality. Comparison of the 1955 ratings with those of 1954 showed that the proportion of behavior disorders and psychopaths rated as "very hostile" did not significantly decrease.

The counselors did note a change in the children's *control* of aggression. In addition to the rating sheet, they filled out a questionnaire dealing with the improvement (or lack of improvement) of the boys.* In regard to control of aggression, the counselors rated 3 of the boys as "markedly improved," 13 as "somewhat improved," and 3 as unchanged.[41]

The aggressive fantasies of the neurotic and psychotic boys did not change significantly.[42] On the Rover Test, the neurotic boys chose 18 per cent aggressive pictures in 1954, 19 per cent aggressive pictures in 1955. On the aggressive stories they increased from 32 to 35 per cent hostile endings. On the cartoons, their aggressive choices increased from 26 to 31 per cent. The counselors did not notice changes in the neurotics' hostility, nor in their control of aggression.

Surprisingly, the psychopaths and behavior disorders had fewer aggressive fantasies in 1955 than did the neurotics. On all three tests, the neurotics made more aggressive choices.

Even more surprisingly, the behavior disorders and psychopaths,

*See Appendix B for the complete "Evaluation of Progress" form.

after a year's treatment, actually had fewer aggressive fantasies than the public school children upon whom the tests were validated.

PERCENTAGE OF AGGRESSIVE CHOICES, 1955

	Behavior Disorders and Psychopaths (n:19)	Psychotics and Neurotics (n:6)	Public School Children (n:79)
Rover	15	19	28
Stories	16	35	—
Cartoons	21	31	48

Wiltwyck, as part of its therapy, is permissive of aggressive "acting out." The aggression is, however, channeled. Fights among boys are supervised or taken to the boxing ring; broken windows must be replaced (partly) with the boy's allowance. The children's aggressive fantasies decrease probably because they have an outlet for their behavioral aggression.

2. *The internalized guilt of the behavior disorders and psychopaths significantly increased* (P <.01). In answer to the Guilt Stories, their "guilty" responses increased from 58 per cent in 1954 to 78 in 1955.

The psychopathic boys increased their "guilty" answers from 50 to 75 per cent. Even though there were only six psychopaths, this increase in guilt was statistically significant at the 5 per cent level.[43]

This growth in internalized guilt should result in greater inhibition of anti-social behavior. The counselors' ratings indicate that this modification does take place. Of those boys whose guilt increased, counselors rated 70 per cent as increasing their control of aggression, 75 per cent as increasing their control of impulsivity, and 80 per cent as increasing their "realistic acceptance of authority."

The neurotic and psychotic boys showed no change in their level of guilt. In 1954 they responded with 68 per cent "guilty" answers, and in 1955 with 64 per cent "guilty" answers.

3. *The boys' tendency to view authority figures as punitive and threatening decreased.* In responding to the Authority Stories, the behavior disorders and psychopaths less often described authority figures as punitive. The proportion of punitive endings decreased from 46 per cent in 1954 to 27 in 1955.[44] This decrease barely missed the 5 per cent level of significance. [45]

The psychopathic boys, taken alone, decreased their punitive views from 60 to 24 per cent.

The punitive responses of the neurotic and psychotic boys dropped significantly, from 42 per cent in 1954 to 22 in 1955 (P <.05).[46]

4. *The neurotic boys' tendency to withdraw from frustration did decrease.* The neurotics' mean number of withdrawn choices on the Rover decreased from 22 per cent in 1954 to 17 in 1955 (P <.05).[47] Yet only 2 of the neurotic boys decreased their withdrawn choices on the Rover, and 4 remained the same.

The withdrawn choices of the behavior disorders and psychopaths did not decrease significantly. In 1954 they chose an average of 16 per cent.

The counselor ratings recorded no significant change in behavioral reactions to frustration. Only 1 of the neurotic boys had decreased his tendency to withdraw from frustrating situations.

The longitudinal study confirmed only shakily the significant difference found when comparing neurotics who had lived at the school for 0–8 months with those who had lived there for 9–23 months.

5. *The realistic self-perception of the behavior disorders increased.* On the counselor ratings of self-perception, the proportion of behavior disorders judged as "realistic" significantly increased, from 25 per cent in 1954 to 58 in 1955 (P <.01).[48] The counselors did not, however, notice a corresponding change in the 6 psychopaths. In 1954 one of the psychopaths was judged "realistic," and in 1955 2 were rated as "realistic."

On the self-perception check list, the proportion of negative qualities admitted by behavior disorders significantly increased, from 10 to 21 per cent (P <.01).[49] The 6 psychopaths decreased (non-significantly) their negative responses from 19 to 13 per cent.

6. *Realistic self-perception of the neurotic and psychotic boys increased.* A comparison of the ratings of the neurotic and psychotic boys showed that the proportion judged as "realistic" significantly increased: In 1954 the counselors rated none of the neurotics as "realistic," but in 1955 50 per cent were judged "realistic" (P <.02).[50]

On the self-perception check list, the neurotics admitted more negative traits. In 1954 the boys admitted negative qualities on 12 per cent of the items, but in 1955 they admitted negative qualities on 21 per cent.[51]

This increase in negative self-descriptions might seem an unfortunate trend. It does, however, reflect greater realism and perhaps greater insight. Admitting negative traits requires a rather high degree of inner security.[52]

7. *The positive ego ideals of the psychopaths and behavior dis-*

orders significantly increased. The proportion of psychopaths and behavior disorders who responded with a positive answer to "What is
a good boy like?" significantly increased from 21 per cent in 1954 to
57 in 1955 (P <.01).[53] The neurotic and psychotic boys did not significantly change their answers.

In response to the question "What are good parents like?" the psychopaths increased their "loving" descriptions. In 1954 none of them
answered with a "loving" response, but in 1955 5 of the boys did
so (P <.01).[54] The behavior disorders did not noticeably change their
responses, but the neurotic and psychotic boys significantly increased
their "loving" answers. In 1954 3 of them answered "loving;" in 1955,
all of them did (P <.05).[55]

Another change occurred in the boys' ego ideals. In response to
"Whom do you admire most?" psychopaths and behavior disorders
answered with a positive ideal significantly more frequently in 1955
than in 1954 (P <.02).[56] The neurotics and psychotics, on the other
hand, answered with a positive ideal significantly *less* frequently
(P <.05).[57]

8. *The boys' reactions to frustration did not change significantly.*
A comparison of the counselors' ratings of June and of February
showed little change:

REACTIONS TO FRUSTRATION

		Realistic	Aggressive	Withdrawn
Psychopaths:	1954	2	3	1
	1955	3	2	1
Behavior Disorders:	1954	2	8	3
	1955	4	5	4
Neurotics:	1954	1	1	4
	1955	1	2	3

Many Wiltwyck counselors felt unable to rate adequately the boys'
reactions to frustration.[58] They pointed out that the child's response
depended on the situation: at one time he might react with aggression; at another time, with withdrawal. The counselors who carried
out "experimental" situations found that the child's reaction to the
test was often quite different from the one anticipated.[59]

The counselors further felt that the number of situations which the
boys found frustrating had decreased. In other words, their tolerance
for frustration may have increased, although their patterns of reaction
had not changed.

9. *Summary of Test Result Changes.* The significant changes, except for the neurotics' decrease in positive ideals in answer to, "Whom do you admire most?" were in a favorable direction:

PERCENTAGE SCORES

	Behavior Disorders and Psychopaths (n:19)		Psychotics and Neurotics (n:6)	
	1954	1955	1954	1955
Rover Aggression:	35	15*	18	19
Guilt Story Aggression:	37	16*	32	35
Cartoon Aggression:	27	21	26	31
Internalized Guilt:	58	78*	68	64
Punitive Views of Authority:	46	27†	42	22*
Rover Withdrawal:	20	16	22	17*
Negative Self-Perception:	10	21*[60]	12	21*

*P<.05 or .01
†P<.10.

PERCENTAGE OF BOYS WITH POSITIVE RESPONSES

Questions	Behavior Disorders and Psychopaths (n:19)		Psychotics and Neurotics (n:6)	
	1954	1955	1954	1955
What is a good boy like?	21	57*	33	50
What is a good parent like?	0	83*†	50	100*
Whom do you admire most?	11	35*	66	17*

*Change is significant at the 5% level or better.
†Figures and significance level are for the psychopaths alone.

IV. CONCLUSIONS

Our test results, as well as comparisons of counselor ratings, showed several major and some minor changes in boys treated at Wiltwyck. In the cross-sectional approach, we assumed that boys who had been in the school between 9 and 23 months had been initially similar to boys then in the school less than nine months. Therefore, differences between the two categories (0–8 and 9–23 months) were ascribed to school therapy. In the longitudinal study we noted changes in the boys who had, when first tested, been in the school less than nine months. On most important traits the two methods coincided in their results. This replication adds substance to our conclusions about the effects of Wiltwyck treatment.[61]

A. *Milieu Therapy's Effects on Neurotic and Psychotic Children*

Wiltwyck seemed to have less effect on neurotic and psychotic children than upon the children in other diagnostic categories.

Wiltwyck's effect upon the *withdrawal fantasies* of neurotics and psychotics is not clear. By comparing the 0–8 month category and the 9–23 month category in the 1954 study, a statistically significant (P <.05) decrease seemed to occur. Yet, when retested after eight months of treatment, the 6 neurotics and psychotics of the 1955 study showed very little change in their withdrawal choices on the Rover. The divergent findings may be due to the small number of cases in the 1955 study or, because in the retested group the mean length of treatment was about a year, they may indicate that changes in withdrawal tendencies appear later in treatment.

Milieu therapy, as practiced at Wiltwyck, seemed to ameliorate the tendency of neurotics and psychotics to have *unrealistic self-estimations*. In both the 1954 and the 1955 ratings, counselors indicated increased self-understanding. On the self-perception check list, the 1955 study showed a significant increase in their negative responses to trait items.*

The neurotics and psychotics seemed to be less fearful of *authority* as treatment progressed. On the Authority Stories, the re-tested children gave fewer punitive endings.* They also gave more "loving" descriptions of good parents.*

We received no clear picture of changes in *anxiety* of the neurotics and psychotics. A comparison of counselor ratings, both in the 1954

---

*Significant trends in the 1955 study only.

and the 1955 studies, indicated no change. Yet, when asked to evaluate progress, the counselors reported decreased anxiety in all of the 6 neurotics and psychotics included in the 1955 study.

In all probability, the therapy achieves changes which our study either did not measure or measured inadequately. We found no significant change in the tendency of neurotics and psychotics to withdraw from frustration (rated by the counselors). Neither the Rover nor the Cartoon Test detected changes in aggressive fantasies. Nor did the level of internalized guilt seem to change.

Surprisingly, the proportion of neurotics and psychotics who "most admired" a positive ideal significantly decreased.* Possibly the association of these, generally non-delinquent, boys with the anti-social children had a negative influence upon them.

At the beginning of this chapter we described a neurotic, "Danny," and a psychotic, "Tommy." By once again looking at these two boys, we can trace the effects of therapy in more individual terms:

When he began treatment, Danny was tense, anxious, and unhappy. He retired from contact with the world, and hid his feelings behind a timid, passive front. His father had deserted the family, and his mother, a prostitute, neglected the child.

During the first months, he kept to himself in the cottage group, and seemed disturbed by his sexual development.

In June, 1954, five months after he entered the school, Danny had not markedly changed. He still had a high level of anxiety, strong withdrawal tendencies, and confused self-perception.

During counseling by his social worker, Danny gave way to "paranoid" fantasies. He accused the school and his parents of attacking him. The social worker gradually counteracted the fantasies by consistent friendliness and warmth.

A Wiltwyck psychologist guided Danny in individual psychotherapy. At first, with the psychologist, Danny expressed "negative" feelings about Wiltwyck, the other boys, and his father. His ambivalent sexual feelings came to the surface. The psychologist found that Danny was bothered by his relation to his mother. The mother, herself a paranoid personality, berated Danny's father, society, and the school.

In the fall of 1954, a rash spread over Danny's face and body. Medical examination did not uncover an organic malfunction. The other boys in the school, who had never been very friendly with Danny, now avoided him completely. Fearful of "catching" the rash, they isolated him.

At Christmas time, Danny expected a visit from his father. Even though his mother hated the father, Danny felt some love for him. Christmas

---

*Significant trend in the 1955 study only.

passed, however, without the father coming to the school. Danny's disappointment was evident.

By February, 1955, Danny seemed to have improved. No longer shunned by the other boys, he often "joined in the fun." He had formed warm relations with his counselor, social worker, and psychologist. His relations with his parents bothered him considerably, but psychotherapy had given him slightly more insight. His counselor reported that Danny's anxiety had decreased slightly, his rash had disappeared, and his paranoid fantasies had ended.

Whenever frustrated, however, Danny withdraws and still spends much of his time brooding. He feels inferior to the other boys and, as his counselor expressed it, "feels very sorry for himself."

When tested in 1955, Danny's aggressive fantasies had decreased, and his view of authority had become less punitive. His self-concept was more differentiated. His withdrawal fantasies, however, had not decreased, and his internalized guilt had not changed.

It appears that Wiltwyck helped Danny in several important ways. It brought him out of his emotional isolation, changed his view of authority, and gave him greater self-insight. The therapy had not, it seems, changed his tendency to withdraw from reality.

"Tommy," a borderline psychotic, had many of the same problems as Danny:

When he entered Wiltwyck early in 1954, Tommy was a severely disturbed child. Voices threatened him, hallucinations pervaded his thinking, and he felt rejected by the world. In public school, Tommy had often thrown aggressive rages in response to teacher discipline. His mother, a paranoid, lived in a mental hospital. His irresponsible father was unable to cope with the boy.

During his first months at Wiltwyck, Tommy posted threatening notes throughout the school and stole from the other boys. A Wiltwyck psychologist took him in treatment. Deep guilt over his mother's commitment to a mental hospital appeared in psychotherapy. Whenever he felt that he was losing the therapist's support, Tommy became aggressive. At the same time, however, he showed a fear of expressing hostility. Testing by the school psychologist showed that Tommy was an "oral character," that he had intense castration fears, and that he felt keen rivalry with his father.

At first, Tommy's social worker had difficulty establishing rapport. Tommy blamed the worker for his coming to Wiltwyck. As his acceptance of the school increased, his hostility to the worker diminished.

In his cottage group, Tommy kept apart from the other boys. The children jibed him as a "fat boy."

In time, Tommy lost weight and his relations with the other boys improved. He was often bullied, but after several months he began to fight back when attacked. His withdrawal from the group gradually decreased.

His "benign" hallucinations continued. Every night as he went to bed, Tommy told himself the story of "Terror Tim," a masked robber. Often the boy identified with the adventurous, imaginary figure. After about eight months of treatment, Tommy fantasied less about Terror Tim.

By February, 1955, Tommy's condition had not markedly improved. He had begun to regain weight, and he was still called "fat boy." He seldom participated in group activities, but spent his time absorbed in fairy tales and comic books. At times he took the role of comic characters. Near his bed, he kept a club which he called "Herman" and endowed with almost human characteristics. His counselors noted feelings of inferiority, particularly concerning his genital development. He was still subject to vast mood swings, although his aggressive explosions had decreased. When frustrated, he withdrew into an emotional shell.

On the 1955 tests, Tommy's aggressive fantasies seemed to have decreased slightly. His withdrawal fantasies had not changed, nor had his view of authority figures. In certain areas, Tommy seemed to have retrogressed: His self-perception was less differentiated than before, he admitted fewer negative qualities concerning himself, and his ego ideals had become more fantastic.

Tommy seemed to have gained less from the Wiltwyck therapy than Danny. Neither boy decreased his withdrawal fantasies. Together, they represent a fairly typical response of neurotic and psychotic boys to Wiltwyck.

B. *Milieu Therapy's Effect on Behavior Disorders*

The behavior disorders at Wiltwyck changed more strikingly than did the neurotics and psychotics. In four important traits, the 1954 and the 1955 studies concurred in finding beneficial trends.

The boys' *aggressive fantasies* decreased significantly. Both the Rover and the Guilt Stories showed that behavior disorders seem to feel less need for hostile attitudes after being in the school for nine months. Furthermore, the ratings of progress, in the 1955 study, marked a decrease in behavioral aggressiveness.

Milieu therapy strengthened the *conscience* of the children. On the Guilt Stories, both studies showed a significant increase in "guilty" responses. In the 1955 study, counselor ratings of progress showed that those children who had increased their internalized guilt also improved their control of impulsivity.

On the Authority Stories, both studies found a significant increase in the recognition of *authority figures* as supportive. The counselor ratings of progress, too, indicated improved attitudes toward authority.

Both studies discerned an increase in the behavior disorders' positive ego ideals. In answer to the questions about good boys and the person whom they admire most, there were significant increases—possibly indicating a shift away from anti-social objectives.

The behavior disorders in the 1955 study also showed greater self-understanding, according to the counselors.* This understanding seemed to be reflected in the larger number of negative qualities which they attributed to themselves on the self-perception check list.*

Other aspects of the boys' characters were not, apparently, affected by treatment. Their views of good parents, withdrawal fantasies, and reactions to frustration showed no significant changes in either study.

The 13 behavior disorders in the 1955 study, when compared with the normal children, illustrate the degree of alteration. When first tested, the behavior disorders had more aggressive fantasies than the normal children. Eight months later, they had *fewer* aggressive fantasies. When first tested, the behavior disorders had significantly less internalized guilt (59 per cent) than the normal children (82 per cent). Yet, after eight months, the behavior disorders had increased their guilt to approximately the level of the public school boys. Behavior disorders began treatment with a more punitive view of authority (43 per cent) than the normal children (36 per cent). By February, however, the behavior disorders had *less* punitive views (27 per cent) than the public school boys. Thus, Wiltwyck seems to socialize these anti-social children.

The progress of one boy, "Bobby," typifies the reaction of behavior disorders to milieu therapy:

> When he came to Wiltwyck, Bobby was a lonely, aggressive child who hated the world. He had a history of stealing, unprovoked attacks on other children, and problem behavior in school. Often anxiety overcame him, and he withdrew from the outside world.
>
> His family had been disrupted by mental disease. His mother and one sister lived in mental hospitals. Another sister was in a foster home. The father had deserted his family.
>
> Interviewed a few months after his arrival, Bobby seemed to repress strong aggressive desires and to feel intense anxiety. He had not adjusted to the Wiltwyck environment. Frustration caused either rage or withdrawal.
>
> In time, counseling by his social worker increased Bobby's feelings of security and acceptance. He formed warm relations with his cottage counselor and gradually became friendly with the other boys. He joined the school choir, and his singing won him applause. His aggression decreased markedly.

---

*The significant increase appeared only in the 1955 study.

His acceptance of restrictions improved and, though he still "talke⟨
he carried out instructions.

In February, his counselor reported that Bobby's anxiety had de⌐___⌐⌐u
greatly. When frustrated, he no longer exploded in hostility, although he
sometimes broke into tears.

In February, 1955, the tests showed several important changes in Bobby.
His aggressive fantasies had decreased. His internalized guilt had increased.
His self-perception was much more differentiated, and he was able to admit
many more negative qualities about himself. His view of authority had
become more friendly, and his withdrawal fantasies had decreased. When
asked what he disliked about Wiltwyck, he replied: "I like everything about
it. There's nothing wrong."

Milieu therapy helped Bobby (as it did most other behavior disorders) in modifying his aggression, in changing his view of authority,
and in controlling his desires in accord with society's restrictions.

C. *Milieu Therapy's Effect on Child Psychopaths*

The psychopathic child, like the psychopathic adult, has a distinct
personality syndrome. Certain of his traits could be distinguished by
the tests we used. The psychopathic children had much less guilt
and a much more punitive view of authority than did the behavior
disorders, the neurotics, or the normal children. The psychopaths had
greater aggressive fantasies and less withdrawal fantasies than did the
neurotics or the public school boys.[62]

The Wiltwyck study clarified two theoretical problems. First, it indicated that the child psychopath's need for love is not extinguished.
The Wiltwyck counselors rated all the psychopathic children as having
a strong craving for attention. In addition, 4 of the psychopaths in
the longitudinal study improved their relations with counselors. Thus,
an affectional bond can be established with the child psychopath.

Second, the study indicated that psychopaths, as children, have no
more intense aggressive fantasies than do other delinquents. The
fantasy aggression of the psychopaths was no greater than that of the
behavior disorders—although it was greater than that of the neurotics and the normal children. Apparently the psychopaths, who
are certainly aggressive in overt behavior, "act out" more than the
other children primarily because they lack internalized controls.

As previous chapters have shown, the psychopath is supposed to
be unresponsive to therapy. Yet both the 1954 and the 1955 studies

showed that milieu therapy improves the child psychopath in many important ways.

In both studies, the psychopaths greatly decreased their *aggressive fantasies* (as measured by the Rover and the Guilt Stories). Although their aggressive fantasies had been no greater than those of the behavior disorders, this decrease marks an important transition, one which was apparently mirrored in behavior. The counselors, in both studies, denoted an increase in control of aggression in their psychopaths.

The psychopaths, notoriously lacking in *conscience,* showed a significant increase in their internalized guilt. This increase appeared in both the 1954 and the 1955 studies and was reflected in the counselor ratings of control over impulsivity.

In both studies, psychopaths who had been in Wiltwyck for at least nine months showed a decrease in their punitive views of *authority figures.* This decrease appeared in the Authority Stories and also in the ratings.

The psychopaths seemed to have changed their orientation toward society. In both studies, the increase in positive *ego ideals* appeared when boys who had been in residence more than nine months answered the questions concerning good boys, good parents, and the person whom they admired most.

Comparison with normal children should again highlight the degree of change. When first tested, the psychopathic children in the 1955 study had lower guilt (50 per cent) than did children of other diagnostic categories. By February, however, their guilt increased to 75 per cent, and closely approximated that of the normal children (82 per cent). Psychopathic children had, originally, a higher level (on the Rover Test) of aggressive fantasy (33 per cent) than the normal children (28 per cent). Eight months later, the child psychopaths had significantly fewer aggressive fantasies (11 per cent) than the normal children. In June, 1954, the psychopaths had the most punitive view of authority (60 per cent) of any diagnostic category. By 1955 the psychopaths had less punitive views (24 per cent) than normal children (36 per cent).

Counselors' judgments showed also that the psychopaths had improved their capacity to maintain affectional relations. Of the 6 psychopathic boys, counselors rated 4 as "somewhat improved" in their emotional relations with other people. The counselors judged 2 boys as unchanged from their consistently poor adjustment. None of the psychopaths, however, was rated as "markedly improved."

In several (comparatively unimportant) areas, the child psychopaths did not seem to change. The counselors did not note improvement in the children's self-perception. Nor did the boys improve their ability to admit negative traits or their realistic acceptance of frustration.

Reviewing the case of "Paul" points up the effects of milieu therapy on the psychopathic child:

Upon entering Wiltwyck, Paul was an extremely aggressive, uncontrolled child. He had been expelled from public school for attacking other children and his teacher. During a robbery, he struck a watchman over the head. Sentenced for the crime, Paul went on a rampage in the children's home.

His parents had severely disciplined Paul, but had been unable to control him. The father openly rejected the boy.

Interviewed in early July, 1954, Paul showed hatred of his parents, strong hostility, and little guilt. He had no friends in the school.

Paul's explosiveness shocked even the Wiltwyck staff, long used to such hostility. During the first months of treatment, he fought constantly, refused to obey authority, and was friendly with nobody.

His counselor tried to guide Paul into activities which would allow harmless release for his aggression. Paul fished in the brook which runs through the Wiltwyck grounds. He caught fish by clubbing them with a stick. His prowess as a fisherman won the respect of the other boys, and his aggression toward human beings decreased.

Paul reluctantly joined a dancing group. At first the instructor allowed Paul to interpret rhythms by himself, releasing his pent-up energy. Later, Paul participated in group dancing. After many months, he appeared in a dancing show given at the school.

Paul's relations with his counselor and the boys in his cottage improved By February, the counselor had established rapport with Paul. Although still impulsive, Paul's control of his behavior had greatly increased. He no longer attacked the other children, and his hostility toward the school had disappeared.

Re-interviewed in February, 1955, Paul's aggressive fantasies had decreased, his view of authority had become more friendly, and his recognition of his own negative traits had increased. His internalized guilt had increased greatly, but still was below the "normal" level. His feelings of rejection were strong. When asked what people liked about him, he replied: "Nothing!"

Although greatly improved, Paul required further treatment. At the end of the interview, Paul talked about a bow and arrow he was making. "I want to put sharp points on it," he said. "What do you think will kill a man faster, a bullet or an arrow?" Obviously, Paul's aggressiveness had not completely disappeared.

Paul had been in the school by February, 1954, only nine months. More striking improvement can be seen in "Miguel," a child psychopath who had been treated for 13 months.

Miguel spent the first nine years of his life in a Puerto Rican orphanage. His parents were divorced immediately after Miguel's birth. Unable to support her children, the mother placed them in an institution.

In 1951, the mother accompanied a male friend to New York. Later she sent for the children. In New York, Miguel displayed destructive, hostile explosiveness. He refused to attend school, stayed away from home at night, stole, and destroyed property throughout the neighborhood.

In late 1953, Miguel's step-father brought the boy before a New York court and complained of his "incorrigibility." The court remanded Miguel to New York's Youth House.

At the House, Miguel pretended that he could not speak English. He formed no affectional relations. He did not control his emotions: during temper tantrums he ran, fought, crawled, yelled, and screamed. Psychiatric examination uncovered "marked feelings of rejection," aggression, "long-standing defiant behavior," and "apprehension about establishing relations."

Sent to Wiltwyck in January, 1954, Miguel had difficulty in adjusting to the school. During the first months, he was hostile, sucked his thumb, and had eneuresis. In June, his counselor reported that Miguel "wanted friends among the boys, but had no close relationships."

In the 1954 interview, Miguel had strongly aggressive fantasies, very low guilt, and a highly punitive perception of authority. He had no clear conception of himself. He admitted few negative qualities, and said he "hated" Wiltwyck.

During the intervening months, Miguel participated both in group therapy and in individual therapy. His aggressive conduct diminished, and his random impulsivity came under more rational control. He became very dependent on the group therapist, and followed him everywhere in the school. His relations with the other boys improved, but he still had no close friends among the boys.

In the 1955 interviews, Miguel's personality seemed to have undergone important alterations. His internalized guilt greatly increased, and his extremely hostile view of authority was almost eradicated. His aggressive fantasies had decreased slightly.

Thus, in milieu therapy, society seems to have an effective instrument for the treatment of psychopathy. Our study indicates that the psychopathic child, if treated in a permissive environment, can be changed. Boys like Paul and Miguel need not become adults like William Cook or Josef Borlov.

D. *Summary of All Changes*

An overview of the changes indicated by each approach may highlight their importance. It should be remembered that many trends of favorable direction occurred which are not included in the table (p. 166).

The increase in guilt, the decrease in aggressive fantasies, and the decrease in punitive views of authority seem to be the most important changes in the psychopaths and behavior disorders. The tests used to measure these traits had high reliability and strong agreement with independent judgments.[64] Moreover, both the cross-sectional and the longitudinal studies showed the same significant trends, and counselors ratings of behavior tended to confirm the findings.

Other apparent improvements cannot be accepted with the same degree of certainty. Such trends as the increased negative answers to the self-perception check-list, the loving answers to "What is a good parent?" and the positive responses to "Whom do you admire most?" appeared only in the longitudinal study.

On a few measures, the lack of change was desirable. The psychopaths and behavior disorders began treatment with almost unanimous agreement with the Wiltwyck code and the general moral code, and a strong interest in Wiltwyck's "constructive" activities. Any significant alteration in these attitudes would have been an unfavorable sign.

In most areas psychopaths and behavior disorders reacted favorably to milieu therapy. Yet our tests uncovered no change in reaction to frustration or in conscious self-perception.

Milieu therapy's effects on neurotic and psychotic children remains uncertain. The longitudinal study, but not the cross-sectional study indicated significant improvements in views of authority and self-concepts. Withdrawal fantasies significantly decreased in both studies —but the decrease appeared in only a few cases.

On the question "Whom do you admire most?" the neurotics and psychotics exhibited an undesirable decrease in positive ideals.

At the beginning of treatment the neurotics and psychotics, like the other boys, agreed strongly with the moral codes. Unlike the other boys, they had few aggressive fantasies, a high level of internalized guilt, and a differentiated self-concept. The positive traits remained unchanged.

With some degree of confidence, therefore, we can conclude that milieu therapy is best adapted to the aggressive child. The treatment decreases aggression, strengthens the conscience, and helps the children's relation to authority.

Tests	Behavior Disorders and Psychopaths		Neurotics and Psychotics	
	1954 Study	1954-55 Study	1954 Study	1954-55 Study
Rover Aggression	Decrease*	Decrease*	No Change	No Change
Guilt Story Aggression	Decrease*	Decrease*	No Change	No Change
Cartoon Aggression	No Change	No Change	No Change	No Change
Internalized Guilt	Increase*	Increase*	No Change	No Change
Hostile View of Authority	Decrease*	Decrease*	Decrease	Decrease*
Rover Withdrawal	No Change	No Change	Decrease*	Decrease*
Neg. Self-Perception	No Change	Increase*	No Change	No Change
Differentiated Self-Percep.	No Change	No Change	No Change	No Change
Positive ans. to "Good Boy"	Increase†	Increase*	No Change	Increase
Loving ans. to "Good Parent"	No Change	Increase*	No Change	Increase*
Positive ans. to "Admire Most"	Increase†	Increase*	No Change	Decrease*
Positive ans. to "Who would you be?"	No Change	No Change	No Change	No Change
Ans. to "Like best (or least) about you"	No Change	No Change	No Change	No Change
Reactions to Frustration	Increase in Realism	No Change	Increase in Aggression	No Change
Perception of Environment	No Change	No Change	No Change	No Change
Agreement with Moral Code	No Change	No Change	No Change	No Change
Agreement with Wiltwyck Code	No Change	No Change	No Change	No Change
Ratings‡	No Change	No Change	No Change	No Change

E. *Why Do the Changes Occur?*

The essence of milieu therapy is that the whole environment is mobilized against the child's disorder. Psychotherapy, group therapy, and art therapy; social workers, counselors, and psychologists converge in treating the child. Consequently, it is difficult to isolate the particular causes of change.

There do seem to be four factors which play primary roles in altering the boys: rapport, non-frustration in the permissive environment, group influence, and individual counseling.

The boy's rapport with Wiltwyck adults seems closely related to his improvement. A quarter of a century ago, August Aichhorn observed: "The most important thing [in curing delinquents] is the child's feeling for the counselor. . . ." In 1925 Aichhorn's assertion seemed startling. Today it is truism. Yet, rarely has there been an attempt to test this theory.

Fortunately, our study offered an opportunity, however imperfect, for checking the effect of rapport on personality. We asked each counselor to denote his relation to the boys:

In the boy's relation with you, do you believe that
___There is no warmth, no rapport
___The boy is friendly, but maintains distance
___There is a warm relation sometimes, other times, cool
___The relation is close, warm, friendly.

Thirty-seven per cent of the boys were judged by the counselors to have "warm" relations with at least one staff member;[65] 29 per cent were designated as having erratic relations ("sometimes cool"); 32 per cent were denoted as having "friendly but distant" relations; and 2 per cent were marked as having "cool" relations. In general, the counselors seemed wary of overrating the degree of rapport.[66]

Comparing these ratings of rapport with the children's performance on the (independent) personality tests uncovers some significant relationships:

Those children with whom any counselor claimed a warm relation had fewer aggressive fantasies than those with whom counselors had distant or cool relations. On all three tests of aggression (the Rover, the Cartoon, and the Stories), those boys who had warm relations with a counselor chose significantly fewer aggressive alternatives. The level of statistical significance ranged from 5% on the Rover to 1%

---

*P<.05.   ‡A few ratings, noted in the text, showed significant
†P<.10.   differences. The majority did not.

on the Cartoon. The mean aggressive score of boys who had "erratic" relations fell between the two extremes.*

Those children with whom any counselor claimed close relations evidenced greater internalization of guilt than those with whom the counselors had erratic, distant, or cool relations (P <.05). On the Guilt Stories, boys with warm relations answered with significantly more "guilty" responses.

Those children with whom any counselor claimed close relations more often viewed authority figures as supportive and friendly than did those with whom the counselors had erratic, distant, or cool relations (P <.05).

Those children with whom any counselor claimed close relations more often had a "loving" ideal of good parents than did those with whom the counselors had distant, cool, or erratic relations (P <.02).

In general, boys who were designated as having close relations with a counselor possessed greater social maturity. They had fewer aggressive desires, "sturdier consciences," and more friendly attitudes toward authority. In these traits, they differed from children who had changeable or cool relations with the staff. The facts gave rise to an interpretive problem: Does the warmth cause these personality traits, or is it the traits themselves which make possible the warm relations?

We used three approaches in attempting to answer this question, and all converged on the conclusion: Rapport may not cause the decrease in aggression, nor the decrease in punitive views of authority; it does, however, seem to strengthen the boys' internalized guilt.

First, when one boy was rated by two or more counselors, the judgments of rapport agreed in only 33 per cent of such cases. Since the majority of the boys maintained differing relations with different counselors, it seemed that a child had no unique quality which appealed to all adults.[67]

Second, taking boys in the 0–8 month category who had *already* established warm relations and comparing them to those boys in the 0–8 month category who had distant, erratic, or cool relations, we found:

a) The children with warm relations *did not* significantly differ from the other boys in their internalized guilt, aggression on the

---

*See Appendix E for a more detailed description of these results and for tables comparing the various scores.

Stories, or their proportion of "loving" answers to "What is a good parent like?"

b) On aggression, as measured by the Rover Test, there was an almost significant difference between those having warm relations and those having erratic, distant, or cool relations.

c) On the Authority Stories and the Cartoon test of aggression, the boys who had warm relations differed significantly from those who had other types of relations.

Since significant differences existed at the beginning of treatment, we assumed that rapport *does not* cause a more friendly view of authority. The relation between rapport and aggression is not as clear; but probably the counselors more easily established rapport with non-aggressive children and thus, less aggression cannot be attributed to the relationship itself.

Third, we analyzed the differences in rapport of those boys in the top and in the bottom quartiles of Rover aggressive scores. Boys with low aggression had significantly warmer relations with their counselors (P < .01).[69]

Using the same procedure with guilt scores, on the other hand, showed that the boys with high guilt did *not* have significantly better relations with their counselors.[70]

Thus, it appears that *close rapport does not significantly decrease aggressive fantasies but that it does fortify, and perhaps cause, a significant increase in the internalization of guilt.* Some confirmation of this came from the counselors who rated the twenty-three re-tested boys on improvement in relations to others. Those boys whose relations improved showed a significantly greater increase in guilt than those boys whose relations had not improved.[71]

We found that particular staff members seemed better able to establish friendships with the boys. During the interviews, the boys were asked, "Whom do you like best at Wiltwyck?" The boys' answers proved interesting:

33% named 7 most popular staff members.
28% named 1 of 21 other staff members.
22% liked "everyone."
12% named another child.
5% of the boys "didn't know."

Of the seven most popular staff members (each chosen at least five times), only one was a woman. All seemed to Wiltwyck's administrators to be secure, self-confident, and contented. They were consistent in their treatment of the boys, though this treatment ranged from extreme permissiveness to semi-authoritarianism. The six men appeared calm, forceful, and masculine in their interests.

Twenty staff members were not chosen at all. Of these twenty, a disproportionate number were women. The boys' lack of rapport with women may be due to their family histories. In many cases, a father had not been present during the boy's early life. He may have deserted the family, served time in prison, or been in a mental hospital. Thus the mother remained, for many of the boys, the symbol of family life. Since the majority of Wiltwyck's children have been brutally treated, they may associate female staff members with unpleasant memories of their mothers.[72]

Wiltwyck's policy of permissiveness, too, probably plays an important role in changing the boys. In part, the establishment of rapport depends on the adult's non-punitive attitude. A child will not identify with the values of a person who continually frustrates him. He may obey, but he will not emulate.

Permissiveness may also account for the children's decrease in aggressive desires. Punishment is, of course, frustrating—and frustration tends to increase aggression. Permissiveness removes at least one cause of the children's hostility. By allowing the boys to "act out" their aggression in socially harmless ways, the school provides an outlet for hostility.

Permissiveness probably influences the child's view of authority figures. Most of the boys had never before associated with a non-punitive, supportive adult. At Wiltwyck the staff is friendly, and the child's view of authority figures is modified.

In addition to rapport and permissiveness, the influence of group living may account for some of the improvements. Before coming to Wiltwyck, many of the boys belonged to street gangs. Group pressures then encouraged anti-social behavior. At Wiltwyck, on the other hand, each group is guided by counselors. Group influence turns the boy in a positive, socializing direction.

The boy leaders themselves seem to be an aid to the "therapeutic" pressure of the group. In the 1953 study, analysis of Wiltwyck's boy leaders (detected by a sociogram) showed them to be low in authoritarianism, anxiety, and aggression. They were secure and well-adjusted in comparison to the other boys.[73]

In the present research, counselor ratings offered a further opportunity for assessing the personalities of the child leaders. The staff named 12 boys as consistently leading at the school. These leaders were bigger and older than the average boy. More importantly, as indicated by our tests, the leaders had significantly lower aggressive scores and significantly greater internalized guilt than the average Wiltwyck child.[74]

The combined influence of the child leaders and the counselors creates a group atmosphere which probably plays an important part in increasing inner controls of the anti-social boys.[75]

Another factor should be mentioned: individual counseling. Throughout his stay, the boy has opportunities for many talks with his counselor, social workers, psychologist, and other staff members. The rapport established is important, but also the talks themselves probably give the boy greater insight into his problems and personality. The children's increased willingness to admit negative traits is probably due to this individual counseling.[76]

These four factors—adult-child rapport, permissiveness, group influence, and individual counseling—best account for the changes which we have traced in the children at Wiltwyck.[77] With each child, one factor may be more important than another. On the whole, however, the relation seems to be this:

Rapport: increases internalized guilt.
Permissiveness: decreases aggression and punitive views of authority.
Group influence: increases behavioral control.
Counseling: increases children's realistic self-perception.

Does milieu therapy permanently change these boys? Only the future will tell. It is axiomatic in modern social science that the situation helps determine behavior and personality. The Wiltwyck environment, a new "situation," causes radical alterations in personality. When the children return to their homes (generally in slum neighborhoods) the "situation" again changes, and their actions and attitudes may change with it. Yet the extent of change in the boys' characters offers substantial hope that the effects of treatment are permanent.[78]

NOTES

1. PAPANEK, ERNST. Training School—Program and Leadership, *Federal Probation,* June, 1953.

2. McCORD, WILLIAM, AND McCORD, JOAN. Two Approaches to the Cure of Delinquents. *Journal of Criminal Law, Criminology and Police Science,* 44 (4) 1953, (Nov.-Dec.).

3. The school wished to remain anonymous.

4. Figures are based on descriptions by King's County and Bellevue Hospital psychiatrists at the time of admittance to Wiltwyck.

5. Case names have been changed.

6. King's County and Bellevue hospitals did not use the psychopathic label. They called such children "active aggressive personalities" or, occasionally, "passive aggressive personalities." They did recognize the character syndrome which we have termed the "psychopathic personality," but preferred the other labels with their less opprobrious connotations.

7. Percentage of boys (rated by two or more counselors) about whom there was complete agreement on a particular trait.

8. ALLPORT, GORDON. *Personality: a Psychological Interpretation.* New York, Henry Holt, 1937. See discussion of this well-known fault of ratings.

9. The "Blackie Test" itself did not fit our requirements since only one of its pictures dealt specifically with aggression.

10. One panel had a different hero in one of the three illustrations. The distribution of choices on this panel did not differ from the other nine.

11. If the subject's name actually was Bob, we changed the name of the stories' hero.

12. For the purposes of this study, only the answers showing definite guilt were computed. Answers dealing with satisfaction were used as a measure of hostility (described in following pages). Answers showing fear of punishment were not specifically computed, but for other types of studies the "fearful" responses might be useful.

13. Using Festinger's formula, $P < .05$.

14. For differences among Wiltwyck's children, $P < .05$.

15. $P < .05$.

16. Home background may be the primary influence upon the child's view of authority. Public school children had a greater proportion of supportive responses. All but two Wiltwyck children were rejected but the records are too incomplete to ascertain whether Wiltwyck children with less punitive views of authority figures also had a reasonably supportive relative.

17. $X^2 = 8.6$, d.f. $= 2$.

18. $X^2 = 3.1$, d.f. $= 2$.

19. $X^2 = 3.9$, d.f. $= 1$.

20. $X^2 = 0.5$, d.f. $= 1$.

21. $X^2 = 3.7$, d.f. $= 1$.

22. Thirty public school children checked 17% negative qualities.

23. The public school boys were significantly more differentiated in their descriptions of themselves: 37%.

24. $X^2 = 5.9$, d.f. $= 1$.

25. $X^2 = 7.3$, d.f. $= 2$.

26. $X^2 = 1.2$, d.f. $= 1$.

27. $X^2 = 5.0$, d.f. $= 1$.

28. See DUNCAN MCRAE: Development of Moral Judgment in Children. Ph.D. thesis in Harvard University Library, dated March, 1950.

29. Seventy-five per cent agreement among counselors rating the same boy.

30. If age, I.Q., race, or religion significantly affected the test, we held it constant in analyzing changes by months of residence. Only changes which remained significant, after holding constant the influencing factor, are mentioned in the chapter.

31. The few neurotics and psychotics in the 0—8 month category made statistically significant changes improbable.

32. Psychopaths in residence more than 23 months scored 63%, holding the increase in guilt more than did the behavior disorders.

33. $X^2 = 4.5$, d.f. $= 1$

34. $X^2 = 5.8$, d.f. $= 1$

35. $X^2 = 3.16$, d.f. $= 1$

36. $X^2 = 3.16$, d.f. $= 1$

37. $X^2 = 2.17$, d.f. $= 1$. Thirteen per cent of the behavior disorders and psychopaths in residence more than 23 months gave positive answers.

38. We had used the 0—8 month group as our base in the 1954 study, and so retested this same group eight months later. The original 0—8 month group contained 35 boys. Seven, all behavior disorders, had been first interviewed upon their arrival in September, 1955, rather than in June. Consequently, in February, they had been at Wiltwyck for only six months. One other child, a psychotic, was released by the school before February. Two remaining boys refused to be re-interviewed.

One of the boys who refused was a neurotic. In the first interview, he scored high on guilt and aggression, average in punitive view of authority. His ideals were all power figures, and he described "good parents" in authoritarian terms.

The other boy was a psychopath. He scored low on guilt and had a fairly punitive view of authority figures. Surprisingly, his aggression was very low. The personality of these two children seems similar to that of the other boys in their diagnostic categories.

39. The level of statistical significance was measured by two formulas. For differences in means, we applied the Wilcoxon non-parametric test for the paired replicates. For differences in proportions, we used the chi-square test for replicates.

41. Of the three boys rated as "unchanged," one was a psychopath; of the three boys rated as "markedly improved," one was a psychopath.

42. The small number of neurotics and psychotics (6) and the small number of psychopaths (6) made statistically significant changes improbable. In order to achieve a 5% level of significance on the Wilcoxon test, whenever change occurs it must be in the same direction. If, for example, 5 boys showed a decrease in aggression and one showed an increase, the change would be non-significant.

43. The guilt of 4 of the psychopaths increased; the guilt of the other 2 did not change.

44. Thirty public school children who answered the Authority Stories scored 36% punitive answers. Thus, after a year's treatment, Wiltwyck's psy-

chopaths and behavior disorders actually had less punitive views than normal children.

45. On the Wilcoxon test for 19 pairs, a T score of 46 is required for 5% significance. The T score of the decrease of the 19 behavior disorders and psychopaths was 44.

46. In the 1954 study, there was no significant difference in the number of punitive endings between the neurotics in the 0—8 month category and those in the 9—23 month category.

47. This decrease, although apparently very slight, was statistically significant according to the Wilcoxon formula.

48. $X^2 = 9.1$, d.f. $= 1$. This increase in realistic self-perception did not appear in the 1954 study.

49. This trend did not appear in the 1954 study.

50. $X^2 = 6.20$, d.f. $= 1$.

51. Five of the 6 neurotics increased their negative judgments, but one decreased. The change is non-significant.

52. Responses to other questions dealing with self-perception did not change. The boys' answers to "What do people like best about you?" "Who would you be, if you could be anyone?" did not significantly change. The proportion of differentiated answers on the check list did not change either.

53. $X^2 = 7.11$, d.f. $= 1$.

54. $X^2 = 7.2$, d.f. $= 1$.

55. $X^2 = 5.33$, d.f. $= 1$.

56. $X^2 = 6.2$, d.f. $= 1$.

57. $X^2 = 5.3$, d.f. $= 1$.

58. Ratings of boys judged more than once, however, agreed 75%.

59. We may have expected too much of the counselors with the rating forms. Except in a few categories, comparison between the 1954 and 1955 ratings showed few changes in the children. Yet when asked specifically to evaluate the child's progress, counselors reported many important changes. In general, it seemed easier to rate changes in a particular child than to compare him to other children or to an abstract standard (of anxiety, aggression, etc.)

60. The behavior disorders changed significantly. The psychopaths did not. Figures given are for the behavior disorders alone, regarding negative self-perception.

61. None of the diagnostic categories showed significant changes in their answers to: "If you could be anyone, who would you be?" "What happens to a boy when he does something wrong?" "What do you like most (and least) about Wiltwyck?" "What do people like best about you?" "What do people like least about you?" None of the diagnostic categories significantly changed the proportion of differentiated answers on the self-perception check list, nor their extent of agreement with the Wiltwyck code or the general moral code.

62. The aggressive fantasies and the withdrawal fantasies of the psychopaths did not significantly differ from those of the behavior disorders.

64. The Rover Test, Guilt Stories, and Authority Stories should be applicable to the study of personality outside the area of delinquency. They might be helpful in studying differences between religious, ethnic, and national groups; between economic classes, and rural-urban areas. Also, the measures might be applicable to various diagnostic problems, especially to differentiating psychopaths from other deviants.

65. With many children, different counselors had different types of relations. For the above summary, the "warmest" rating given each child by any counselor was used in assigning him to a category.

66. Recent studies have shown that therapists often overestimate their rapport with a patient. Teuber and Powers, for example, analyzed the counselor-child relations in the Cambridge-Somerville Study. They found that the counselors' reports were often inaccurate. See HANS-LUCAS TEUBER and EDWIN POWERS: Evaluating Therapy in a Delinquency Prevention Program. *Psychiatric Treatment,* Vol. 21, Baltimore, William and Wilkins Co., 1955.

67. This might also indicate that a child wants only one parent substitute.

68. d value on the Festinger table was 2.96; 3.05 is necessary for the 5% level of confidence.

69. $X^2 = 7.6$, d.f. $= 1$.

70. $X^2 = 0$, d.f. $= 1$.

71. $X^2 = 4.90$, d.f. $= 1$.

72. The study furnished further evidence concerning the effect of family ties upon boy-staff relations. Of those boys who answered with a parent to: "Whom do you admire most?" a significantly higher proportion were rated as having erratic relations with their counselors ($P < .05$). Sixty-nine per cent of those boys who admired their parents had erratic relations, 24 per cent had distant or cool relations, and only 7 per cent had warm relations. The child who admires his parents most may be transferring from his parents to his counselor the expectation of erratic treatment.

73. New England's leaders were tough, anxious and aggressive.

74. Mean aggressive score of 10% on the Rover; mean score on the stories of 70% guilty answers.

75. Group therapy is also conducted at Wiltwyck. Guided by skilled leaders, the pressures in this situation probably exert a socializing influence.

76. Inner security is also necessary before a child can admit his negative qualities. Apparently, the boys have this feeling of being accepted. The boys were asked their opinions on statements concerning the school. To the statement: "There is always someone at Wiltwyck who likes you," 105 of the 107 boys agreed.

77. In 1955, we asked the counselors to signify factors which they believed accounted for improvements in the boys. They tabbed "experience of group living," "relations with adults," and "non-punitiveness" as most important. Individual therapy and classroom experiences were also mentioned.

78. Wiltwyck became a therapeutic institution a few years ago. Only in late 1953 did it reach the present level of policy and personnel. Therefore, a follow-up study of released boys cannot be completed for several years.

Currently, students from the New York School of Social Work are conducting a follow-up study of children who have been released from Wiltwyck within the last 10 years. While the results of the study will be interesting, they will not accurately measure Wiltwyck's present effect on the boys. Both policy and personnel have greatly changed in the last 10 years.

It is planned that the 107 boys investigated in the present study will be traced during the next 10 years, as they return to their original environments.

7

The Psychopath, The Law, and Society

Psychopathy represents the most expensive and most destructive of all known forms of aberrant behavior . . .

ROBERT LINDNER.

On April 20, 1931, two men accosted the driver of a Baltimore milk wagon. The middle-aged driver, John W. Anderson, stopped his truck. The two men climbed aboard and asked Anderson for his money. The driver resisted, and there was a brief struggle. Although both bandits carried guns, only one used his—to shoot and kill the driver.

John Anderson left a wife and three children.

His murderer, Herman Webb Duker, was a psychopath. As a child, Duker had been rebellious and vicious. He had served nine months in the New York City Reformatory. Released, he went to Baltimore, broke into apartments and stole $2000.

At eighteen, Duker was committed to the Maryland School for Boys. Psychiatrists diagnosed him as a "psychopath of the chronic delinquent type, with some sexual psychopathy and with a marked tendency toward the runaway reaction."[1] But the laws of Maryland did not recognize psychopathy as "insanity." Thus Duker could neither receive mental hospital treatment, nor could he be permanently segregated from society.

Duker escaped from the Maryland school.

While committing another crime in New York City, he was apprehended and sentenced to 18 months in the Elmira Reformatory. Because of his aggressive, belligerent behavior, Duker's term was stretched to 31 months. Once again, a psychiatrist diagnosed him as a "psychopathic personality."

177

Like Maryland, New York laws did not recognize psychopathy as "insanity." Duker missed another opportunity for treatment.

In January, 1931, Duker was released.

On April twentieth, he shot and killed John Anderson in Baltimore.

Duker's case illustrates the inadequacy of present social and legal policy, with its blindness to the facts of psychopathy. If Duker could have been cured while incarcerated, or if he had never been released, Anderson might still be alive.

At his trial, Duker stood before the court in brazen, guiltless defiance. On advice of counsel, he pleaded guilty to first degree murder. His lawyer did not use insanity as a defense, for Duker "knew the difference betwen right and wrong."

The testimony of five psychiatrists and a voluminous report on his past life, however, marked the defendant as a pathologically deformed person. Judge Joseph Ulman, recounted:

> Duker's twenty-two years of life unfold types and degrees of activity that indicate a grossly distorted personality. He is not merely a youthful delinquent who has achieved a precocious maturity in crime. As a small child he exhibited an appalling and inhuman cruelty to animals which persisted for many years. The full record of his robberies and like crimes will never be known. He confesses many for which he was never apprehended; and says that after committing them he experienced an unusual sense of peace and satisfaction—almost of exaltation—a release from his nervous restlessness. This is certainly not the common experience of normal criminals. He has for years suffered from serious abnormalities in the sex sphere. None of these peculiarities is at all obvious to superficial examination. On the witness stand he presents the picture of an alert, courageous and peculiarly plausible individual. His apparent normality, coupled with his abnormal career, is itself an evidence of his pathological condition.

> What is that condition? With a degree of unanimity that reflects credit upon every medical witness in this case, the Court is assured that Duker is a "psychopathic personality." This is the conclusion reached by the present and former medical officers of the Supreme Bench, whose freedom from bias was to be presumed. It is the conclusion reached in 1928 by Doctor Partridge, then psychiatrist of the Maryland School for Boys, and in 1930 by Doctor Christian and the late Doctor Harding, Superintendent and Psychiatrist, respectively, of Elmira Reformatory—long before the murder had been committed. It is the same conclusion reached by Doctor Truitt, employed by the defense, and by Doctor Tanyhill and Doctor Gillis, employed by the State, for the purposes of this hearing. The "battle of experts," so often and so properly denounced as characteristic of American criminal trials, did not occur in this case."

Under contemporary law, Duker was fully responsible for his actions. Yet the trial evidenced the incongruity of a test based on "the knowledge of right and wrong":

> To paraphrase the views expressed by every expert witness in this case, the psychopathic personality is emotionally unbalanced so that he does not respond normally to what his conscious mind tells him. He knows the consequences of wrong-doing, but impulses beyond his control sway his actions regardless of the result to himself or to others . . . Every witness in this case agreed that Duker has not the normal emotional and moral impulses and controls—and every witness concluded that he is "not fully responsible" for his actions.[3]

The jury convicted Duker of first-degree murder. Judge Ulman, in sentencing the defendant, had only two choices: life imprisonment or execution. Every psychiatric witness testified to the peril of imprisoning Duker:

> Doctor Guttmacher says of Duker that he is potentially one of the most dangerous types of individuals that society knows; that in a penal institution he would not be amenable to authority, and would be among the leaders in rebellion against it. Doctor Truitt, interrogated by the Court specifically as to how he thinks Duker would respond to the discipline of imprisonment for life in the Maryland Penitentiary replied that "the outlook would be unfavorable." The court had, then, to decide between life imprisonment and hanging for a man who is legally sane, medically of abnormal psychology, and socially extremely dangerous. Moreover, he is socially dangerous and a menace to the life of others whether he be at large or confined in prison. And it must not be forgotten that prison guards are human beings—and that administration of law "for the protection of society" applies to them as well as to other citizens.[4]

Convinced of Duker's extreme dangerousness, Judge Ulman sentenced him to be "hung by the neck until dead." As he passed sentence, Ulman stated: "This action is a confession of social and legal failure."[5]

Society had had the opportunity of giving Duker the intensive treatment which he so obviously required. In New York, in Elmira, in Maryland schools, Duker's life might have been changed; but it was not. Even admitting a failure in treatment, different laws might have segregated Duker early in life.

Knowing that Duker was legally, but probably not morally responsible for his crimes, Judge Ulman was well aware of the implications of his decision:

> Duker is a mentally abnormal person, and I knew him to be so when I sentenced him to hang. There is something very ugly about that bald state-

ment. Even a judge who believes in capital punishment would hesitate a long time before he imposed the death sentence upon a person known to be mentally irresponsible. I do not believe in capital punishment . . . society confesses its own failure every time it exacts a life for a life.⁶

Neither the public nor Maryland's Governor understood the reasoning of Ulman's decision. People showered the Judge with letters, praising him for a courageously vindictive punishment. The Governor, Albert C. Ritchie, perhaps with justification, questioned the fairness of hanging a man who was "not responsible" for his crime. The Governor commuted Duker's sentence to life imprisonment, stating: "What I cannot understand is how the Court could first decide—as it did—that Duker's mental disorder should be considered in mitigation of punishment, and that he should not be hanged; and then sentence him to be hanged anyhow, not for his crime, but because the penitentiary is the only place to which he could be committed."⁷

I. The Psychopath and Legal Policy

The Duker case highlighted two questions which have long puzzled legal philosophers. Is the psychopath responsible for his acts? And, how can we best protect society from his depredations?

Non-responsibility for an act due to mental disorder was first introduced into the common law in 1724. An English court held that a man was irresponsible if "he doth not know what he is doing, no more than . . . a wild beast."⁸

A century later, the quaint "wild beast test" was superseded by the famed M'Naghten decision, a case which set the bounds for contemporary standards of legal responsibility. In 1843 M'Naghten, a paranoiac, murdered Sir Robert Peel's secretary. The killer mistakenly believed that the secretary was the statesman himself. The courts judged M'Naghten mentally irresponsible. The House of Lords attacked the court's decision.

The judges' reply constitutes the precedent upon which American and English law now bases its standard of criminal responsibility: a plea of insanity depends on establishing that "at the time of committing the act, the party accused was labouring under such a defect of reason, from disease of the mind, as not to know the nature and quality of the act he was doing, or, if he did know it, that he did not know he was doing what was wrong."⁹

Thus, in modern America a man, although insane, is considered legally responsible unless he is found by the jury not to know the difference between right and wrong. In fourteen states, the criminal is assumed legally irresponsible—even if he does know that his act was "wrong"—if the crime was committed under the influence of an "insane, irresistible impulse." In most cases, a psychopath is tabbed as legally sane and responsible.

These criteria seemed more plausible before modern science discarded the theory of faculty psychology. At that time, man's brain was sometimes depicted as a conglomeration of independent compartments, each recording or controlling a different species of idea or action. Some facultative theories held for a special "moral sense" which enabled the individual to distinguish right from wrong. If functioning correctly, "moral reason" controlled or repressed "irrational impulse."

Contemporary research, on the other hand, has inseparably linked the conscious and the unconscious, the rational and the irrational. Man's nature is an interdependent, interrelated structure. One Federal judge graphically stated the current position: "The modern science of psychology . . . does not conceive that there is a separate little man in the top of one's head called reason whose function it is to guide another unruly little man called instinct, emotion, or impulse in the way he should go."[10]

Moreover, the criminal law ignores the complexity of causes which prompt man's behavior. Probably no criminal, whether mentally disordered or not, deliberately decides to commit an "evil" act. His behavior cannot reasonably be depicted as the conscious choice of an independent free will. Rather, the actions of all criminals come from a complicated interplay of biological, social, and psychological causes. Thus it is unrealistic to try arbitrarily to distinguish the "sane" from the "insane" criminal on the basis of these criteria. The impracticality of this task has been pointed out by Hervey Cleckly: "The law, at least theoretically, operates on the assumption of an absolute contrast, an either-or standard by which one must pronounce patients totally insane (irresponsible) or totally sane (responsible). This, as nearly all psychiatrists will admit, is neither in accordance with reality nor conducive to fair and useful action.[11]

Based as they are on such faulty premises, the tests of responsibility become, in practice, highly confused. Neither the lay jurist nor the trained psychologist can abstract "moral faculty" and trace its functioning. The result is that confused testimony makes the issue of responsibility a legal quagmire.

In theory, the tests of insanity are unrealistic; in practice, they are unwieldy. The psychopath, together with other criminals, is punished by imprisonment although imprisonment rarely changes him. Later he is released, and he repeats his patterns of behavior.

If the psychopath were declared irresponsible, two new possibilities would be open. He would, in all probability, be sent to a mental hospital where the best instruments of modern treatment could be applied. Even in a therapeutically advanced hospital, as our review of treatment showed, the psychopath might still be unreformed. In the event that treatment failed, the psychopath could be permanently segregated by commitment. His release would be dependent, not upon the crime he had committed, but upon the cure of his disorder.

If treated early in life, Herman Duker might have been cured. Milieu therapy, as the Wiltwyck study indicates, could probably have lessened his aggression, increased his inner controls, and helped him to internalize the standards of society. He might, if treated correctly, have formed relationships which would have broken through his callousness.

If treatment failed, Duker should not have been returned to society. Yet he "served his sentence" and, under present law, he had to be released. Legal recognition of Duker's mental abnormality and "irresponsibility" would not have been "softness"; it would have been a realistic, necessary step in the protection of society.

Unfortunately, many judges hesitate to abandon the prevailing standards of responsibility for fear of destroying punishment's effectiveness as a deterrent of criminal behavior. This position arises from the theoretical premises of the criminal law. As Roscoe Pound has commented: " . . . historically, our substantive criminal law is based upon a theory of punishing the vicious will. It postulates a free agent confronted with a choice between doing right and doing wrong and choosing freely to do wrong. It assumes that the social interests . . . are to be maintained by imposing upon him a penalty corresponding exactly to the gravity of his offense."[12]

Punishment does not, as we have seen, deter the psychopath. He is incapable of moral control, and rational weighing of consequences is alien to his nature. In any case, the risk of permanent commitment in a mental hospital seems a reasonably stronger deterrent than the threat of a few years in prison.

Causative research has shown that psychopaths have rejectant, childhoods and, in all probability, brain structures incompatible with the inhibition demanded by society. The psychopath's neurological and environmental background creates a mental disorder which makes him dangerous. Both for the safety of society and in fairness to the psychopath, he should be "treated" instead of "punished."

Acknowledging irresponsibility of action assumes that human beings have a varying capacity for free choice. Some men, unhampered by biological, social, or psychological defects, can utilize this potentiality to its highest degree. In the psychopath, the sphere of conscious choice has been diminished by restrictions of environment and neurological structure.[13] The psychopath does not choose to be a wicked man. His margin of freedom is slight.

For years, social and medical scientists have recognized the dangerous inadequacies in the existing tests of criminal responsibility. Even in 1838, five years before the M'Naghten decision became the accepted standard, psychiatrist Isaac Ray called moral knowledge a "fallacious" test of criminal responsibility.[14] Modern psychiatric groups have repeatedly recommended the abandonment of the standard.[15]

Increasingly, the legal profession agrees. In 1928, Sheldon Glueck stated: "It is evident that the knowledge tests unscientifically abstract out of the mental make-up but one phase or element of mental life, the cognitive, which, in this era of dynamic psychology, is beginning to be regarded as not the most important factor in conduct and its disorders."[16] In the same year, Justice Cardoza concurred: "Everyone recognizes that the present [legal] definition of insanity has little relation to the truths of mental life."[17]

Glueck and Cardoza advanced beyond the legal thought of the 1920's. Only recently has the profession as a whole begun to adopt their viewpoint. A recent Federal court decision marks the first official recognition of this trend.

Monte Durham, the defendant in this historic trial, had for many years been in and out of hospitals and prisons. At seventeen, the Navy discharged him with the comment that he suffered "from a profound personality disorder which renders him unfit for Naval Service."[18] Two years later, car-stealing netted him a probationary sentence. He attempted to commit suicide. After a short sojourn in Washington mental hospitals, Durham returned to society and began passing bad checks.

Arrested for forgery and sentenced to jail, Durham exhibited signs of mental disorder. Examination at St. Elizabeth's hospital resulted in diagnosis of "psychosis with psychopathic personality." After 15 months of hospital treatment, he was released as "recovered" and returned to jail to serve the remainder of his sentence.

Paroled from jail, Durham broke the conditions of his release, headed for the South and again forged checks. He was returned to St. Elizabeth's hospital, and this time diagnosed as a psychopathic personality, "without mental disorder." Eventually discharged, he broke into a home and was returned to the hospital. After insulin shock treatments and sixteen months of hospitalization, he went on trial.

During the trial, Durham's mother testified that he "seemed afraid of people" and had asked her to enclose his windows with steel bars. Durham's own testimony was confused and hallucinated:

Q: Do you remember writing it?
A: No. Don't you forget? People get all mixed up in machines.
Q: What kind of a machine?
A: I don't know. They just get mixed up.
Q: Are you cured now?
A: No, sir.
Q: In your opinion?
A: No, sir.
Q: What is the matter with you?
A: You hear people bother you.
Q: What? You say you hear people bothering you?
Q: Yes.
Q: What kind of people? What do they bother you about?
A: (No response.)[19]

A psychiatrist, called as an expert witness, repeatedly testified that Durham was "of unsound mind." Yet he could not absolutely certify that the defendant was legally insane. "If the question of the right and wrong were propounded to him," the psychiatrist said, "he could give you the right answer."[20] By any other standard, however, Monte Durham suffered from a mental aberration.[21]

Nevertheless, the trial judge held Durham legally responsible, and imprisoned him.

In 1954, Durham's case was carried to the United States Court of Appeals. Circuit Judge Bazelon, recognizing the issues involved, asked the prosecutor, the defending counsel, and a "friend of the court" to file complete briefs on the problem of criminal responsibility. Because of several legal errors, Judge Bazelon reversed the lower court's decision.[22] Most importantly, the Court formulated a new test of criminal responsibility: " . . . an accused is not criminally responsible if his unlawful act was the product of mental disease or mental defect."[23]

The Judge hoped that the new standard would avoid a "misleading emphasis on cognitive" abilities. He reflected: "In attempting to define insanity in terms of a symptom (i.e., irresistible impulse or moral knowledge), the courts have assumed an impossible role, not merely one for which they have no special competence."[24]

This test of criminal responsibility would clarify the legal issues. Courts would no longer ascertain the defendant's "moral knowledge." Nor would they determine his exact state of mind while he committed the crime. Yet the court would be faced with deciding whether the defendant's crime was *caused* by "mental disease" or "mental defect." This, too, is a complex problem. During the Durham case, for example, the psychiatric witness responded to the Judge's persistent questions: ". . . I can't tell how much the abnormal thinking and the abnormal experiences in the form of hallucinations and delusions —delusions of persecution—had to do with his anti-social behavior."[25] Yet the witness was convinced that Durham was of "unsound mind."

In an attempt to simplify further the legal problem of responsibility, the American Law Institute has proposed another test. Formulated by Sheldon Glueck, the new standard recognizes the pervading influences of mental disorder on crime. "A person is not responsible for criminal conduct," this criterion states, "if it was committed substantially under the influence of a mental disease or defect." The advantage of the test is that it does not require exact specification of the role played by mental disorder in a particular crime. Although no state is bound to accept proposals of the American Law Institute, its recommendations exert a wide influence over the profession.

These proposed tests of criminal responsibility, though striding across a mire of confusion, leave the status of the psychopath undetermined. Is he mentally diseased? Asociality, aggression, guiltlessness, and lovelessness set the psychopath apart from the normal human being— just as hallucinations or delusions characterize the psychotic. Yet many lawyers and psychiatrists argue that the psychopath— like the neurotic, the confirmed alcoholic, and the drug addict—is not "diseased."[26]

Judge Ulman, in rendering his decision to hang Herman Duker, expressed the practical problem:

> "Responsibility," whether mental responsibility or moral responsibility or social responsibility, is a concept about which it is useless to argue. Opinion concerning it is not the result of reason, but rests in emotion or belief. To me it was clear that a judge pronouncing sentence had to disregard altogether this kind of philosophical consideration. When an individual is attacked, his right of self-defense is absolute, and he need not stop to inquire whether his attacker is acting voluntarily or by reason of compulsions beyond his control. When society is subjected to attack, either actual or potential, and whether by one who is responsible or by one who is irresponsible, those charged with its protection *must* repel the attack, using such means as are available for the purpose.[27]

The problem of responsibility, a vital philosophical issue, still hinders the criminal law in its task of protecting society from the psychopath.

A revolutionary proposal by Sheldon Glueck would, in practice, by-pass the problem of responsibility. Glueck has proposed the establishment of a "treatment tribunal" as society's most effective defense. His revision would separate the two functions of criminal law: determination of guilt, and imposition of sentence. During the trial, the judge and jury would ascertain only the guilt or innocence of the defendant. If found guilty, the criminal would be remanded to a treatment tribunal. This board, composed of behavioral scientists, would then handle the disposition of the case. The individual's sentence would depend, not upon an arbitrary definition of "responsibility," but rather upon a scientific evaluation of the nature and causes of his behavior.

This legal dichotomy would leave the complicated issue of treatment to experts who have training and experience. Most judges, while highly capable of deciding the issues arising during a trial, are unqualified for the difficult task of prescribing differential treatment. Indeed, recent research has repeatedly demonstrated that judges impose sentence inconsistently.[28]

Under our present system, as Sheldon Glueck discerned, judges must "prescribe in advance the length of time the patient should be kept in the hospital and then hold him there the full period or discharge him ahead of time, whether cured or not."[29] The treatment tribunal would eliminate prescription of the exact period of time required for reformation. Sentences would be, within broad statutory limits, indeterminate. The nature of the criminal's disorder, his response to treatment, and his danger to society would be reviewed periodically by the board. A prisoner would be released when he seemed likely to make a satisfactory adjustment to society.

The treatment tribunal would fit the sentence to the criminal and not to the crime. Contemporary law imposes a specific punishment for a specific crime: the more serious the crime, the greater the punishment. Often, dangerous individuals receive light sentences because they are caught while committing minor crimes. This prevailing "pay as you go" plan neither protects society nor prevents crime. The long range interests of society require that sentencing be based, not on the nature of the crime, but on the nature of the criminal.

Such a fundamental change in the administration of law naturally depends on a revision in our concept of justice. Western criminal law seems now to be based largely on a pattern outlined, in 1764, by Cesare Beccaria, a Milanese nobleman. Revolted by the favoritism and brutality of European justice, Beccaria attempted to establish a universal standard. "Pleasure and pain are the only springs of actions in beings endowed with sensibility,"[30] he wrote. Therefore, by instant infliction of pain on the wrong-doer, crime could be stopped. The punishment, he believed, should not be erratic: "If an equal punishment be ordained for two crimes that injure society in different degrees, there is nothing to deter men from committing the greater as often as it is attended with greater advantage."[31]

Beccaria's theory, enlightened and laudable for his times, conflicts with modern knowledge of human nature. Crime, particularly the crimes of a psychopath, does not come from the decision of a "vicious will." Criminal acts are not reasoned calculations of the degrees of pleasure and pain involved. The criminal, when he commits a crime, rarely thinks of being caught.[32]

Severe punishment neither reforms the criminal, nor does it prevent crime. Wisconsin has a mild criminal code; yet it ranks among the lowest in number of violent crimes committed. Southern states, possessing highly punitive laws, have the highest rates of violent criminalism. George Bernard Shaw detected the inadequacy in the Beccarian theory: ". . . the flaw in the case of Terrorism is that it is impossible to obtain enough certainty to deter. The police are compelled to confess every year, when they publish their statistics, that against the list of crimes reported to them, they can set only a percentage of detections and convictions."[33]

The establishment of a treatment tribunal, though contravening the Beccarian standard of "justice," would protect society more thoroughly, particularly from the psychopaths.[34] Its aim would not be to punish a man for his crimes; it would be to rehabilitate the individual.[35]

Glueck explained: "The legal and institutional provisions for the protection of society must be based not so much upon the gravity of the particular act for which an offender happens to be tried, as upon his personality, that is, upon his dangerousness, his personal assets, and his responsiveness to peno-correctional treatment."[36]

Bringing about such a revolution in legal thought is not impossible. Indeed, California has already established a system which, in some ways, resembles the treatment tribunal. After the courts sentence a felon to prison, California's Adult Authority assumes responsibility for his treatment and release. Every sentenced criminal passes through a reception center, where he undergoes thorough social-psychological examination. Officials recommend a general treatment plan for the individual. On the basis of this plan, the prisoner is assigned to an institution which best meets the needs of his maladjustment. His release date, roughly set by statute,[37] is dependent on the Authority's judgment of his progress. Recently, Maryland has copied many aspects of California's system; its courts now sentence the criminal, not the crime.

In the treatment of juvenile delinquency, several states have revised their methods in recent years. California, Massachusetts, Minnesota, Texas, and Wisconsin have established "youth correction boards."[38] After appearance in court, delinquents are remanded to the administrative board. Each youth's sentence and treatment is then determined, and his release date set, at the board's discretion. Many of the states are, however, hampered by insufficient treatment facilities.

Americans are beginning to recognize that our legal system does not furnish adequate protection. Treatment tribunals, in one of several forms, may offer a more effective instrument of social control. Nevertheless, the combination of public apathy and prejudice hinders their further development.

By themselves, of course, treatment tribunals will not eliminate crime. Nor do they offer a final answer to psychopathy. It would be useless for a treatment tribunal to commit a psychopath to an institution which could do nothing to cure him. The psychopath needs special attention. Intensive and patient therapy is essential for his rehabilitation.

Well-trained personnel, public cooperation, and the effective utilization of scientific knowledge, together with a reoriented criminal code, could do much to alleviate criminality.

II. THE PSYCHOPATH AND SOCIAL POLICY

Our laws can be changed to protect society from psychopathy. Declaring the psychopath irresponsible, preferably with the additional establishment of treatment tribunals, would be beneficial and realistic protective measures. Yet legal changes are not enough. We must apply more effective methods of treatment—and treatment is contingent upon accurate diagnosis. In the control of psychopathy, progress in social science must accompany or precede progress in the law.

Social science has moved slowly forward. Measures have been developed for distinguishing the psychopath—the conscienceless, aggressive, asocial individual—from other deviants. For the adult pschopath, unfortunately, cures are difficult. Psychotherapy and hypnoanalysis have, apparently, rehabilitated some psychopathic personalities. The needs of the time require a great increase not only in the application of these methods, but in thorough evaluation of their results.

If every means of treatment has been tried and has failed with a particular individual, there seems to be only one sound alternative for the protection of society: unlimited custody. This is an expensive alternative, and one which civilized man hesitates to adopt. But Billy Cook, Josef Borlov, and Herman Duker have shown the dangers of this hesitation. Exile need not be irrevocable. Examinations might indicate important changes which would justify release.

Many states have already enacted "habitual criminal" laws which allow permanent incarceration after a certain number of felonies have been committed. The "habitual criminal" is frequently a psychopath; but, all too frequently, such criminals have already cost society dearly.

Unlimited custody should be used only in those cases where extensive treatment has failed, and where every predictive instrument indicates the dangerousness of the individual. Society should not condemn a man to life custody unless it has exhausted all other resources.

Some social commentators, like Judge Ulman, advocate execution of the hardened psychopath. Lifetime imprisonment, they believe, would be taking a risk: the psychopath endangers his warders and fellow convicts.

George Bernard Shaw saw no greater cruelty in executing the "incurable criminal" than in incarcerating him for life. Execution, Shaw declared, would end the suffering of the convict, protect the lives of the guards, and offer true safety to society. After describing some psychopathic personalities, Shaw added:

> Now you cannot get rid of these nuisances and monsters by simply cataloguing them as subthyroidics and superadrenals or the like. At present you torment them for a fixed period, at the end of which they are set free to resume their operations with a savage grudge against the community which has tormented them. That is stupid. Nothing is gained by punishing people who cannot help themselves, and on whom deterrence is thrown away. Releasing them is like releasing the tigers from the Zoo to find their next meal in the nearest children's playing ground . . . .
>
> . . . . It was a horrible thing to build a vestal virgin into a wall with food and water enough for a day; but to build her into a prison for years as we do, with just enough loathsome food to prevent her from dying, is more horrible: it is diabolical. If no better alternatives to death can be found than these, then who will not vote for death? If people are fit to live, let them live under decent human conditions. If they are not fit to live, kill them in a decent humane way. Is it any wonder that some of us are driven to prescribe the lethal chamber as the solution for the hard cases which are at present made the excuse for dragging all the other cases down to their level, and the only solution that will create a sense of full social responsibility in modern populations?[39]

Despite Shaw's arguments, his suggestion that the psychopath's life be extinguished seems unjustified. Execution is irrevocable; custody can be ended. New treatments may be developed, or misdiagnoses occur.

Perhaps the case described by Raymond Corsini, San Quentin psychologist, was misdiagnosed. Or perhaps, as many "prison hands" believe, a spontaneous and inexplicable transformation took place:

> The prison psychologist often sees the processes of change where the uncontrollable psychopath finally becomes mature. There is a sudden influx of insight, remorse, and conscientiousness . . .
>
> One particular inmate diagnosed as a psychopathic personality, explained

that while engaged in a conversation with some prison associates he became suddenly aware that their conversation was distasteful. He realized in a flash of insight the consequences of his past actions and the nature of his present attitude. He backed away from the group, feeling a revulsion for them. He walked around the prison overwhelmed by the intensity of the insights he was experiencing. He literally changed overnight in his psychological make-up, becoming an earnest, seeking, conscientious, ambitious person.[40]

This spontaneous recovery seems in conflict with contemporary knowledge of psychopathy. Yet it serves to illustrate the dangers of execution. Diagnoses, like all human judgments, can be mistaken. Execution of psychopaths, because they are psychopaths, would end all possibility of correcting fallacious diagnoses or mistaken predictions.

In future years, effective treatment for psychopathic personalities may be discovered. Psychotherapy, aided perhaps by hypno-analysis and drugs, shows promise. Further development may prove that these or other methods can cure even the most hardened cases.

Since execution precludes the possibility of better treatment, spontaneous "conversion," or correcting mistaken diagnoses, it hardly seems a just solution to society's problem. Thus, permanent custody represents the most effective and the fairest protection for society. Tragically, one hundred years of scientific research have not produced a more satisfactory answer.

Fortunately, social science has developed a more successful treatment for child psychopathy. If present knowledge were applied extensively, the delinquent child need not become the dangerous adult.

The Wiltwyck project indicates that "milieu therapy" can do much to countermand psychopathy. The aggressive drives of the psychopathic children markedly declined, their friendly acceptance of authority gained, and (most importantly) their internalized guilt significantly increased. Combined psychological therapy, sustained acceptance, and realistic punishment in the form of "consequences" changes the psychopathic child into a more socialized individual. Some of the children's personalities underwent basic transformation.

Apparently, the reorientation of child psychopaths requires a complete change in environment. Possibly, in a few cases, schools, guidance clinics, or social work could provide the prolonged therapy necessary for socializing the child. For most child psychopaths, nevertheless, curing the pervasive disorder depends on total reorientation of the environment.[41]

Unfortunately, there are few schools which approximate the Wilt-wyck climate. To make deep inroads on the problem of psychopathy, the milieu therapy "idea" must be extended. Public reformatories have the physical facilities, but neither the philosophy nor the staff for accomplishing this task. Wider application of effective treatment requires an alteration in the reformatory and in the public attitude toward child psychopaths. The emphasis must be placed on "curing" —not punishing, "training," or "educating"—such children.

Effective treatment also requires money. And the public is loath to open its pocketbook. When financial troubles forced the closing of Detroit's Pioneer House, Fritz Redl justifiably exclaimed: ". . . we are still having trouble in recovering from our amazement that, in one of the richest cities in the U. S. with its pride and world-wide fame in the non-human aspects of engineering, it would remain impossible to create adequate treatment channels to rescue these five lives."[42]

Milieu therapy is expensive; very expensive. The cost of treating one boy for one year at Wiltwyck is over $4500. Thus, for the average length of residence, treatment costs $7000. Nevertheless, this is a small price to pay when compared to the financial toll which the uncured psychopath exacts. Here, for example, is the record—and its cost to society—of one San Quentin psychopath:[43]

AGE	ITEM	COST
6	Arrest, trial, and probation for stealing from mail boxes.	$ 300
7-12	Arrests, trials, probation, and losses from many petty thefts.	$ 1,000
14	One year's maintenance in California reform school and cost of repairs to school property.	$ 2,400
17	Trial, psychiatric examination, arrest for assault with intent to kill.	$ 400
	One year's maintenance in mental hospital and treatment.	$ 2,000
19	Losses, trial, and arrests for several burglaries.	$ 2,000
	Maintenance for four months in county jail.	$ 400
	One year of probation.	$ 400
20	Losses from burglaries. One year's maintenance in Iowa's mental hospital.	$ 2,000
22	Faked enrollment in Maritime Service, then Air Corps. Discharged from both as unfit for service.	$ 400
23	Maintenance in Colorado prison for one year; losses from robberies.	$ 3,000

25-29	Losses from burglaries; maintenance for four years in San Quentin.	$ 9,000
	Total:	$23,100

In less than three decades of life, this psychopath cost society $23,100. As the years pass, this sum will multiply. Add conservative estimates of the cost of police services and of losing the man's constructive labor, and the estimate soars.

For one-third the financial burden, society might have changed the life of this man.

Effective treatment, assuming its availability, probably depends upon spotting the disorder early in the person's life. Identifying the child psychopath is a problem too long ignored by students of the disorder.

In the last twenty years, however, Sheldon and Eleanor Glueck have been developing predictive instruments for use with adult criminals and juvenile delinquents. Although not specifically aimed at the prediction of psychopathy, these tests should work as well, perhaps better, for psychopathic criminals. Certainly their use with psychopaths should be intensively investigated.

The Gluecks have constructed actuarial tables for adult prisoners, relating backgrounds and prison records to post-incarceration behavior. They discovered that a variety of factors distinguished the convicts who later committed crimes from those who did not.[44]

In 1944 the Army used these tables with 200 prisoners in military rehabilitation centers.[45] Applying the Glueck scales retrospectively, Army researchers discovered that 170 of the inmates had a 60 per cent chance of failure at the time of their induction. Twenty more had a 50 per cent chance of failure.[46] If the tests had been used before induction, a majority of the delinquents would probably have been rejected.

The Glueck instruments could be of great value in the handling of adult psychopathy. If the test had, for example, been applied to Herman Duker before parole from the reformatory, he might not have been released. The test, when used retrospectively, predicted that Herman Duker had had a 95 per cent chance of total failure.[47] The murder of John Anderson proved the "prediction" correct.

The correct prediction of psychopathy in children has even greater importance. The effectiveness of treatment, many studies have shown, apparently diminishes with increasing age. The most recent of the Gluecks' work, *Unraveling Juvenile Delinquency*, offers strong hope that the disorder can be detected early in life.

From their comparison of delinquents with non-delinquents, the Gluecks selected the social and psychological factors which most clearly demarcated the two groups. Choosing independent factors which were present early in the child's life, the Gluecks constructed three statistical tables. The tests consisted of weighted scores based on the incidence of delinquency in relation to each trait. One table drew its materials from the boys' social backgrounds; another, from psychological traits on the Rorschach test; and a third, from traits diagnosed through psychiatric interviews.

In the last few years, several studies have demonstrated the high predictive value of the social scale. Bertram J. Black and Selma J. Glick applied the test to 100 boys at the Hawthorne Cedar-Knolls School. Tracing the backgrounds of the children, the researchers assigned each boy a weighted score. They studied five factors in making the judgment: paternal discipline, maternal supervision, paternal affection, maternal affection, and family cohesiveness. The authors concluded: "It could have been determined very early in the lives of the 100 boys that they were headed for delinquent careers, in other words, that in over 90 per cent of the instances they were likely to develop into serious delinquents."[48]

In 1952 Harvard researcher Richard E. Thompson furnished further evidence of the test's predictive value. Thompson chose 100 case studies from the Cambridge-Somerville experiment. Using the five social factors, Dr. Eleanor T. Glueck made judgments on the behavior of each boy. Since the Cambridge-Somerville experiment included a follow-up study, it provided an independent check of the Glueck scale. In 91 per cent of these cases, Dr. Glueck correctly predicted whether the boy became delinquent in later years. Moreover, as Thompson noted: "(The scale) maintained its high reliability when specifically applied to boys as young as six years. Its predictive power was maintained on boys of ethnic origin that was different from that of the series on which it had originally been constructed; on a group whose intelligence quotients were higher than those in the original group; on boys of somewhat better economic status than in the original sample . . .; and it was just as effective when checked on boys residing in more privileged city areas."[49]

These studies have done much to confirm the value of the Glueck scales.[50] Now for the first time, prediction is being attempted on the basis of the Gluecks' work. In New York, the Glueck tables are being applied in slum areas as children enter school. Half of the children whom the test predicts will become delinquent are receiving extensive counseling; the other half, used as a critical test of the scales' validity, are left to the usual school and community devices.

In other areas, researchers are measuring the predictive value of such instruments as the Minnesota Multiphasic Personality Inventory.[51] Interim reports indicate that these tests, too, can weed out future criminals—particularly when the tests are applied to adolescents.

Closely allied with the study of prediction is the study of causation. At present, it seems logical to presume that a combination of loveless-ness in childhood and a defective brain produces psychopathy. The growth of guidance clinics, social work, and early medical care may possibly aid in preventing the disorder. An effective preventive policy depends, however, on extending our knowledge of causation.

Every improvement in social policy, whether it be altering the legal structure, expanding "milieu therapy," or increasing research into various phases of the disorder, depends on changing the public atti-tude. The present atmosphere is supercharged with aggression. Re-venge, in its most primitive form, pervades both the theory and the application of our modern instruments of social control. The criminal law and the prison often serve as legitimized outlets for society's re-pressed aggression.

The heinous crimes perpetrated by psychopaths call forth bitter savagery from the public.[52] After a recent murder by two psycho-pathic boys, a prominant newspaper columnist thundered: "From the record so far you would just have to say that these punks are plain bad, poison mean, inhuman little animals who deserve no consid-eration, no clemency. Society didn't make them that way, either. The rottenness must dwell within a man who kills strangers for fun when the killer himself is not insane." The columnist advocated im-mediate execution of the boys. Obviously, the writer made his judg-ment not on the basis of a reasoned knowledge of psychopathy's causes, its nature, or its treatment—but on the basis of counteraggression.

The author's outburst is not uncommon. In fact, most of our social and legal structure is based on vengeance. Unfortunately, vindictiveness does nothing to solve the problem. It only impedes realistic solutions. Revising the legal system and providing effective treatment of the disorder depends on altering the public's attitude. Society's protection from psychopathy requires realism, not vituperation.

The control of psychopathy obviously demands several important changes in contemporary social policy. Some of these improvements only the trained lawyer or the social scientist can initiate. Others can be aided by every individual in his role as citizen. All of the changes depend on the cooperation and support of the public. These seem to be the minimum requisites of an effective policy:

> The criminal law must be revised in consonance with our knowledge of the causes and nature of psychopathy. Tests of criminal responsibility should be adopted which recognize that the psychopath has a serious, pervading mental disorder.
> Criminal law should abandon its emphasis on the nature of the offense and concentrate instead on the nature of the offender.
> The sentencing of psychopaths should, ideally, be placed in the hands of a "treatment tribunal" which would emphasize rehabilitation rather than punishment.
> Experimentation in the treatment of adult psychopathy should continue. Until an effective therapy is developed, the hardened adult psychopath should be placed under custodial care.
> The use of milieu therapy for the treatment of child psychopathy should be expanded.
> Research into causation, as well as treatment and prediction, must be stepped up.
> The public must be weaned from its vindictive attitude and brought to one of realistic appraisal of its own best interests.

Many of these improvements are interdependent. Legal changes without effective treatment are inadequate; research discoveries, if unimplemented, do little good. Gordon Allport's observations on conquering the problem of racial and religious prejudice apply equally to psychopathy: "Since the problem is many-sided, there can be no sovereign formula. The wisest thing to do is to attack on all fronts simultaneously. If no single attack has large effect yet many small attacks from many directions can have large cumulative results."[53]

Perhaps the most practical place to start the task would be in changing reform school practices. The decreased fantasy aggression, increased acceptance of society's standards, and newly formed consciences developed through milieu therapy indicate that we do have methods for successful treatment of child psychopathy (as well as for milder forms of delinquency). With changes in philosophy, with increased financial support, and with an improvement in personnel, many reform schools could reproduce the effectiveness of milieu therapy.

Some final words about the seriousness of the psychopathic problem: It cannot be stated too often that the disorder takes a costly toll in money, in corrective efforts, and in lives. We have already discussed, very cursorily, the financial burden of psychopathy. One psychopath in his twenties has already bled society of $23,100; his older comrades, in a full lifetime, cost probably three times that much.

How prevalent is this critical disorder? Because of the confusion over diagnosis, no one can give an accurate answer. Many estimates have, however, been made. Some scientists believe that psychopaths constitute a large proportion of all criminals. San Quentin psychologist Raymond Corsini reckoned: "Psychopaths make up the bulk of prisoners."[54] Sheldon Glueck places the proportion lower, at around 20 per cent of all criminals.[55] Ecuadorean psychiatrists found 13 per cent of Quito prison convicts were psychopathic.[56] Eighteen per cent of British inmates were so diagnosed.[57] United States Naval officials calculated that their training centers contained 26 per cent psychopaths.[58]

In 1952, 166,950 criminals were incarcerated in American prisons. Using a conservative estimate of 10 per cent, it would seem that 16,600 of these were psychopathic.

Fewer estimates have been made of the proportion of psychopaths among juvenile delinquents. In their most recent study, Glueck and Glueck found that 7 per cent of incarcerated juvenile delinquents were psychopathic.[59] In the Wiltwyck study, 14 per cent of the boys suffered from the disorder. Using the mid-point, 10 per cent, 3,000 juvenile psychopaths should be added to the 16,600 adults.

Finally, psychopaths can be found in mental hospitals as well as in prisons. Kirson Weinberg believes that 2.6 per cent of all hospital admissions are psychopaths.[60] Other scientists have found a higher incidence: Royal Naval Hospitals admissions include 5 per cent psychopathic patients[61]; American Army hospitals, in 1938, contained 36 per cent psychopaths[62]; and Hervey Cleckly figured that psychopaths accounted for 31 per cent of the psychiatric beds in a Georgia hospital.[63] Again using a conservative figure, 5 per cent, 24,000 psychopaths reside in American mental hospitals.

By adding these figures:

    16,600 adult imprisoned psychopaths
     3,000 juvenile psychopaths
    24,000 hospitalized psychopaths

we arrive at the estimate that, in 1952, over 43,000 psychopaths were in the custody of American institutions. Admittedly, this is only a reasonable guess. Since this includes no judgment on the number of psychopaths outside institutions, the true incidence is undoubtedly higher.

Such gaugings of the cost and extent of psychopathy only begin to measure the danger of the disorder. The psychopath commits twice as many crimes as the average convict, and his crimes are of the most critical nature.[64] His guiltlessness creates an unsual propensity for bizarre sexual activities.[65] He often uses drugs, and more often peddles them.[66] Thus his pernicious activities affect many lives, and unhappiness follows in his wake.

An additional danger lies in the psychopath's relation to the political order. We have discussed briefly the criminal's preference for an authoritarian regime.[67] In Herman Goering's life, we have shown what can happen when a fertile political situation and a psychopathic personality concur. The malignancy of a psychopath who gains political power can hardly be overemphasized.

The American political structure is not immune. The life of political boss David Stephenson warns Americans of the danger of psychopathic demagogues.

Born in 1892, in a small Texas town, Stephenson participated in petty crimes and carried a gun as a young child. He gained a reputation for flamboyance, lying, and pleasure-seeking exhibitionism. During drinking sprees, he liked to orate in the town square.

Stephenson hated his parents. His father died when the boy was young, his life ruined by oppressive manual labor. Stephenson's mother detested her son. The antipathy between them never ceased. In later life, when Stephenson was making over $900,000 a year, he refused to send a penny to his mother—who worked as a waitress.

Stephenson married twice. At twenty-two, he wedded the winner of an Oklahoma beauty contest. Three months later he deserted her and their unborn child. She divorced him on grounds of sadistic cruelty. Stephenson's other marriage ended also in divorce. The second wife complained of his sadistic sexual activities and his thievery from her mother.

During World War I, Stephenson served in the National Guard, but never went overseas. After the war, he bragged about fictitious war experiences. He lived from day to day, skipping from job to job.

In the early 1920's, Stephenson had a stroke of luck. A friend of his, a petty Indiana politician, hired him as assistant in establishing a state Klu Klux Klan. Stephenson relished the work. When his friend died, Stephenson inherited the Klan leadership with its enormous power.

Within the next few years, he built an extensive machine. He extended honorary memberships to seven hundred Indiana clergymen. He formed the "Horse Thief Detectives" to carry out the bullying work of the organization. Hundreds of thousands of Indianans flocked to join the Klan. If they did not, the "detectives" exerted pressure.

Throughout the state, Stephenson held rallies giving vent to his uninhibited drives. At a meeting in an open field, he flew over the people in a red airplane, painted with gold crosses. The airplane swept to a landing in the middle of the crowd. Stephenson gave a brief rabble-rousing speech and then flew back into the clouds.

This new power allowed Stephenson to acquire a palatial house. He gave raucous parties, attended by "the best people" in Indiana. During the parties, Stephenson had photographers weaving among the crowds. To the pictures taken by the photographers, Stephenson added faked pornographic details and used the negatives to blackmail his guests.

Stephenson's power extended over the political structure of the state. Even though reports of his graft, robberies, and strange sexual behavior persisted, Stephenson suppressed them before they reached the courts. At the height of his influence, Stephenson jokingly declared: "I'm the embodiment of Napoleon." In Indiana, at least, no one laughed at the joke.

In 1925 Stephenson kidnapped Madge Oberholtzer, a worker in the Department of Public Institutions. In his private railroad car, he raped her. Afterwards, Miss Oberholtzer tried to poison herself with bichloride of mercury. Stephenson and his chauffeur took her from the train and placed her in an automobile. For hours, the two drove the girl around. She pleaded to be taken to a doctor. Stephenson refused, and watched with curiosity as she died.

The story of her death leaked out, but Stephenson was unafraid. "My word is law," he declared. His power, however, could not stop the public uproar, and Stephenson was indicted.

No Indiana lawyers wanted to handle the case, and the courts were frightened. An honest prosecutor was finally discovered, but the state refused to pay his traveling expenses to the trial.

After his arrest, Stephenson gave way to an almost paranoid episode. The Imperial Wizard of the Klan, he believed, was persecuting him. Evidence began to pile up against Stephenson as witness after witness overcame timidity.

A final piece of testimony convicted Stephenson of murder. The medical report showed that Madge Oberholtzer had died, not from the bichloride of mercury, but from an infection caused by teeth wounds on her body. Stephenson was sent to prison.[68]

In 1955, at age sixty-three, David Curtis Stephenson was paroled from prison, his power gone, his fortunes at their nadir. Stephenson ruined himself, yet he remained in power long enough to trail agony through the state.

The crimes of a Stephenson, of a Duker, of a Cook revolt society. Psychopathy, and all of its execrable consequences, has plagued every human society. Dostoyevsky's inspired portrait of Fyodor Karamazov testifies that psychopathy is not confined to modern America.

It is the part of wisdom to understand the problem of psychopathy and not to give way to emotion. We have the tools to solve the problem: we know the nature and character of the psychopath's affliction; we know how to distinguish him from other "mentally diseased" people; we know, at least rudimentarily, what causes psychopathy. And, if the Wiltwyck study is a true indication, we know how to change the psychopathic child and avoid the vicious fruits of his maturity.

If society has the will, it can protect itself against this most dangerous, and, at the same time, most lonely of human beings.

NOTES

1. ULMAN, JOSEPH. *A Judge Takes the Stand*. New York, Knopf, 1933. p. 211.

2. *Ibid.*, 215-216.

3. *Ibid.*, 217.

4. *Ibid.,* 218.

5. *Ibid.,* 219.

6. *Ibid.,* 229.

7. *Ibid.* The Governor also questioned the validity of sentencing a man because of a prediction concerning his peril to society. See *Ibid.,* appendix.

8. GLUECK, SHELDON. *Mental Disorder and the Criminal Law.* Boston; Little, Brown, 1927, 138-130. (Cited from: Rex vs. Arnold, 16 How. St. Tr. 695, 764, 1724.)

9. GLUECK, SHELDON. *Crime and Justice.* Cambridge, Harvard University Press, 1945, p. 99.

10. Durham vs. United States, 1954. U.S. Court of Appeals, Wash. D. C., 214 F. 2d, 862, Federal Reporter, West Publishing Co., St. Paul, p. 864.

11. CLECKLY, HERVEY. The Psychopath Viewed Practically. In ROBERT LINDNER and R. V. SELIGER: *Handbook of Correctional Psychology.* New York, Philosophical Library, 1947, 395-412.

12. POUND, ROSCOE. Introduction to F. B. SAYRE: *Cases On Criminal Law,* 1927, pp. xxxvi-xxxvii.

13. For a discussion of the complicated issue of criminal responsibility and free will, see Glueck, *op.cit.* (note 8).

14. See ISAAC RAY: *Medical Jurisprudence of Insanity.* Boston; Little, Brown, 1838.

15. Both a report made by the Royal Commission on Capital Punishment and an American report by the Committee on Forensic Psychiatry of the Group for the Advancement of Psychiatry agreed that the M'Naghten rule should be abandoned.

16. Glueck, *op. cit.* (note 8).

17. CARDOZA, B. *What Medicine Can Do For The Law.* New York, Harper, 1930, p. 32.

18. Durham vs. United States, *op. cit.* (note 10), p. 864.

19. *Ibid.,* 865.

20. *Ibid.,* 868.

21. At times Durham was labelled "psychopathic," at other times, "psychotic." Almost all psychiatrists who examined him agreed, however, that he was mentally abnormal.

22. Among other errors: the lower court did not recognize that the burden of proof of Durham's sanity lay with the prosecution; incorrectly dismissed as "no evidence" all psychiatric testimony, because the witness could not certify that the defendant failed the right-wrong test; and did not weigh the "whole evidence."

23. *Ibid.,* 874-875.

24. *Ibid.,* 872.

25. *Ibid.,* 873.

26. In the discussions at the American Law Institute, Manfred Guttmacher wished to add "major [mental disease]" to the criterion for irresponsibility. This addition, depending upon its interpretation, could rule out psychopathic personality.

27. Ulman, Joseph, *op. cit.* (note 1), 230-231.

28. GAUDET, FREDERICK J. Sentencing Behavior of Judges. In VERNON BRANHAM and SAMUEL KUTASH: *Encyclopedia of Criminology*. New York, Philosophical Library, 1949.

29. Glueck, *op. cit.* (note 9), p. 100.

30. BECCARIA, C. *An Essay on Crimes and Punishments*. London, F. Newburry, 1770.

31. *Ibid.*

32. A treatment tribunal would not eliminate whatever element of deterrence punishment exerts. Men would still be incarcerated, and often for longer periods.

33. SHAW, GEORGE BERNARD. *The Crime of Imprisonment*. New York, Philosophical Library, 1946, p. 36.

34. Beccaria's work deserves credit, for it modified the brutality of his times and controlled the favoritism of the courts. Voltaire described a typical criminal case of the century. A young man, the Chevalier de la Barre, sang some sacriligious songs in a tavern one night. Vindictive neighbors complained. As punishment, the "criminal" had his tongue pulled out at the roots, his right hand cut off, and was burned at the stake by a slow fire.

35. Under a treatment tribunal, the rights of the criminal would be protected: statutes might roughly determine sentences, counsel and witnesses might appear at the tribunal, annual reviews of each case would be required, and an appellate tribunal would have to be established. See Glueck, *op. cit.* (note 9), 227-229.

36. GLUECK, SHELDON. Principles of a Rational Penal Code. *Harvard Law Review*, 41:453-482, 1928.

37. Ideally, the sentence of a treatment tribunal would depend entirely upon the character of the offender. In practice, the public would not tolerate such a complete revision in the law. Consequently, the Glueck proposal allows broad indeterminate sentences, set by law. Crimes which particularly revolt the public would still require longer punishment than would "minor" offenses.

38. See THOMAS C. DESMOND: Youth Correction Authority Plan. Branham and Kutash, *op. cit.* (note 28).

39. Shaw, *op. cit.* (note 33), pp. 50-51, 54-55.

40. CORSINI, RAYMOND. Criminal Psychology. In Encyclopedia of Criminology, *op. cit.* (note 28), p. 112.

41. The fact that the Cambridge-Somerville counseling failed in treating psychopaths, while Wiltwyck succeeds, supports this assertion. Such a position runs counter to the social-work theory that children should never be removed from their parents. Apparently, with psychopathic children, a separation is advisable.

42. REDL, FRITZ AND WINEMAN, DAVID. *Controls From Within*. Glencoe, Free Press, 1954, p. 315.

43. Estimates of the cost of arrests, trials, and incarceration are taken from the World Almanac's average figures for 1954. Estimates of cost of losses are taken from the convict's records.

44. See SHELDON and ELEANOR GLUECK: *500 Criminal Careers*. New York,

Knopf, 1930. Also *Criminal Careers in Retrospect*, New York, The Commonwealth Fund, 1943. Also *After-Conduct of Discharged Offenders*, London, Macmillan, 1945.

45. SCHNEIDER, ALEXANDER J. N.; LA GRONE, CYRUS W.; GLUECK, S.; AND GLUECK, E. Prediction of Behavior of Civilian Delinquents in the Armed Forces. *Mental Hygiene*, 28(3), 1944 (July).

46. The Army designated 130 of the inmates as "psychopathic personalities." Of these, 88% received highly delinquent predictive scores on the Glueck scales.

47. Ulman, *op. cit.* (note 1).

48. BLACK, BERTRAM J. AND GLICK, SELMA J. *Recidivism at the Hawthorne-Cedar-Knolls School*. Research Monograph No. 2, Jewish Board of Guardians, New York, 1952, p. 22.

49. THOMPSON, RICHARD E. A Validation of the Glueck Social Prediction Scale for Proneness to Delinquency. *Journal of Criminal Law, Criminology and Police Science*, 43:469, Nov.-Dec. 1952.

50. D. Tiedman has noted that the Glueck scales were constructed on the basis of a population in which there were 50% delinquents. In normal areas, with other proportions of delinquents, Dr. Tiedman believes that the scales will not accurately differentiate the non-delinquents.

51. For a discussion of current predictive devices, see L. E. OHLIN: *Selection for Parole*. New York, Russell Sage Foundation, 1951. Also ELIO MONACHESI: Prediction of Criminal Behavior, in Branham and Kutash, *op. cit.* (note 28).

52. *The Authoritarian Personality* research has demonstrated that, ironically, criminals themselves are the most intemperate in their condemnation of crime, advocacy of stern punishment, and acceptance of conventional moral values.

53. ALLPORT, GORDON. *The Nature of Prejudice*. Cambridge, Addison-Wesley Publishing Co., 1954, p. 507.

54. Corsini, *op. cit.* (note 40), p. 112.

55. GLUECK, SHELDON. Introduction to ROBERT LINDNER: *Rebel Without A Cause*. New York, Grune and Stratton, 1944.

56. CRUZ, J. Estudio de las Personalidades Psicopaticas en Nuestra Criminalidad. *Arch. Crim. Neuropsiquiatry*, 3:38-50, 1939.

57. HYLAND, H. H. AND RICHARDSON, J. C. Psychoneuroses in the Canadian Army Overseas. *Canadian Medical Association Journal*, 47:432-442, 1942.

58. CURRAN, D. AND MALLINSON, P. Psychopathic Personality. *Journal of Mental Science*, 90,266-286, 1944.

59. Glueck, Sheldon and Eleanor, *op. cit.* (note 44).

60. WEINBERG, KIRSON. *Society and Personality Disorders*. New York, Prentice Hall, 1952, p. 264.

61. EAST, W. N. Psychopathic Personality and Crime. *Journal of Mental Science*, 91:426-466, 1945.

62. Curran and Mallinson, *op. cit.* (note 58).

63. CLECKLY, HERVEY. *Mask of Sanity*. St. Louis, C. V. Mosley, 1941.

64. See R. B. VAN VORST: An Evaluation of the Institutional Adjustment

of the Psychopathic Offender. *American Journal of Orthopsychiatry,* 14:491-493, 1944.

65. The term "sexual psychopath" has gained wide currency in recent years. Many social scientists have pointed out that the label is a misnomer. Most sexual deviants are not psychopaths. The true psychopath, while sexually uninhibited, is not the sex "maniac."

Recently, "sexual psychopath" laws have been enacted which permit the permanent imprisonment of offenders. Edwin Sutherland suggested that these laws are unnecessary: the sexual offender usually does not repeat his crime; imprisonment does not cure him; and the states which have instituted the laws have not witnessed a drop in sexual crimes. See EDWIN SUTHERLAND: Sexual Psychopath Laws. *Journal of Criminal, Criminology, and Police Science,* 40:545-554, 1950.

66. AUSUBEL, DAVID P. The Psychopathology and Treatment of Drug Addiction in Relation to the Mental Hygiene Movement. *Psychiatric Quarterly Supplement,* 22:219-250, 1948.

67. See T. W. ADORNO, ELSE FRENKEL-BRUNSWICK, DANIEL J. LEVINSON, and R. NEVITT SANFORD: *The Authoritarian Personality.* New York, Harper, 1950.

68. ZINK, H. A Case Study of a Political Boss. *Psychiatry,* 1:527-533, 1938.

Appendix A: Wiltwyck's Population

A statistical breakdown of Wiltwyck's boys in the summer of 1954 showed:

RACE: 72 were Negro; 35 were white.

RELIGION: 68 were Protestant; 39 were Catholic.

AGE: Median age was eleven. Distribution was as follows:

Age	Number of Boys
7-9	11
10	21
11	32
12	27
over 12	16

INTELLIGENCE: Median I.Q. was 90. This figure is based on intelligence tests given during the intake examination and is probably well below potentiality. Distribution was as follows:

I.Q.	Number of Boys
below 81	30
81—90	30
91—100	32
over 100	15

There was no significant difference in I.Q. among the diagnostic categories.

TIME IN RESIDENCE: Median period of treatment was 10 months. The average treatment span for all children who pass through Wiltwyck is 18 months. Distribution of months in residence was as follows:

Number of Months in Residence	Number of Boys
0—8	35
9—23	45
over 23	27

Appendix B: Tests and Ratings

STAFF RATINGS

Please check the phrase which best describes the boy. If none of the descriptions are adequate, please write in your answer.

1. *Hostility:*
   Extreme, often physically violent___
   Very hostile, sullen___
   Occasional outbursts of hostility___
   Active, assertive, not hostile___
   Retiring, withdrawn, not hostile___
   Other _____

2. *Destructiveness:*
   Extreme, no concern for property___
   Often destructive___
   Occasional destructive outbursts___
   Little or no destructiveness___
   Other _____

3. *Anxiety:*
   Extreme, always fearful___
   Usually very anxious, but sometimes relaxes___
   Very anxious in some situations, usually not anxious___
   Little or no anxiety___
   Other _____

4. *Impulsivity:*
   Extreme, no control over impulses___
   Very impulsive, but at times controls himself___
   Not markedly impulsive, normal for his age___
   Other _____

5. *Narcissism:*
   Extreme, entirely self-centered___
   Self-centered, but sometimes considers others___
   Not self-centered, usually considerate___
   Other _____

6. *Knowledge of General Social Code:*
   Has no understanding of society's moral code___
   Understands society's code concerning some areas, not others___
   Has adequate knowledge and understanding of moral code___
   Other _____

7. *Knowledge of Wiltwyck Code:*
   Has no understanding of moral code unique to Wiltwyck___
   Understands the Wiltwyck code in some areas, not in others___

Has adequate knowledge and understanding of Wiltwyck's code___
Other _____

8. *Guilt.* When the boy violates either Wiltwyck's code or the general social mores, does he:
Feel no guilt___
Feel little guilt___
Feel guilty only for certain violations, not for others___
Feel considerable remorse for all types of violations___
Other _____

9. *Rapport With Rater.* In the boy's relation with you, do you believe that:
There is no warmth, no rapport___
Boy is friendly, but maintains distance___
There is a very warm relation sometimes, other times very cool___
The relation is close, warm, friendly___
Other _____

10. *Boy's Perception of Himself:*
The boy has a highly unrealistic estimate of himself, his abilities, and personality___
The boy is partly unrealistic, partly realistic in his self-conception___
The boy is usually realistic in his self-estimate, but is seriously disturbed by this concept___
The boy is usually realistic in his self-concept and is generally satisfied with himself___
Other _____

11. *Boy's Perception of the World:*
The boy views his world as hostile, threatening, evil___
The boy views his world neutrally___
The boy views his world as friendly, helpful, good—
Other _____

12. *Boy's Perception of Authority* (Parents, staff, judges, etc.):
Hostile and fearful to all forms of authority___
Hostile and fearful to some forms of authority___
(Please specify) _____
Normal attitude towards authority, usually respectful___
Friendly, usually unafraid___
Other _____

13. *Reaction to Frustration.* When the desires or expectations of the boy are frustrated, he:
Reacts by withdrawal, retires___
Reacts with fury, hostility, or destructiveness___
Reacts sometimes with hostility, sometimes realistically___
Reacts sometimes with withdrawal, sometimes realistically___
Reacts realistically, meets situation calmly___
Other _____

14. *Relation to Other Boys:*
He is almost universally disliked by the other boys___

He is disliked by most, friendly with a small group___
He is liked by almost all the other boys___
Other _____

15. *Leadership:*
He never leads the other boys___
He leads the other boys sometimes, usually in destructive activities___
He leads the other boys sometimes, usually in constructive activities___
He is generally regarded as a leader___
Other _____

16. *Desire for Recognition:*
He has a strong craving for approval and recognition___
He sometimes demands recognition and approval, but usually he is
    satisfied with normal amount___
He has no strong drive for recognition___
Other _____

17. *Suggestibility:*
He is highly suggestible___
He is moderately suggestible___
He is independent, not markedly suggestible___
Other _____

EVALUATION OF PROGRESS
[Filled out by counselors]

Please check the phrase which best describes the changes in the boy's personality and behavior since June, 1954. If any important changes occurred before that date, please note them. If a specific trait (e.g. anxiety) was not one of the boy's problems upon entering Wiltwyck, please omit it.

1. *Control of Aggression:*
In controlling his aggressive outbursts, temper tantrums, destructiveness, or hostility, the boy has . . .
_____ Not changed
_____ Increased his control somewhat
_____ Increased his control markedly

2. *Anxiety:*
The boy's anxieties, fears, and unreasonable worries have . . .
_____ Not changed
_____ Decreased somewhat
_____ Decreased markedly

3. *Insight into Personality:*
The boy's understanding of his own motives, attitudes, and character traits has . . .
_____ Not changed
_____ Increased somewhat
_____ Increased markedly

4. *Relation to Others:*
In his relations with other people at Wiltwyck, the boy's friendliness and rapport have . . .
_____ Not changed (consistently poor)

_____ Improved somewhat
_____ Improved markedly

5. *Relation to Authority:*

In his relation to various authority figures (parents, counselors, etc.), the boy's realistic, friendly acceptance of them has . . .

_____ Not changed (consistently poor)
_____ Improved somewhat
_____ Improved markedly

6. *Impulsivity:*

In controlling erratic, unplanned, impulsive behavior, the boy has . . .

_____ Not changed
_____ Increased his control somewhat
_____ Increased his control markedly

7. *General Impression:*

In the last eight months, the boy's behavior and personality . . .

_____ Have not changed
_____ Have changed beneficially in some ways, not in others
_____ Have changed beneficially in many ways
_____ Have undergone a transformation

8. *Reasons for Improvement:*

If the boy has improved in the Wiltwyck environment, what factors do you believe were most responsible for bringing about this change? (If possible, please number the factors in the order of their importance):

_____ Relations to counselor
_____ Relations with other adults
_____ Group therapy
_____ Individual therapy
_____ Art therapy
_____ Relations with boys
_____ Experience of group living
_____ Experience of non-punitiveness
_____ Athletics
_____ Classroom experience
_____ Other _____

9. *Other Comments:*

INTERNALIZED GUILT STORIES

Bob took a piece of cake that was for dinner. His mother walks in. How does Bob feel?

Bob ran into another boy on his bicycle. The other boy is hurt. How does Bob feel?

Bob was in a ten-cent store. He took a rubber ball and put it in his pocket. How does Bob feel?

Bob was in a fight. The other boy had two teeth broken. How does Bob feel?

Bob's teacher helped him with his reading. One day he said, "I don't want help. I don't like you." The teacher was hurt. How did Bob feel?

Bob's friend was mean to him. Bob stole the friend's marbles. How did Bob feel?

Bob left his clothes on the floor. Bob's counselor tripped and hurt himself. How does Bob feel?

Bob was playing with matches one day. He set the house on fire and a man was killed. How did Bob feel?

Bob was angry. He broke the school's movie projector out of spite. How does Bob feel?

Bob and Jack fought one day. Bob pulled a knife and stabbed Jack. How does Bob feel?

AUTHORITY STORIES

Bob and Jack were fighting. Bob was hurt. Bob's mother walked up. What did she do?

Bob came home very late one night. He had fallen down and hurt himself. What did his father do?

Bob could not do his arithmetic. The teacher saw his blank paper. What did the teacher do?

Bob was playing baseball. He hit a ball into a yard. The wall was too high for him to climb. A policeman came along. What did the policeman do?

Bob ran away from Wiltwyck (camp, for public school boys). He came home the next day dirty and tired. What did Bob's counselor do?

SELF-PERCEPTION QUESTIONNAIRE

What do people like best about you?
What do people dislike most about you?
If you could be anyone in the whole world, who would you be?
Whom do you admire most in the whole world?
What is a good boy like?

Check-list

Are you:

Afraid	Smart
Bad	Mean
Brave	Kind
Clean	Nice
Cruel	Neat
Dumb	Always honest
Generous	Well-liked
Dirty	Selfish
Good	Scared
Ugly	Strong

"PERCEPTION OF THE ENVIRONMENT" QUESTIONNAIRE

What do you like most about Wiltwyck?

What do you like least about Wiltwyck?

What are good parents like?

What happens to a boy when he does something wrong? Is what happens right?

Whom do you like best at Wiltwyck?

MORAL CODE QUESTIONNAIRE

Code of general society: (Do you agree or disagree?)

Stealing is always wrong.

You should always be kind.

It is always wrong to kill.

You should never tell a lie.

You should always be generous.

Code of Wiltwyck: (Do you agree or disagree?)

It is always wrong to run away from the school.

You should always think of the good of the school.

If you do something wrong, you should take the consequences.

There is always someone at Wiltwyck who likes you.

You should go to class whether you want to or not.

If a boy can't go home, it's not his social worker's fault.

Going home would not solve everything for a boy.

RATINGS OF REACTIONS TO FRUSTRATION
[Filled out by counselors]

Please check the best description of the boy's response to the frustrating situation. If no alternative fits the boy's behavior, please write in your own description.

(Withdrawn)

The boy was saddened, withdrew from the situation. _____

(Aggressive)

The boy was extremely angry, reacted with hostility, fury. _____

The boy was extremely angry, reacted with destructiveness. _____

The boy was angry, reacted first without hostility or destructiveness, then gradually adjusted to the situation. _____

(Hyperactivity)

The boy was hyperactive, agitated, but not destructive. _____

(Realistic)

Although angry, the boy immediately adjusted to the situation, accepting it realistically. _____

The boy was not particularly angry, adjusted to the situation, accepted it realistically. _____

The situation was not at all frustrating to the boy. His manner did not change at all. _____

[This page shows the information gathered from case records for each boy.]

Name   Age

Date of Arrival   Religion

Cottage and Counselor

Recorded I.Q.

Personality Characteristics

Personality Diagnosis

Behavioral Background

Reason for Entering Wiltwyck

Family Characteristics

Additional Information

Appendix C: Measurement Procedure, Validity and Reliability

In the following pages, we present our methods of constructing the tests used in the Wiltwyck study and for establishing their reliability and validity.

In many of the areas we wished to measure, tests had not been previously developed. We could find no standardized measures of, for example, internalized guilt, reactions to frustration, or withdrawal tendencies.

Certain projective tests (e.g., the Thematic Apperception Test, the Rorschach, and the Blackie tests) can measure some relevant traits. They were not, however, suitable for our research. We wished to measure specific traits and these projective tests were designed primarily to give a gestalt impression. Moreover, recent studies have indicated certain deficiencies in these tests—particularly in those areas that we most wished to examine.*

Established self-report tests (e.g., the California Test of Personality) measure specific qualities, but they demand a degree of insight, literacy, and honesty which we could never expect of our delinquent children.

Consequently, for the 1954 research, we had to reject existing psychological tests. This left us with the task of developing new measures—measures which we hoped would tap unconscious processes, conscious values, and actual behavior.

Some of our measures seem to detect characteristics of the delinquent not previously measured. It is our hope that these tests might be of use in other studies of personality.

1. The Rover Test

Trial testing with 30 public school children and an item analysis resulted in the elimination of all but 12 panels. Originally, we had asked the children, "What does Rover do?" Many children commented, "Rover does this, but he wants to do that." Asking the child, "What does Rover want to do?" tapped more directly the child's aggressive desires.

Before applying the new test to the Wiltwyck boys, we gave the Rover to 79 boys, aged nine to twelve, in a Massachusetts public school. The public school teachers, who had worked with their students for eight months, rated each child's aggressive and withdrawal tendencies. For each trait they designated the upper and lower thirds of their classes.

---

*For cogent criticism of projective techniques, see GORDON ALLPORT: The Trend in Motivational Theory. *American Journal of Orthopsychiatry, 22,* 1953. Also, ROBERT GOLDWYN: Some Investigations of the Validity of the Rosenzweig Picture-Frustration Study. (Unpublished honors thesis at Harvard University.) In 1953, we had used the Adult-Child Interaction Test and found it difficult to separate aggression from assertiveness in the protocols.

The teachers made three separate judgments of aggression: aggressive fantasies, aggressive behavior, and "composite" aggression. With each, they divided their children into high, medium, and low aggressive groups. The teachers based their "composite" judgment on the hostile desires of the child as revealed in his compositions, art work, and handicrafts, as well as in his actual relations with the teacher and other students. Some of the children, for example, showed intense hostility in their themes, but only occasionally in their actual classroom behavior. They would be judged highly hostile in fantasy and "composite" ratings, low in behavioral ratings.

Because of the difficulty in rating fantasy withdrawal, the teachers' judgments of this trait stemmed primarily from the child's behavior. If the student frequently withdrew in response to actual frustration, the teachers marked him as exhibiting strong withdrawal tendencies. Judgments were of strong, moderate, or slight withdrawal tendencies.

After administering the test to the 79 school children, we compared the teachers' ratings to the Rover results. In 71% of the cases the Rover aggression score agreed with the teacher's judgment of behavioral aggression; in 99%, with the judgments of fantasy hostility. *In 94% of the cases* the Rover aggression score agreed with the teachers' "composite" judgments. Chance agreement would be only 33.3%. In other words, if the teacher rated a child as being among the upper third of her students in aggression, the number of his aggressive choices on the Rover also fell in the upper third.

In 86% of the cases, the Rover withdrawal score agreed with the teachers' judgments. A child who usually withdrew from troubling situations generally made a greater number of withdrawn choices on the test.

A split-half reliability coefficient of .74 (on odd-even scores of all responses) for the Rover Test indicates that the test measures with adequate consistency.
The standard deviations on the test:
Public school aggression: 2.27
Wiltwyck aggression: 2.77
Public school withdrawal: 1.54
Wiltwyck withdrawal: 1.47

The distribution of scores by age, at Wiltwyck, was as follows:

Age		Percentage of Aggressive Choices
7—9	(11 boys)	27
10	(21 boys)	19
11	(32 boys)	19
Over 11	(43 boys)	10

The distribution of scores by intelligence, at Wiltwyck, was:

I.Q.		Percentage of Aggressive Choices
Below 81	(30 boys)	20
81—90	(30 boys)	26
91—100	(32 boys)	20
Over 100	(15 boys)	19

2. *The Cartoon Test*

Before giving the Cartoon Test to the Wiltwyck children, we presented the 10 panels to 30 school students in Massachusetts. Teachers had rated their children's aggressive fantasy, aggressive behavior, and "composite" aggression.

The Cartoon Test scores agreed with the fantasy ratings in only 36% of the cases, with the behavioral ratings in 58%, and with the composite judgments in 61% of the cases. Chance agreement would be 33.3%. The Cartoon Test seemed a less valid measure of aggressive fantasies than the Rover. The Rover and Cartoon aggressive scores had a positive correlation of .29. The standard deviation of the public school boys' responses was 3.25; the standard deviation for the Wiltwyck population was 2.4.

3. *The Guilt Stories*

Because we had defined conscience as the inner quality which prevents violations of social rules, we again turned to teachers' judgments as an approach to validation. We administered the stories to 30 public school children. Their teachers divided the children into 3 groups, according to the degree to which they adhered to rules of "polite" classroom behavior. By taking the distribution of the children's answers to the stories (and dividing these into high, middle, and low guilt), we found 66% agreement with teachers' judgments. Chance agreement would be 33.3% The mean score of the non-delinquents was 82%—high enough to warrant application of the test at Wiltwyck, where we expected to find a larger range and perhaps lower initial guilt.

At Wiltwyck, we again tried to assess the test's validity by asking the counselors to rate each child on this form:

When the boy violates either Wiltwyck's code or the general social mores, does he:

 Feel no guilt _____
 Feel little guilt _____
 Feel guilty only for certain violations, not for others _____
 Feel considerable guilt for all types of violations _____

After administering the Guilt Stories to 107 Wiltwyck children,* we compared the results to the counselors' ratings. Using a chi-square analysis, we related the highest and lowest guilt scores to the rating categories. The children rated as having no guilt did not significantly differ from those judged as having considerable guilt. On the 45 children who were rated by two or more counselors, the judgments agreed on only 33%.

Less directly, we found some validation in another area of the counselors' ratings: judgments of the boys' hostility. The counselors divided the boys into 5 categories:

 Extreme, often physically violent
 Very hostile, sullen
 Occasional outbursts of hostility
 Active, assertive, not hostile
 Retiring, withdrawn, not hostile

Regarding hostility, counselors agreed in 85% of the ratings on the 45 children judged by more than one.

---

*Standard deviation, 2.56; mean score, 63.6%.

A chi-square comparison of the ratings and the Guilt Story scores* revealed: children who showed the greatest internalized guilt on the stories had significantly less behavioral aggression than those who showed little guilt.† Lack of hostility cannot, of course, be equated with internalized guilt; yet theoretically, conscience should inhibit hostile actions (at least in American culture).

A split-half reliability of .76 showed that the stories measured a single quality with adequate consistency. The Spearman-Brown correction gives a reliability score of .86 if the test were twice as long.

The distribution of guilt scores by age, at Wiltwyck, was:

Age		Percentage of Internalized Guilt
8–9	(10 boys)	65
10	(21 boys)	66
11	(32 boys)	60
12	(27 boys)	65
Over 12	(16 boys)	60

4. Authority Stories

We sought validation from the Wiltwyck counselors, who rated their children's view of authority as:

Hostile to, and fearful of, all forms of authority

Hostile to, and fearful of, some forms of authority

Normal attitude toward authority—usually respectful

Friendly, usually unafraid of authority

When more than one counselor rated a child, the judgments agreed in 75% of the cases.

Chi-square comparison of the ratings and the boys' story responses showed: boys rated as hostile to all authority gave significantly more punitive answers to the stories than did boys rated as hostile to only some forms of authority; boys with some hostility responded with significantly more punitive answers than those judged as friendly to authority.‡ The high level of statistical significance ($P < .01$) indicates that the stories successfully differentiate punitive from supportive attitudes toward authority.

The split-half reliability of the stories was .74. Correction by the Spearman-Brown formula for a test twice as long gave a reliability of .85.

The distribution of scores by intelligence, at Wiltwyck, was:

I.Q.		Percentage of Punitive Answers
Below 81	(30 boys)	28
81–90	(30 boys)	35
91–100	(32 boys)	38
Over 100	(15 boys)	35

---

*The scores were divided into upper and lower halves.

†$X^2 = 3.99$, d.f. $= 1$; $P < .05$.

‡Story responses divided into high and low halves of punitive responses; $X^2 = 12.43$, d.f. $= 3$.

The distribution of scores by age, at Wiltwyck, was:

Age		Percentage of Punitive Answers
7—9	(11 boys)	59
10—11	(53 boys)	42
Over 11	(43 boys)	21

5. *Self-Perception Questionnaire*
Answers to the questions, "What do people like best about you?" and, "What do people dislike most about you?" were divided into 3 categories:
   Answers concerned with internal traits
   Answers concerned with behavior, not character
   Inability to name any quality
Two independent judges agreed 96% on the scoring.
Answers to the question, "If you could be anyone in the whole world, who would you be?" were divided in 4 categories:
   Myself
   A power figure (e.g., God, Samson)
   A positive ideal (e.g., a counselor, G. W. Carver)
   An inability to name any figure
Two independent judges agreed 92% on the scoring.
Answers to the question, "Whom do you admire most in the whole world?" were divided into four groups:
   Parents
   A power figure
   A positive ideal
   Inability to name any figure
Independent judges agreed 83% on scoring.
Answers to the question, "What is a good boy like?" were divided into three categories:
   Positive (e.g., "He takes care of others.")
   Negative (e.g., "He does *not* steal.")
   An inability to give any answer
Independent judges agreed 99% on the scoring.
The percentage of differentiated answers to the self-perception check list was distributed by age as follows:

Age		Percentage of Differentiated Answers
7—9	(11 boys)	5
10	(21 boys)	15
11	(32 boys)	22
Over 11	(43 boys)	24

The difference in score between "7—9" and "Over 11" was significant at the 5% level.
The relation between intelligence and self-perception can be seen in the following chart:

I.Q. AND SELF-PERCEPTION

I.Q.	Percentage of Differentiation	Percentage of Negative Traits	Percentage of Positive Ideals
Below 81	12	12	20
81–90	24	14	19
91–100	18	16	28
Over 100	22	17	32

6. *"Perception of the Environment" Questionnaire*

Answers to the question, "What do you like most at Wiltwyck?" were divided into four categories:*

"Everything"

"Nothing"

Constructive activities (e.g., sports, class)

Destructive activities (fighting, running away)

Answers to the question, "What do you like least about Wiltwyck?" were of three types:†

Unrealistic (conditions that could not be changed)

Realistic (conditions which could be corrected)

20% of the children said they liked everything connected with Wiltwyck

Answers to the questions, "What are good parents like?" were divided into three categories:‡

Loving ("They take good care of their children.")

Authoritarian ("They *don't* allow you to steal.")

Unclear ("They're nice.")

Answers to the question, "What happens to a boy when he does something wrong?" were divided into three categories:§

Punishment ("He gets socked.")

Consequences ("He has to make up for what he did.")

Inability to give any answer

After the boy answered the preceding question, we asked, "Is what happens right?" Answers were divided into three categories: ‖

"Yes"

"No"

"Differentiated (e.g., "It depends on what he did.")

7. *Moral Code*

The agreement with the moral code was distributed as follows by age and intelligence:

---

*Two independent judges agreed 98% on the scoring.

†Two independent judges agreed 85% on the scoring.

‡Two independent judges agreed 95% on the scoring.

§Two independent judges agreed 92% on the scoring.

‖Two independent judges agreed 100% on the scoring.

Age	Percentage of Agreement	I.Q.	Percentage of Agreement
7—9	100	Below 81	96
10	92	81—90	92
11	89	91—100	89
Over 11	80	Over 100	82

8. *Reactions to Frustration*

At the beginning of their treatment the Wiltwyck boys responded to frustration in the following ways:

Response	Behavior Disorders and Psychopaths, %	Neurotics and Psychotics, %
Aggression	39	20
Hyperactivity	8	0
Realistic Acceptance	39	40
Withdrawal	14	40

SUMMARY OF VALIDITY AND RELIABILITY OF TESTS

1. *The Counselors' Ratings*

Reliability: At least 70% agreement on behavior; little agreement on attitudes

Use: assessment of behavior and validation of other instruments. Only reliable ratings were used

2. *The Rover Test:* measured aggression and withdrawal

Scoring: percentage of aggressive and percentage of withdrawal choices out of twelve situations

Reliability: split-half coefficient of .74

Validity:

94% agreement with teachers' judgments of aggression of public school boys;

86% agreement with teachers' judgments of withdrawal of public school boys

3. *The Cartoon Test:* measured aggressive fantasy

Scoring: percentage of aggressive pictures chosen

Reliability: split-half coefficient of .78

Validity: 61% agreement with teachers' judgments of "composite" aggression of public school boys.

4. *The Internalized Guilt Stories*

Scoring: percentage of guilt responses.

Reliability: split-half coefficient of .76; Spearman-Brown correction gave .86

Validity:

66% agreement with teachers' judgments on "polite" behavior of public school boys;

Significant difference (P < .05) between public school boys and Wiltwyck boys

Differentiated (P < .05) between very hostile and non-hostile boys at Wiltwyck

Significant difference (P < .05) between personality types in Wiltwyck at beginning of treatment

5. *Authority Stories*

Scoring: percentage of punitive and of supportive responses

Reliability: split-half coefficient of .74; Spearman-Brown correction gave .85

Validity:

High level of agreement (P < .01) with counselors' ratings at Wiltwyck

Significant difference (P < .05) among personality types at beginning of treatment

6. *Self-Perception Questionnaire*

Scoring:

concern with internal and external traits

degree of positive ideals

ability to admit negative qualities

ability to differentiate descriptions

Reliability: Agreement in scoring between two judges ranged from 83% to 98%

7. *Perception of Environment Questionnaire*

Scoring:

constructive vs. destructive appetites

unrealistic vs. realistic complaints

loving vs. authoritarian views of good parents

punishment vs. "consequences" as a result of "wrong" behavior

Reliability: Agreement in scoring ranged from 85% to 98%

8. *Moral Code Questionnaire:*

Scoring: agreement or disagreement with generalized statements of ethics.

9. *A Test of Reactions to Frustration:* judged by counselors

Scoring: responses of aggression, hyperactivity, realistic acceptance, or withdrawal

Reliability: 75% agreement when boys were rated more than once

The Usability of the Tests

We should, perhaps, add a note concerning the uses of the tests developed in this study. Because of their high reliability good correspondence to independent measures, and ability to differentiate various disorders, the Rover Test, the Guilt stories, and the Authority stories seem to be our best instruments. Because they directly measure basic traits like guilt, withdrawal fantasies, and views of authority, the tests may well be applicable to other problems in social and psychiatric science.

In general, most of our direct questions proved ineffective either in differentiating between the children or in uncovering the effects of treatment. Particularly for delinquents, the projective method or open-ended stories seem more applicable.

Only one test, the Cartoons, proved entirely useless. It uncovered no meaningful differences among normal boys and the delinquents, nor did it detect any of the effects of treatment.

Like others in the past, we ran into difficulty in using behavioral ratings. Counselors often disagreed in judging internal qualities and even in rating actual behavior. For a high degree of reliability, the observers of behavior should be trained to look for the same qualities in the same way—a requirement that we did not fulfill.

It is our hope that the tests used in this project will be helpful not only as measures of the results of treatment, but in other areas of behavioral science.

Appendix D: Results of the 1954 Study

On the following pages, we have listed in statistical tables the results of the 1954 study of Wiltwyck boys. In reading the tables, the important relationship to note is, of course, the change in scores between the 0–8 month category and the 9—23 month category.

ROVER TEST: Percentage of Aggressive Choices*

Months	Behavior Disorders and Psychopaths (n:51)	Psychotics and Neurotics (n:25)
0–8	33	17
9–23	15 (P<.05)	19

GUILT STORIES: Percentage of Aggressive Endings†

Months	Behavior Disorders and Psychopaths (n:51)	Psychotics and Neurotics (n:25)
0–8	37	35
9–23	25 (P<.05)	28

CARTOON TEST: Percentage of Aggressive Choices

Months	Behavior Disorders and Psychopaths (n:51)	Psychotics and Neurotics (n:25)
0–8	32	34
9–23	29	36

GUILT STORIES: Percentage of Guilty Endings‡

Months	Behavior Disorders and Psychopaths (n:51)	Psychotics and Neurotics (n:25)
0–8	50	67
9–23	76 (P<.01)	71

*Behavior disorders and psychopaths in residence more than 23 months scored 24%; neurotics and psychotics in the same category scored 35%.

†Behavior disorders and psychopaths in residence more than 23 months scored 38%; neurotics and psychotics in the same category scored 27%.

‡Behavior disorders and psychopaths in residence more than 23 months scored 50%; neurotics and psychotics in the same category scored 74% guilty answers.

§Of the psychopaths and behavior disorders who had resided at the school for over 23 months, the counselors rated 63% as having adequate knowledge, 37% as having some knowledge, and none as having no understanding of the code.

222

AUTHORITY STORIES: Percentage of Punitive Endings*

Months	Behavior Disorders and Psychopaths (n:51)	Psychotics and Neurotics (n:25)
0–8	45	38
9–23	26 (P<.05)	32

ROVER TEST: Percentage of Withdrawn Rover Choices†

Months	Behavior Disorders and Psychopaths (n:51)	Psychotics and Neurotics (n:25)
0–8	20	26
9–23	20	12 (P<.05)

Counselor Ratings on Self-Perception‡

Months	Behavior Disorders and Psychopaths (n:47)			Psychotics and Neurotics (n:20) (P<.05)		
	Realistic	Some Realism	No Realism	Realistic	Some Realism	No Realism
0–8	24%	56%	20%	0%	83%	17%
9–23	26%	54%	20%	54%	33%	13%

Counselor Ratings: Knowledge of the Wiltwyck Code§

Months	Behavior Disorders and Psychopahts (n:47) (P<.02)			Psychotics and Neurotics (n:20)		
	None	Some	Adequate	None	Some	Adequate
0–8	7%	50%	43%	0%	33%	67%
9–23	4%	23%	73%	5%	25%	70%

*Behavior disorders and psychopaths in residence more than 23 months scored 33%; neurotics and psychotics in the same category scored 44%. Psychopaths in residence for more than 23 months scored 32%.

†Behavior disorders and psychopaths in residence more than 23 months scored 16%; neurotics and psychotics in the same category scored 8%.

‡Chance agreement would have been 33.3%. The counselors agreed on 50% of the boys rated by two or more staff members. When the disagreement was major, the ratings on the boy were not used. Behavior disorders and psychopaths who had resided at Wiltwyck for more than 23 months were judged by the counselors as being more realistic: 32% rated as realistic, 56% as showing some realism, 12% as unrealistic. Since only 4 neurotics and psychotics were included in the over-23-month category, we did not compute their ratings.

Reaction to Frustration*

Behavior Disorders and Psychopaths* (n:48)

Months	% realistic	% aggressive	% withdrawn
0—8	39	46	15
9—23	50	45	5

Psychotics and Neurotics* (n:22)

Months	% realistic	% aggressive	% withdrawn
0—8	40	20	40
9—23	47	42	11

---

*Of the boys in residence more than 23 months, counselors rated 40% of the behavior disorder and psychopaths and 50% of the neurotics as reacting realistically.

Appendix E: Counselor-Boy Relations and The Effect on Personality

In the following tables a comparison is made between the boys' relations to their counselors and the boys' scores on various tests:

Relation of Boys	Percentage of Aggressive Choices		
	On Rover	On Stories	On Cartoon
warm (n:34)	18	23	25
erratic (n:30)	23	38	41
distant or cool (n:27)	35	39	47

Percentage of Guilty Endings on Stories
Boys with:

warm relations (n:34) 71
erratic relations (n:30) 57
distant or cool relations (n:27) 60

Percentage of Punitive Endings to Authority Stories
Boys with:

warm relations (n:34) 29
erratic relations (n:30) 43
distant or cool relations (n:27) 40

Percentage of "Loving" Parent Descriptions
Boys with:

warm relations (n:34) 57
erratic relations (n:30) 37
distant or cool relations (n:27) 23

Responses of Boys in the 0—8 Month Category

	% of Aggressive choices on Cartoon	% of Punitive Endings on Authority Stories	% of Aggression On Rover	% of Guilty Answers	% of Story Aggression	% Answering "Loving"
Boys With Warm Relations (n:15)	15	24	15	61	28	43
Boys With Other Relations (n:19)	33	42	27	53	30	35

Index

227